EVEN WORSE THAN WE HAD HOPED

EVEN WORSE THAN WE HAD HOPED

A Journey Through the Weird Wild World of Local TV News

Paul B. Spelman

ISBN 978-0-615-27970-1 (softcover)

Learn more about the book at evenworsethanwehadhoped.com

This book is dedicated to Erin, Billy, and Jeremy, who make everything so much better than I had hoped.

Contents

Introduction (and Disclaimer) 13

Prologue: Fall of 2000 18

Chapter 1 The Minor Leagues 26

Chapter 2 Dienst, Koto and Colorado – Beginnings 34

Chapter 3 Christie Brinkley and Deciding to
Leave Telluride 52

Chapter 4 TV and Making a Tape 59

Chapter 5 The Great Paul Spelman Job Tour 67

Chapter 6 Whiteville 82

Chapter 7 The Daily Grind 113

Chapter 8 Help and the Human Boomerang 129

Chapter 9 Creative Fabrication and Fair Play 141

Chapter 10 Don't Go Back to Whiteville 165

Chapter 11 Life Is a Festival 171

Chapter 12 Newsrooms 179

Chapter 13 Photogs 196

Chapter 14 All in the Family 217

Chapter 15 Life as a Quasi-Celebrity 228

Chapter 16 Pay, Perks, and Parking Tickets 239

Chapter 17 Hurricanes and Heading for
Higher Ground 259

Chapter 18 Moving Up and the Name Game 266

Chapter 19 Knoxville and the Nightside 283

Chapter 20 When Bad Live Shots Happen
to Good People 297

Chapter 21 Death, Dogs, and Racking Up the Points 311

Chapter 22 The News of the Day 338

Chapter 23 The Spaces Between the Trees 357

Chapter 24 Farewell Knoxville 366

Epilogue: Fall of 2000 371

Aftermath 376

Acknowledgments 387
About the Author 389

EVEN WORSE THAN WE HAD HOPED

Introduction (and Disclaimer)

Most people really don't have any idea what it's like to be a TV news reporter. I know this because people ask me all sorts of weird questions about it, and because the depictions of TV reporters in books, TV shows, and movies are woefully inaccurate. This is probably because most people have little experience or exposure to what goes on behind the scenes in TV news. Most people merely see the end product, and either envision a life of glamour or one of narcissistic superficiality. As rock singer Don Henley put it in his scathing commentary on TV news, "Dirty Laundry," the bubble-headed bleach blonde comes on at five and she'll tell you about the plane crash with a gleam in her eye. There is some of that in the business, of course, but the truth is that TV news is a lot more complex than it appears, and nowhere near as glamorous.

This is particularly true for smaller TV markets. Markets such as Lexington, Kentucky, and Tallahassee, Florida; or Wilmington, North Carolina; Portland, Maine; Lincoln, Nebraska; or Knoxville, Tennessee. This is not the TV news of Brian Williams and Diane Sawyer. But Brian Williams started in a small market, and so do most of the other reporters and anchors who eventually make it to the network news. More importantly, most of America actually gets its news from local markets like these.

I did not enter the TV business with the idea of writing a book about it. In fact, the genesis for this book was my desire for parental approval. I was a few years out of college and working as a reporter for a small newspaper in Telluride, Colorado, and wanted my parents back in New York City to know that I was not a degenerate ski bum wasting a costly college education. My parents dutifully subscribed to my

13

newspaper, the *Telluride Times-Journal*, but the *TTJ* was the kind of paper where each reporter wrote four or five stories in each issue. Not wanting to appear as though the paper was the work of a few overworked staffers, the *TTJ* didn't put bylines on many of its articles. That way, if I'd written every story on the front page, it wouldn't appear as though the entire paper was "Brought to you by Paul Spelman."

This made it difficult for my parents to know which stories were mine. To remedy this, I started sending a list of headlines for my stories, and soon after, I started including short notes about the stories, and about the stories behind the stories. These notes were often much more interesting than the articles they were about. I titled these notes to my parents, "Headlines & Comments," and they often went on for several pages. They essentially chronicled the education of a cub reporter.

Later on, after I switched into TV reporting, I stopped sending headline lists every month but kept taking notes. I did this for several years, writing down observations and anecdotes; sometimes in my reporter's notebook, sometimes on newspapers or envelopes or whatever scrap paper was nearby. I stashed these notes in a big box under my bed. For a long time, they just sat there as a potential fire hazard. Organizing them into a coherent structure took a distant back seat to my learning how to be a TV reporter, and I had my hands full with that task. Eventually, though, I realized that I had accumulated a lot of interesting information about the TV news business. I realized I had a book.

I should say right off that anyone looking for a scholarly analysis of TV news is not looking in the right place. I'm not a journalism professor, and my goal here is not to dissect how and why the media is corrupting America and undermining our democracy. That may be the case, for all I know, but I'm not the one to say so. And while I have reservations about the profession, for the most part I enjoyed it and found it interesting.

The reason I feel the need for this sort of disclaimer is because the media, and especially the TV media, is a very easy target. There seems no limit to the number of critics eager to lambaste TV news reporting as sordid, sensational and self-serving. Fortunately, there are plenty of capable authors around to provide this sort of criticism, and some have written exhaustive treatises on the subject. I'm sure much of what they say is correct, but my goal isn't to repeat or contest their findings. I am not a crusader out to change the system. Instead, what I have written is an insider's "tell-some" — an account of what I consider revealing recollections, ruminations, and insights on what it is really like working as a TV reporter in local media.

The "local media" part is an important distinction. I worked for a few years as a local newspaper and radio reporter, and then spent a decade in TV news, most of that for local stations. I have been on the air thousands of times, and had my stories appear on dozens of TV stations around the country. However, I've never been on *60 Minutes* or *Dateline*, or worked for a national network broadcast. I've never been to Iraq, stalked "Deep Throat," or peppered the president with tough questions as he stepped onto Air Force One. In fact, my only encounter with a U.S. president was a humiliating experience. He mistook me for an intern.

What I have written is therefore an account of *trying* to make it to the top in TV news; an insider's view of what it's really like working your way up the TV ladder. When I wrote most of this, I had just moved to Washington, D.C., from Knoxville, Tennessee, a medium-sized market. Prior to Knoxville, I worked in a smaller market in Wilmington and Whiteville, North Carolina, and before that, I was in the really minor minor leagues, working as a print and radio reporter in Telluride, Colorado.

This low-level experience may actually be a benefit, however, because the journalistic trenches can be much more entertaining, amusing, and revealing than life at the top of the media food chain. There's certainly more fly-by-the-seat-of-your-pants reporting and unusual encounters with odd individuals. The small markets are where you experience the nitty-gritty of the news business and get to see life outside of the media fishbowl of Washington, New York, and Los Angeles.

That's what I wanted when I entered the TV news business — to see and experience America at ground level. Quite simply, I got more than I bargained for. I never would have imagined that I'd have to knock on the door of a suspected murderer, confront a rifle-wielding county judge accused of growing marijuana, do twenty-seven live shots in a single day, or have to ride out two hurricanes in two months. I also never imagined that I'd be a full-time TV reporter and still earn less than most kindergarten teachers.

I am certainly not the first reporter to embark on this kind of journey. Small markets are where many of the top network stars honed their craft. But even many who did seem to have forgotten what it was like. Perhaps they block it out as an unpleasant memory. Many seem to recall their early years through a nostalgic haze that turns days of struggle and frustration into a time of innocence and wonder. When I wrote most of this, I was in the midst of that struggle and frustration, and there wasn't much innocent or wonderful about it. That's not to say it was a terrible experience. The truth is that while life in small TV markets can be a rough road, it is also extremely funny, fascinating, and educational. I learned much more about America and its inhabitants than I ever would have had I remained in my hometown of New York City and taken a sane, sober job that paid the bills and had some semblance of a future.

One thing I do wish, though, is that I had had a better idea what I was getting into when I started down this path. That's where this book comes in. It is not directed at others in the news business, although many will find the scenes and stories familiar. This book is aimed, rather, at anyone considering an on-air reporting career, and anyone curious about what it's like. Curious about the good and the bad, the funny and the sad, and all the other things that you experience when you enter the wild and weird world of local TV news.

Prologue: Fall of 2000

It is often said that right before you die, your whole life flashes before your eyes. You spot the meteor hurtling toward you and the next thing you know you are reliving your childhood. This sounds very dramatic, although I do wonder how well I would appreciate such a split-second recap of my existence. It sounds more like a rap video than a fulfilling documentary about my life and accomplishments. Then again, my accomplishments probably don't merit a full-length feature.

Hopefully, I won't find out about near death experiences, at least not for a while. But I do know what it's like to have your career flash before your eyes. To have your professional dreams and aspirations appear before you, along with the grim realization that they aren't going to come true. This happened for me at six o'clock in the morning on a beautiful sunny day in the fall of 2000, as I drove my old pickup truck toward Washington, D.C.

I'd been on the road just a few minutes when a warning light came on, bright and red on my dashboard. The stereo made a peculiar popping sound and started cutting in and out, giving National Public Radio the sound of a distant radio transmission from outer space. "I'm Bob Edw...cough...and ...cough cough crackle pop ...is morning ...snap cough ...ition."

Uh oh. Houston, we have a problem.

I glanced down and noticed that the battery light on my dashboard was blinking on and off like one of those hi-fi monitors no one pays any attention to. That sort of flickering sound-level indicator looked pretty cool to me back when I was a teenager listening to Pink Floyd in the dark, but here I was 20 years later and this didn't look cool at all.

Glancing at the dash, all sorts of explanations went through my head – the alternator's broken, a blown fuse, KGB sabotage. All seemed equally plausible. I normally ignore the warning lights in my truck. The truck is from 1985, and its warning signals seem to go on and off at will. I stopped trying to figure them out, and accepted that after 200,000 miles, the truck had earned the right to random displays of emotion. It is not like there was much I could do anyway. Living in an apartment in New York City, my family did not own a car, and to say I know little about automotive maintenance is an understatement.

Despite the mileage on my truck, it normally ran pretty well. It had taken me all around the country in search of my first TV news job and had rarely let me down. On the rare occasions when it had mechanical difficulties, I always took it to a professional mechanic. Popping the hood and glancing underneath is about the extent of my repair ability. If the engine were missing, or the brakes were on fire, I might be able to spot the problem. Otherwise, I'm stumped.

But when the lights started flickering on this day, I did have an inkling of what was wrong. That's because I had experienced something similar six months earlier. What had caused it then, according to the repairman who explained it all to me, was that the truck's battery had come loose and was sliding around, ripping apart the wires connecting it to the engine. The battery did this because I had smartly forgotten to replace the engine's oil cap, allowing 10-W-30 to spew all over the front of the truck and creating a slick surface tailor-made for battery sliding.

The odd thing about when this happened was that even after the wires broke loose, the truck could keep running so long as it was moving at a relatively good clip, 30 or 40 miles an hour or faster. But once I went below that, forget it — the engine, steering wheel, brakes, and everything else shut down completely. The battery wires are not especially hard to reattach, even for me, but on this morning I didn't have much to work with. I didn't have any clamps, jumper cables, wrenches, screwdrivers, or other handy instruments for do-it-yourself automotive work. I was also decked out in my finest suit and tie, and didn't have a lot of time to fool around. This morning I was en route to a tryout as a TV reporter in Washington, D.C. This, I believed, was my shot at the big time.

I had moved to the D.C. area after nine years of paying my dues as a news reporter, working my way up through bigger and bigger markets. I started out at a small public radio station in Colorado; moved up to a TV bureau in a North Carolina farming community; then on to a relatively small city on the North Carolina coast; and finally to a station in Knoxville, a medium-sized market in East Tennessee. I spent about three and a half years in Knoxville, which is enough for anyone not an avid fan of the University of Tennessee football team. I was not, and was ready to leave after a year or two but had difficulty finding another job.

I tried the normal route of calling up big market TV stations and sending my on-air resume tape, but I rarely got so much as a reply. So after more than a year and a half of fruitless searching, I took a chance and moved to the Washington area without a job lined up in hopes of finding freelance TV reporting work. It was a gamble, but seemed better than sitting in Knoxville waiting for the phone to ring. The Knoxville area code didn't seem to be on the quick-dial lists of most big market news directors.

There is a fair amount of freelance TV work in and around D.C. There are five or six local stations in Washington, plus a number of national news bureaus that use freelance reporters. Then there's the Baltimore TV market just up the road. It seemed like an abundance of opportunity for a reporter with my experience.

I did have experience. I'd spent several years in radio, newspaper, and TV news. I had performed hundreds of live shots, written thousands of stories on tight deadlines, and covered everything from capital murders to cave rescues to circus openings. Sometimes all three on the same day. I firmly believed that I was ready for the big time; I just needed a chance to show it.

So after moving to D.C., I called every local station I could find, and walked my tape into newsrooms and bureaus all over the area. I did everything I could to get their attention, short of taking hostages. That would come later, I figured, when things got really desperate. All I wanted was for one reporter opening, even just a temporary one, to give me a shot. Maybe a reporter would take a long summer vacation, a leave of absence, or suddenly fall ill. Nothing fatal required, just an extended bout of mono or an unexpected pregnancy would do the trick.

But so far, either D.C. and Baltimore reporters were a remarkably healthy bunch or my resume tape simply wasn't impressive enough, because I hadn't received a nibble. Most of the news directors wouldn't even take my calls. Or if they did, they'd simply tell me, "Send us another tape. If we're interested, we'll get in touch." From long experience, I knew that meant good luck getting a job somewhere else. A bit more of this and I would have to seriously reevaluate my TV dreams.

21

I should explain about those dreams. Like most reporters in TV news, I harbored visions of making it to the big time. I dreamed of breaking the big story, covering important events, chronicling history in the making. I imagined myself reporting for *60 Minutes*. I could see Brian Williams tossing to me in the field; Diane Sawyer deferring to my expertise on foreign affairs. It sounds silly, but I could picture it in my head. Unfortunately, nobody else could. Instead of *Dateline*, *Nightline*, or *Frontline*, I was much closer to the unemployment line.

With my communications background, I probably could have found a job in public relations, crafting press releases about product launches or a new hospital wing, but that really wasn't what I wanted to do. Nothing against PR, but my dream was to make it as a news reporter, and it's hard to give up on something you've sacrificed so much for.

By that point, I had sacrificed quite a lot. I had changed cities four times in six years; worked innumerable nights, weekends, and holidays; braved hurricanes, blizzards, mudslides, and murderers; and all for near-starvation wages. But that didn't seem to be of much help in Washington; the TV market seemed impenetrable. Even the one supposed "contact" I had before I arrived, the D.C. bureau chief at Tribune Broadcasting, Cissy Baker, hadn't exactly welcomed me with open arms.

Cissy Baker was an influential woman in Washington. The daughter of former Tennessee Senator and White House Chief of Staff Howard Baker, Cissy ran the Washington bureau for all of the Tribune Company stations that carried TV news. I had met her a year before and kept in touch, occasionally calling to inquire as to the health of her reporting staff. When I had called from Knoxville she had always been friendly and encouraging on the phone, but since I'd actually moved to the

D.C. area, I had had a lot of trouble getting through to her. I called six or seven times, leaving several messages on her voice mail and with her staff. I was fast approaching that fine line that separates dedicated persistence from prosecutable harassment. Most rational people might have concluded that perhaps Cissy did not desire my services. But with nothing else showing the slightest glimmer of possibility, I tried her one more time.

"Cissy Baker," came the voice on the other end. Amazing. I had reached the real person. Frankly, I was a bit taken aback, and didn't know what to say.

"Hi, this is Paul Spelman." Good opening line, now what?

"Hi, Paul Spelman," she responded in a friendly manner that didn't reveal whether she knew who I was or thought I was about to offer her discount phone service.

"Um … I just thought I would check in with you and let you know I was available in case you needed any reporting help."

"Yes, I got your messages," she replied. "I have your number."

This was followed by a fairly lengthy pause during which there didn't seem much else to discuss. I figured that was about it. A career in PR was beckoning. But right before I said thank you and hung up, she broke the silence by adding, "How would you like to work on Wednesday?"

It was now Monday afternoon, so not a lot of advance notice. But it wasn't like I had anything else planned. Nevertheless, I pretended to check my schedule. "Wednesday, let's see … Yes, I should be available."

"Good. Be here at 7:30 in the morning. See you then. Bye."

This was it. My big break. Put up or shut up time. Now I had to show that I had what it takes as a TV reporter in a big market. Prove that I could handle the prime time. If I did okay, it would lead to more freelance work, both with Tribune and the other D.C. news outlets. Once you get your foot in the door it all falls into place, that's what everyone told me about the D.C. news market; it's very clubby, you need to get in the loop.

So after two days of obsessing over every last detail of my suit, tie, nose hair, etc., I awoke early Wednesday morning and headed for my big tryout. I left my apartment very early because I was living far outside of the city. Not having a job when I moved to the area, I couldn't afford a place closer in to Washington. As a result, I was actually living nearer to Pennsylvania than to D.C. My commute to D.C. thus involved driving rural back roads for 25 minutes to reach an interstate, then another 15-minute drive to a subway station, and finally a 35-to-40 minute Metro ride. Yet even with my early start, I hadn't factored in truck troubles. Now, as I watched the dashboard put out its S.O.S. signals, it went through my head that I might not make it.

I immediately felt a surge of panic and desperation. What could I do? I couldn't just call in and say, sorry, you'll have to get someone else today. For one thing, at this point I was the last remaining person in America still lacking a cell phone, and there weren't any pay phones around. I was out in the country. There weren't even a lot of houses nearby.

Besides, what sort of impression would that make, calling in with an excuse on my very first day? When you are a small-time reporter getting a shot in the capital of the free world, it's not as though they're going to give you the benefit of the doubt. They're taking a risk letting you walk in the door.

It may have been a bit melodramatic, but I thought to myself, well, that's it. My years of striving, of sacrifice, all for naught. My TV dreams will die on a small country road just out of reach of the nation's capital. Everything had seemed to hinge on this one big chance, and it looked as though it was about to slip away, the victim of an oil-slicked battery and a torn metal wire.

Sure enough, about 10 minutes after my dashboard lights began flickering, I had to slow down for a stop sign and the truck flat out died. The whole vehicle shut down, and I was lucky to coast to the side of the road. Turning the ignition didn't even spark a slight purr. It looked like a decade of work was about to go to waste.

Chapter 1

The Minor Leagues

If I weren't as stubborn, I would have given up long before I moved anywhere near D.C. It is very hard to make it in TV news, and quite simply, the odds are against you. Literally hundreds of thousands of people start out with the same dreams I had of making it to the big time in TV news, and most end up getting out of the business long before then. Most either realize that working in TV news isn't what they envisioned, or decide that instead of paying dues for a decade or longer with little guarantee of success, they'd rather have:

> a) an income that enables you to afford a few luxuries, such as furniture and a toaster;
> b) a stable home life and family, or at least a job where you don't have to move every two or three years;
> c) a job that doesn't require working nights, weekends, holidays, and hurricanes;
> d) a job where you don't have to deal with criminals, politicians, and other unsavory sorts;
> e) all of the above

Of course, I could have done what some people do: stay as a reporter in TV but stop trying to move up to the big markets. Some people remain in small or medium-sized TV markets, like Tallahassee, Florida, or Richmond, Virginia. But the number that remain is minute compared to the sixty-thousand plus communications, broadcasting, and journalism majors who graduate every year with dreams of becoming the next

Stone Phillips or Katie Couric. Quite simply, there is a tremendous attrition rate. Of the various news organizations I've worked at, I'd guess that three out of four of my former colleagues are now in another line of work, and that is a conservative estimate.

The reason for this is because, as I found out, it is a long, bumpy, and often exasperating road to the top in TV news. While you do sometimes hear about rapid rags-to-riches stories, most reporters remain in rags for a long time. I'm not talking about the glamorous network life of Mike Wallace and Barbara Walters; I'm talking about the TV news that much of America actually relies on for its information – local stations, often in small to medium-sized cities. According to one recent poll by the Radio and Television News Directors Foundation, twice as many people rely on local TV news than watch the network big wigs; and four times as many people watch local news as rely on local newspapers for information. That's millions and millions of people watching their local news.

Life at these local stations isn't at all like what most people think it is after watching movies and television shows that portray TV news. In *Up Close and Personal,* Robert Redford and Michelle Pfeiffer were not at a small station in New Bern, North Carolina, they were in Miami; and I doubt William Hurt and his *Broadcast News* buddies have ever set foot in a station in Bangor, Maine, or Harrisonburg, Virginia. But I have, because these sorts of stations are still the best way to break into the business.

I landed my first on-air TV job in Whiteville, North Carolina, a tobacco- and hog-farming community of about 5,000 people. I earned that job after working for three years as a radio and newspaper reporter in a town so small it didn't have a TV station. In fact, it barely got TV reception.

Local TV news in America is divided into markets, ranked 1 to 210. The lower the number, the bigger the market. New York City is market 1, Los Angeles is 2 and Chicago is 3. Kansas City is market 29, Omaha, 73, and Helena, Montana, 208.[*] I grew up in market 1, and wasn't going to land an on-air job there without any experience. I had to go small. And when I say small, I don't mean Miami, as *Up Close and Personal* would have you believe. Miami is not an entry-level city, that's the major leagues. Mary Tyler Moore was playing for keeps in Minneapolis, a top 25 market, whereas TV news in Macon, Georgia won't be mistaken for prime time. TV news is a lot like pro baseball, you start in the minors and work your way up.

The good thing about this process is that the smaller the market, the more mistakes you're allowed to make. And boy do you make mistakes. I've made so many I could have my own blooper show, *Paul Spelman's Funniest Semi-Pro Videos.* Of course, I don't need my own show since my mistakes have already been seen by thousands of people.

Like the time I reported that arson investigators were searching for signs of suspicious skin moisturizer. I didn't actually say that, but not far from it. What I did was mistakenly say the word *emollients* when I should have said *accelerants*. Accelerants are things like gasoline and kerosene, very useful in starting suspicious fires, and very suspicious when found in useful fires. Emollients on the other hand, are moisturizers and face creams. Not quite the same thing. But with the hot lights shining down on me and a producer jabbering away in my ear, I mixed up the word accelerant with another fire-related word, immolate, and fused them together

---

[*] Market numbers are recalculated every year or two, so a TV market might go up or down a few slots based on changing demographics. It is rare to move more than three or four positions.

into the word emollient. So with the utmost gravity, I informed thousands of viewers to be on the lookout for arsonists with dry skin.

Try making that mistake in a top TV market. You may not enjoy the view very long. But when I did it in Knoxville, a medium-size market, no one said a word. I actually figured out myself that I had made a mistake and mentioned it to one of the anchors (off air, of course). He replied that it had seemed odd to him at the time, but said I delivered the line with such conviction that he figured I must know what I was talking about. "Hmmm. Maybe Lubriderm does cause fires ...."

That's not to say mistakes don't get noticed in smaller markets, but, and here's the big difference, stations usually don't demote or fire reporters because of them. The smaller the market, the more mistakes reporters are *expected* to make. Most reporters who get better and stop making mistakes don't stay in small markets, so small markets usually have reporters with little experience, or reporters for whom experience doesn't seem to help.

Just as pro baseball in the U.S. has four different classes (A, AA, AAA, and the major leagues), TV news can be divided into small markets, medium markets, larger markets, and the "major leagues." The major leagues in TV news probably equates to the top 20-25 cities. Mind you, I'm still talking about local TV news. Being on national network news is so high up it doesn't even rank, it's like being on the Dream Team.

A quick way to gauge TV market size is to look at a city's pro sports teams. Big markets have more teams. Atlanta has major league baseball, football, basketball and hockey, not to mention the Olympics and Ted Turner. It's market 9. Portland, Oregon has one major league team, the NBA Trailblazers, and a few minor league teams. It's market 23. Knoxville didn't have any major league teams, but did have a minor league hockey team and an AA class minor league baseball team. It's market 62.

I should note that similar sized TV markets don't always provide similar quality newscasts. Some small markets are known for having relatively high quality newscasts (Charlottesville, Virginia, for instance, and Ft. Myers, Florida), while plenty of big markets have a reputation for overly sensational slop (LA and Miami, for instance). But in general, the smaller the market, the less impressive its TV news will be. That's because smaller markets reach fewer people and thus charge less for advertising and thus have less to spend on staffing, equipment, and salaries. Especially salaries. While a reporter in Tampa might earn $65,000 a year, a reporter up the road in Panama City is lucky to get $20,000. When I started in TV in 1994, I was paid $17,000. By 1997, I was up to $17,500, although I actually took home less because I had to reimburse the station for any equipment I lost or damaged. The longer I worked there, the more I owed.

Many people have the idea that TV is TV and it's a glamorous profession wherever you are. I wish I could say this were true. In small markets the pay is low, the equipment old and unreliable, and the news events themselves not all that captivating. Covering the 12th city council hearing devoted to whether the courthouse needs a new parking garage is not something you want to brag about to friends and family. But you do learn the craft in small markets, you make your mistakes, and, hopefully, you get better and move up.

Some people, of course, even talented ones, stay in small markets permanently if they have family in the area or prefer a more relaxed lifestyle. Most small-market stations have one or two staffers who have been there for decades even though they could have moved up long ago. A few brave ones even move back. At the Wilmington station I worked at, our chief photographer (technically they are "videographers" since they shoot video, but almost everyone in the business refers to them as photographers, or "photogs") had worked for a station in Charlotte (market 28, right on the cusp of the majors), before returning to Wilmington to be closer to his family. In Knoxville, a reporter named Don Dare (one of the great true TV names) had worked in St. Louis, Los Angeles, and Miami, all major league markets, but moved back to a middle market because he said he didn't want to raise his family in a large, urban setting.

This is rare, though, especially for on-air people. Most of the time, the only on-air people who remain in small markets are the main anchors, because they're the only ones who earn a decent salary. For everyone else it's like the military, up or out.

But if you leave TV news, it's very difficult to get back in. And there are some genuinely good reasons to stay. For one thing, local news is consistently interesting and entertaining. In all my time in local news, I can't recall more than two or three days where I found myself wishing the clock would move faster. Usually I was praying for a few more minutes before deadline.

There's also something about TV reporting that is enormously instructive. People who would never talk to me had I not been a reporter would open up and share everything they knew about a subject. You also get to experience all sorts of different activities. TV reporters are like professional dilettantes; you get to try lots of different things without ever knowing anything in depth. After a decade as a reporter, I was the quintessential generalist. Put me in a stadium with 50,000 people and I could find something to talk about with nearly every person there, because at one point or another, I'd probably done a story that would relate.

Oh, you're a hairdresser? I once did a news-you-can-use piece about the dangers of running a blow-dryer while standing in the shower with the water running. You're a firefighter? I just did a story about how fire poles are on their way out because too many oversized firefighters are breaking their ankles on the way down. You used to run a sanitation company in New Jersey and seem reluctant to talk? No kidding, I once did a story about the federal witness protection program.

As a TV reporter, I learned to become an extremely quick study because every day it was something new that I had to master and explain to viewers. It's a bit like being a substitute teacher in a different subject every day. I once saw a newspaper comic that captured this perfectly. It was captioned "How Reporters Start Their Day," and showed a blindfolded man tossing a dart at a board covered with different subjects: politics, science, the economy, etc. Above the dartboard was a sign that declared, "Today I am an expert on _____. "

There's a lot of truth to that cartoon. It is a unique aspect of journalism, and much truer for local TV reporting than for newspapers, because in TV, you don't usually have a "beat." Print journalists may become experts in a particular subject, such as politics, health, or education. Local TV stations, on the other hand, need so many more supporting staffers (photographers, tape editors, directors, sound engineers, etc.) that they can't afford as many reporters as a newspaper in the same market. A typical station in a small- or medium-sized market may have only three or four reporters working each day, and just one on a weekend. Local stations rarely get the luxury of assigning a reporter to focus on one type of subject matter to the exclusion of all others. That's why Monday I might show up as the "News 6 Crime Reporter," the next day I'd be the "News 6 Science Correspondent," and two days later I'd be live from the circus doing an "up close and personal" on Sara the Tiger Whisperer. TV reporters rarely become specialists, at least until they make it to the network level.

This is great if you're the reporter. You get to see an enormous variety of things. It's what I enjoyed most about the business. It was like having a license to learn about anything and everything. Which is why, even though I often felt it was time I moved into a career that was more productive, or at least more lucrative, another part of me always wanted to keep on reporting, shooting for the big time, and giving it a go in this very strange business.

Chapter 2

Dienst, Koto, and Colorado —Beginnings

Had I really known exactly how strange it would be, I might never have gotten into TV in the first place. It is a bit odd that I did, anyway, since I came late to the idea. Most TV reporters major in journalism, communications, or broadcasting, and intern at local news stations to get experience. I never did a TV internship, and instead of attending one of the 300-plus colleges that offer a degree in journalism, I selected a liberal arts school that didn't have a single journalism class. While Colgate University can count several noted journalists among its alumni (celebrated curmudgeon Andy Rooney probably being the most prominent), the school wasn't geared toward turning out future newscasters.

To this day, the only journalism class I ever took was in high school. It was one of the few high school classes in which I got a decent grade (a B+), which should have clued me in to something, but at the time, the class seemed too unstructured to be a genuine subject. I wrote "articles" for homework while riding the subway to and from school, which made for some interesting penmanship but hardly seemed like something that would translate into a lifelong vocation. I figured I'd stumbled onto an easy instructor.

In fact, my main understanding of what reporters did came from *The Year of Living Dangerously,* a stylish Australian film starring a young Mel Gibson as a foreign correspondent in Indonesia in the 1960s. Mel got to hang out in exotic locales, smoke unfiltered cigarettes, and bed the beautiful Sigourney Weaver. This seemed like something to aspire to. Even so, it wasn't enough to make me set on a career in TV. Besides, I was under the mistaken impression that Mel's character, Guy Hamilton, was a newspaper reporter. It was only when I viewed the film again years later that it dawned on me that "Guy" worked for the Australian *Broadcast* Service, carried around a microphone, and had an assistant shooting a motion picture camera. Since I had become a TV reporter myself by that point, this late realization served as utter validation for my own career choice.

But, as I noted, I really wasn't planning on a career in news, TV or otherwise. My few forays into journalism in college consisted of a couple of travelogues for the student newspaper and an editorial I wrote explaining why undergraduates should be allowed to have bigger parties and drink more beer. Hardly heady material to launch a media career. To be honest, I don't think a journalism career would seriously have occurred to me if I hadn't roomed with Jonathan Dienst. Dienst is to blame.

Jon is now a big-market reporter for WNBC-TV in New York City, but when I met him he was just another Colgate student. He was a year younger, and at first we weren't especially close. But when both of us signed up for a semester in London, we decided to room together. Little did I know how that would influence my life.

Unlike me, Jon is one of those types who grew up dreaming of being on TV. He's been addicted to TV news since infancy, and I can imagine him giving live reports from the playground whenever a playmate fell off the jungle gym. Jon may even have pushed kids off so he could break the story.

At Colgate, Jon immersed himself in what meager broadcasting opportunities our school offered. In particular, he became a radio announcer for several school sports teams, including hockey, one of the best college programs in the country. Doing play-by-play for hockey is no easy task, since it is an extremely fast-paced game. Furthermore, the Colgate squad was almost entirely Canadian. Eighteen of the team's 24 players hailed from north of the border, and the Canadian anthem was played at every home game, although dutifully played second, following the Star Spangled Banner. Every other player on the team seemed to have a tough-to-pronounce name such as Rejean Boivin or Hugues Rivard.

Despite these challenges, Jon had a gift for describing the action. In fact, Jon's only real failing was that he had difficulty keeping his emotions in check, and at times the other announcers would have to shut off Jon's microphone when he went off the deep end following a heroic play by a Colgate skater. This made for some amusing exchanges that went something like this,

"DARTMOUTH HAS A BREAKAWAY UP THE ICE, SHOT ON GOAL! OH MY GOD, HE SAVED IT!!! HE SAVED IT! SAVE BY COWLEY!! SAAAAAAAVE BY COWLEY!!! I CAN'T BELIEVE IT!! NO, DON'T TOUCH MY MICROPHONE! I'M OKAY! I'M OKAY!"

Jon's enthusiasm later became something of a handicap when he switched into more serious news reporting, because his reports retained that energetic style even while recounting horrific events. "MURDER!! – IN THE BRONX! TWO DEAD!! I CAN'T BELIEVE IT, LET'S GO TO THE VIDEOTAPE ..." Of course, in some markets, that might play pretty well. Maybe that's why Jon's been so successful in New York.

Jon also did a few summer news internships, and it was one of these that indirectly led to my getting into the business. That's because, after an internship with a TV station in New York, Jon arranged it so that he would be a news stringer for the station during our semester in London. Being a stringer meant Jon would keep his eye on the British newspapers and notify the New York station of any interesting stories. Why a local New York station would want a news stringer in England remains a mystery to me, but Jon arranged it so that we received free subscriptions to several British newspapers. Free to us, anyway. I never completely understood Jon's arrangement, and I'm not sure the station did either, at least until they got the bills several months later. But the end result was that Jon and I received five newspapers a day, seven on Sundays, delivered to the door of our London flat.

So instead of studying Yeats, touring Stonehenge, or visiting Big Ben, Jon and I spent much of our semester abroad reading the newspaper. Or I should say newspapers. We read all of them. It was the only diversion we had without venturing outside, and England isn't known for its balmy climate. We also didn't have a lot of spending money, couldn't afford a TV, and had telephone service that was so basic we couldn't dial out. We could receive phone calls, but to actually place a call we had to walk down to the corner pay phone with a bucket of coins. For long distance calls you needed two people: one to feed coins into the slot while the other talked on the phone. So most of the time, we sat around and read the papers.

You might think we'd get bored reading multiple papers since we'd see the same stories over and over again. That wasn't always the case. In England, newspapers are politically aligned (they are in America too, but less openly), which meant that each paper had its own distinct slant. We'd read the "conservative" Tory papers, the "left wing" Labour papers, the tabloids with their page-three girls and sports star exposes ("Tart Has Sex With Manchester Midfielder, Left Unsatiated"), the "serious" papers and their accounts of

37

Parliamentary strife, and everything in between. Then, when Jon and I had used up our reading material, we'd sit around and argue over which paper provided the best coverage.

At the time, I was something of a journalistic snob, favoring detailed analyses on what I regarded as important issues of the day. This was a holdover from my upbringing. My family read the *New York Times* and rarely watched TV news, much less local news. Jon, on the other hand, was, is, and always will be, a fan of more sensational fare. So while I might be perusing an exhaustive article about the impact of the exchange rate on indigent potato farmers, Jon was apt to be enthusing over a story about spiritual weightlifters pumping iron for Jesus. The more they lifted, the better their chance for salvation. Pounds for piety, or something like that.

I remember that story, by the way, because I believe it was the only piece Jon sent back that actually made it on the air in New York. At the time, the story seemed ludicrous to me, and it seemed ludicrous that a station would want to put it on the air. It was only later when I got into TV myself that I came to see the true significance of those weightlifters, and why they really were worth a three-part series during sweeps. But, as I said, that understanding came much later.

Still, all that reading and arguing about news really piqued my interest in journalism. I got far more enjoyment out of it than anything I was studying in school. I really liked reading about real issues and everyday lives. It was much more interesting than the detached musings of mostly dead authors I was required to analyze as an English major. Even weird weightlifters seemed more appealing than the poetry of Sylvia Plath. I was much more intrigued by Plath's suicide-by-gas-oven than by her use of rhyme and meter.

So I started to consider journalism as a career option. Even then, TV news wasn't in the picture. After all that time with the newspapers, I figured print reporting would be my route. I viewed newspapers and magazines as *true* journalism. TV reporters, I thought, were just good-looking talking heads that spoke clearly and used plenty of hairspray.

After graduating from Colgate in 1989, I tried submitting articles to newspapers in New York, but none of them seemed interested. I also tried to get a job in the magazine industry as fact checker, a copywriter, and even a secretarial assistant, but most magazines didn't have a lot of jobs available. As a marginally skilled typer, I really wasn't qualified for a secretarial position anyway. So instead, I worked a number of part-time jobs, including jobs as a restaurant host and as an elementary school gymnastics instructor — jobs for which I was probably less qualified than the secretarial position. But it was all I could find. Basically, I was floundering, and New York City is a tough place to flounder. Were it not for the fact that I lived at home with my exceptionally tolerant mother and stepfather, I would have found myself broke and applying for government assistance.

Jon Dienst, meanwhile, was having more success. He enrolled at the Columbia Journalism School and, while still in school, had managed to get an article published in the *New York Post*. I briefly considered following his lead and applying to Columbia, but journalism school is costly, and it would have meant waiting another year to get in (if I even could) and then another year of classes and academics. I was not a good student and couldn't stomach the idea of going back for more.

Jon explained to me that the other way to get a reporting job is to latch on with a newspaper in a small market. This seemed a better option. To do that, I'd have to leave New York, so when another friend announced that he was planning a trip across country, I decided to join him. I figured this might be my entree into news. Follow newspaperman Horace

Greeley's advice and go west, young man. Maybe I could land a job with a small-town paper and get my foot in the door.

We stopped in a number of towns and I ended up in Telluride, a stunning mountain resort in the southwestern part of Colorado. The town used to be a gold mining mecca, and legend has it that Butch Cassidy robbed his first bank here, escaping into the mountains with more than $10,000 in mine payroll funds. When I arrived, the town still looked a lot like it probably did back in Butch's day, making it something of a western "Brigadoon." But it now also had a popular ski resort, which led to a great deal of turnover in the workforce as post-collegiate twenty-somethings came through for a few years of fun on the slopes before getting serious about a career. It was sort of like college in that every year the senior class departed, opening up promising slots for underclassmen. I was told that to get work at the local newspaper, all I had to do was get in line and wait. Eventually, one of the paper's reporters would decide to return home, leave for graduate school, or go into the family insurance business.

So I got a job as a waiter and bided my time, stopping in at the local paper every two or three weeks to remind the editor that I was available. It took about four months before she gave me a shot, but even before then, I'd begun reporting for the local radio station, KOTO, a National Public Radio affiliate that had a daily local newscast. I didn't know anything about radio reporting, but KOTO needed part-time people and they were willing to teach.

KOTO was about as far removed as you can get from big-time commercial broadcasting. It was a small station, just a six-room Victorian house converted into a 10,000-watt radio station. Some college stations have more watts than that. KOTO's entire operating budget when I arrived was $141,000, enough for four paid staffers and a host of volunteer disc jockeys. But it did have a news "department," basically one guy named Jon Kovash.

Kovash was a tall, thin hippie holdover with a shaggy beard, shaggy hair, and a shaggy demeanor. He had a deep resonant voice and a very relaxed on-air speaking style. Perhaps a bit too relaxed, since most suspected it was not the product of legal means. Every now and then Jon would emerge from the station equipment room accompanied by an aroma that would undoubtedly be grounds for a search warrant.

But whatever he was doing, it didn't seem to interfere with his work. If anything, it gave him the serenity to remain calm in the face of a daily deadline, a heavy workload, and constant sniping from local leaders and real estate developers, often upset with what they felt was his anti-growth reporting. Jon never seemed to get stressed or disturbed by anything. So much so that I sometimes wondered if he fully grasped what was going on. I recall one day when the computer erased nearly the entire newscast five minutes before airtime, and Jon's only comment was, "Well, some days are like that."

I guess the pressure eventually got to him, however, because a few years after I left, he had to step down as news director following an incident involving dog excrement and one of his more persistent critics. I wasn't there and don't have all the details, but according to a newspaper account, Jon dumped "a large pile of fresh dog feces" on the hood of the other man's car.

When I was there, though, Jon was always a stable and fearless leader despite a challenging job. Jon was almost single-handedly responsible for putting out a daily newscast five days a week; a newscast that was expected to cover everything newsworthy to the entire area. If a lot was going on (by Telluride standards, of course), Jon would have to do five or six stories in a day, sometimes more. On the other hand, if it

41

were a slow news day, Jon would have to dig up enough stories to fill the newscast.

To help him out, Jon was allowed to hire half a person. In other words, he was given about $7,000 to spend on part-timers. So Jon enlisted several young reporters who each did a few stories a week for about $15 each. One of these reporters was a young Duke graduate from Atlanta named Lynn Heinisch, who also wrote for the newspaper. Lynn was (and is) a very friendly and engaging person, and when I told her I wanted to be a reporter but hadn't been able to get work at the paper, she suggested I try the radio and offered to help. I'd never even considered doing radio reporting, but figured I could give it a try, so I stopped by KOTO one day while Lynn was working.

Lynn was busy hammering away on her computer but welcomed me warmly and gave me a story to do. I still remember it, of course. It was a feature piece about an upcoming mountain bike race, and it didn't require any research on my part because Lynn had already interviewed the race organizer. All I had to do was listen to her taped interview, pick out a couple of sound bites, and write a passable script. It was my first "professional" story, and hopefully, I am the only one with a copy.

I didn't have the slightest idea how to write a radio story. Not having studied broadcasting, I wasn't familiar with the technique of selecting ten-second "actualities," as sound bites are technically called, and framing a story around them. Instead, I selected sound bites that were 45 seconds long and repeated what I had written in my script. "The race organizer says the race should be a lot of fun," I'd write, followed by a sound bite of the race organizer stating, "I expect the race should be lots of fun." This hails from journalism's school of redundancy school, and leaves the impression that there is an echo emanating from your set.

Lynn, however, was patient, and helped me clean up my copy as best she could. But even then, my problems were far from over because I had to voice the story onto tape for broadcast. I found I had difficulty breathing while talking. I wasn't used to speaking into a microphone and became very self-conscious. I tensed up and started gasping for breath, a bit like a seal having an asthma attack.

The only possible explanation for anyone who heard my story later that night was that I must have been trying to ride the bicycle race myself while delivering the report, a new standard for journalistic verisimilitude. "The ... (breath) ... race will start ... (breath) ... at the end of town ... (gasp ... breath) ... and go up and over ... (breath, slight choking sound) ... the mountain pass." I'm surprised listeners didn't call 911 and send help. Lynn was nice about it, though, and tried to explain all she could about how to do radio news. She spent so much time instructing me that it would have been far faster had she done the story herself. But she helped me through it, and after a two or three dozen takes, I got to hear myself delivering this breathless two-minute piece about an upcoming mountain-bike race.

Hearing my voice on the radio made me both proud and horrified. Proud to think I was a "newscaster," and horrified because my voice sounded so different from what I had imagined. As anyone knows who's ever heard his or her own voice on tape, there's something odd about hearing yourself. Even with the finest audio equipment, you sound different than you do inside your head. Even now, years later, I'm still not used to it. And in Telluride, I was far from smooth.

Even after I had a lot more experience under my belt, my on-air performances were always a crapshoot. Once, while doing another newscast with Lynn, this one live, I stumbled over the word "Towaoc" with unfortunate results. Towaoc is a Native American word and the name for a well-known canal in southwestern Colorado. I'm told it is properly pronounced TOY-yahk. Unfortunately, I hadn't been told that at the time. I meant to check the pronunciation before the broadcast, but it slipped my mind, something I only realized when I got to the word while reading my script live on the air. I should have just confidently picked a pronunciation and kept going, but instead I hesitated mid-word. "Tow ... twa ... towawa ..."

Lynn started laughing. She continued laughing as I fumbled for a pronunciation. Her laughing started me laughing, which made it harder to read the script. My voice took on a strange, high pitch as I tried to stifle my laughter and keep reading. At this point, Lynn was laughing so hard she had slid over into the corner of the studio and bent down to get as far away from the microphone as possible. I continued reading in a halting squeaky manner that sounded as if I was being force-fed helium while choking on a chicken bone. Just when I finally managed to get my voice under control, I came to the word "Towaoc" again in my script. I paused for a full second or two and then skipped it entirely, stating simply "the ...um ... canal." This started Lynn laughing again. It was the longest 60-second story I have ever had to deliver. Thankfully, our station tape recorder failed to work properly that night, so there is no official record of it.

Despite incidents such as this, I found that I enjoyed radio reporting immensely. There was something wonderful about being able to speak directly to listeners, and about using ambient sound and sound bites to tell a news story. It made the story come alive and tell itself. It was so much more fun than I had expected it didn't even feel like real work. The fact that I got paid $15 per story was a bonus; I would have done it for free. This is an attitude common among young reporters, and one most quickly get over. I did too, but at the time, I loved the experience and the stories, even though most weren't nearly as exciting as the mountain bike race or my Towaoc Canal piece. Most of what I covered fell into the category of Extremely Boring Stuff.

That's because most of the news in Telluride came from meetings. Dozens and dozens of them. There were City Council meetings, County Commission meetings, Town Planning and Zoning meetings, School Board meetings, meetings of the Telluride Housing Authority, the Joint Town/County/Mtn. Village Planning Commission, the Telluride Chamber Resort Association, and a host of others that have mercifully faded from memory. My job, once I became a full-fledged reporter, was to attend these gatherings and look for a story. This wasn't the kind of journalism I'd seen from Mel Gibson, but it was here that I learned my first important lessons about reporting and, in particular, about reporting in a small market.

Most significantly, I had to learn that a meeting did not amount to anything in and of itself. The fact that someone holds a meeting isn't news, so beginning my story with, "The county commissioners met today ... " wouldn't tell anybody anything. This sounds pretty self-evident, but you'd be surprised how many reporters make this mistake. Lynn and Jon had to drum it into me repeatedly that other than the officials themselves, and possibly their appointment secretary, nobody cared whether they got together to chat. What was important was what they said and did.

I didn't fully grasp this concept until Lynn and I came up with what we called the ten-second rule. This involves imagining that you have just come from a meeting and run into some friends who want to know what happened. You have 10 seconds to tell them. Would I say, "Well, the commissioners got together and spoke for three hours on all sorts of topics" or would I tell them, "They raised your taxes and outlawed the sale of salami on Sundays." It's kind of like asking, "What happened in Philadelphia in 1776?" Did some guys in wigs make speeches and practice their signatures, or did they declare independence from a tea-taxing monarch?

One reason this concept was difficult for me was because in some ways it clashed with the second, and equally important, lesson I learned as a small-market reporter: that there is *always* a news story. This isn't something you will learn in big-market news. In big cities, there are plenty of genuinely interesting things going on. New York City reporters often have more news then they can cover, and get to choose between covering the big subway track fire or the nun who held up the liquor store (I'd go with the nun). Big-market reporters are often excellent journalists, but they don't have to scrape and scrounge for stories like you do in such news hotbeds as Lafayette, Louisiana, and Yuma, Arizona. And since Lafayette and Yuma are many times larger than Telluride, you can imagine what sort of stuff I was covering. I had to develop a heightened sense for finding something, anything, I could write about. I got so where if the town mayor scratched his nose, I could turn it into a two-minute radio piece. If a finger ventured inside, I had a three-part series.

The key to performing this journalistic magic trick was to recognize that what *didn't* happen could be as newsworthy as what did. Kovash explained this to me one day when I returned from a meeting and informed him that nobody did anything.

"There's your story," he replied.

He was right. When there's nothing going on, trumpet the nothing. "EVERYTHING STILL THE SAME! STATUS QUO CONTINUES!! HEAR ALL ABOUT IT ...."

I tried to be subtler than that, of course, but not by much. Something on the order of, "Despite growing concern, the city council again failed to act on ...." Other useful ones were, "It will be another week of waiting before we learn the fate of ..." and, "The pressing question of such and such remains unresolved ...." I learned to write stories about nothing that would make Seinfeld proud. What I was really saying was that no news is still news. While this may seem to clash with the idea that meetings aren't news by themselves, it doesn't, because what I learned was that it can be news when nothing happens so long as that nothing might affect somebody. In other words, if someone is concerned about the nothing, than it can be something. If the tree in the forest doesn't fall, but someone wants it to, or is worried that it might, then it still makes a noise. Make sense? Not always, but it did fill airtime.

Even while learning these invaluable lessons at the radio, I still had it in mind that I really wanted to be a newspaper reporter. Oh, this radio stuff was fun, but it was just fooling around, I thought. Print reporting, that was true journalism. So every few weeks, I'd drop by the *Telluride Times-Journal* to check whether any staffers had died, departed, or become otherwise too incapacitated to work. By this time, the *TTJ*'s editor, Marta Tarbell, had heard me on the radio, and while she was undoubtedly concerned about my breathing difficulties, she may also have been impressed by my ability to cover nothing so effectively. Or maybe it was just evident I wasn't going to go away. Whatever the case, after four months of radio reporting, and repeated visits and harassment on my part, Marta relented and said she had a story I could do for her. Of course, it would be a meeting.

My big opportunity would be to cover an early-morning session of the Telluride Chamber Resort Association, a local organization whose job it was to market the region to tourists. TCRA meetings involved reams of statistics about skier days and per-capita spending on t-shirts, key chains and other tourist-related bric-a-brac. The meetings were excruciatingly boring, and Marta offered me this opportunity because nobody else wanted it. But where others had scorn, I saw glory. I saw this as a way of finally getting into the newspaper. I said yes before Marta finished telling me what I had to do.

The meeting turned out to be as unexciting as promised, but I still recall how proud I felt when I saw my first published article with the byline "by Paul Spelman." I walked around with my head held high all afternoon, figuring everyone would compliment me. No one did. No one ever notices a byline. The only people who notice bylines are other reporters or irate readers who call to complain. Later on, I would take to gift-wrapping Christmas presents in my bylined newspaper articles as a joke, and still no one noticed. My family just thought I was too cheap to buy wrapping paper.

Even so, I was immensely proud. Getting into the newspaper business had been my goal when I left New York, and I had succeeded, even if the newspaper was just a small weekly in a town of 1,500 people. I proceeded to take every assignment I could. I covered town and county government, the ski area and the courts. I wrote about new businesses, old businesses, and businesses going out of business. I covered environmental issues, crime, and even tried my hand at sports and entertainment. And most of all, I covered real estate and development.

I probably learned more about land-use issues than I would have had I gone to school to become a city planner. As it was, the actual city planners became my most important sources. I doubt a week went by when I didn't call them five or 10 times. I'd end up writing detailed stories about how the new development on lot 161-B on Coonskin Ridge received final approval from the county commission while lots 161-D and 161-A received preliminary approval and 161-C had been sold to another developer who planned to build a 34,000 square foot log cabin with a six-car garage.

You would think architects and real estate agents were the only ones who cared about this kind of news, but in Telluride it was hard to find someone who didn't. Half the town would be up in arms over some new land development proposal, with the other half planning to sell it. At some meetings, the more lively sessions, residents and developers would actually scream and yell and threaten each other with bodily harm over whether a new condominium complex could be 25 feet tall or 27 feet tall, whether it should have a 12- or 16-foot setback from the street, and whether the proposed hanging gables meshed with the town's Victorian mining heritage.

There was something about the whole thing that was slightly evocative of *The Treasure of the Sierra Madre*, but with land instead of gold. The beauty and value of the terrain seemed to turn some otherwise good people mean and self-centered. Sometimes I'd look around at Telluride's stunning vistas and think, "Well, time to go listen to people be really nasty to each over all this beauty."

I don't want to give the impression that people in Telluride weren't friendly or nice. Some of the nicest people I've ever met were in Telluride, and I still think of it as a wonderful place. But some of the real estate fights got down and dirty. I spent a lot of time interviewing very angry people, and often the disputes ended up in court. At one point, Telluride had one lawsuit for every 36 residents, the second highest rate in Colorado (behind Aspen). For one controversial land

49

development, I wrote 29 different stories over two years, and I was the second or third reporter assigned to cover the project.

Covering these issues was a good experience though, in that I learned some valuable lessons about how to get people to call you back. This is important, because people have a tendency not to return reporters' calls. So I had to develop some sneaky techniques. One was to leave an erroneous message on their answering machine, so the person would feel the need to correct the mistake. "Hi, this is Paul Spelman from the *Times-Journal*. I'm calling to confirm a report that you're planning to dedicate 200 acres of your slope-side property for use as a development-free town park. We're doing a story about this generous gift to the community and wanted your comments." Another technique was to leave a message as if the other person's answering machine had malfunctioned. So instead of announcing my name and newspaper, I would act as though I had already identified myself. I came up with this technique one day when I desperately needed a comment from the ski company. Ski company officials had a reputation for not returning media phone calls, so when I got the person's answering machine, I simply started speaking as if the voice mail had cut off the beginning of my message.

"(Beep) … and so I think you'll see it's pretty important, and if you could give me a call it should help both of us out. Here's my number …."

The guy called back within the hour, explaining with a somewhat worried tone that his answering machine hadn't recorded the entire message.

"Really," I replied. "Could be the altitude. You should get that fixed. But listen, the reason I was calling was that … ."

Of course, it is possible he would have called me back anyway, but I doubt it. He didn't sound happy when he learned I was a reporter. I was starting to learn the tricks of the trade.

This didn't make my Telluride stories any more interesting, but it would serve me well when I moved into TV news later on.

Chapter 3

Christie Brinkley and Deciding to Leave Telluride

In the nearly three years I spent in Telluride, I recall only one genuinely riveting "Stop The Presses!!!" news story. It involved cover girl Christie Brinkley, who was out heli-skiing with a group of friends, including her soon-to-be husband (and soon-after-that-to-be-ex-husband) Ricky Taubman. The helicopter they were in got hit by a gust of wind as it was touching down near the top of a 13,000-foot mountain, slid several hundred feet down a steep chute, and flipped over. Somehow, everyone on board survived, although there were several injuries, most relatively minor. Brinkley and the others were then plucked off the side of the mountain by the Telluride search and rescue squad.

To say I was unprepared to cover something of this magnitude would be an understatement. I knew how to attend meetings, not cover stories involving helicopter accidents and supermodels. I wish I could say I rose to the task. I did not. I did a terrible job.

I was working at the radio station when word started to filter in about some sort of helicopter crash. There was no indication who was on board or what had happened, but for some reason, the county sheriff's department would not even confirm that there was an accident, nor would the heli-ski operation, Helitrax. Then someone called the station and told me that the day before, they'd heard an employee of Helitrax bragging that he was going up skiing with Christie Brinkley the next day. Which meant that if a Helitrax chopper had crashed, so had Christie Brinkley.

I didn't know what to do. I tried calling the home number of one of the Helitrax owners and got a family member, but she wouldn't confirm that Christie Brinkley was on board or that a helicopter had crashed. "I'm sorry, I can't say anything right now," was all she would say, and I did not press. I felt bad for bothering her. How often have you heard a reporter say that?

I tried driving out toward where the crash was rumored to be, but the road was blocked off and I couldn't see anything. Thirteen thousand feet is way, way up; you can't see it from the valley level. So I went back to the radio station and sat around. By this point, the phones were lighting up, as CNN, the networks, and even a few local stations from Denver, New York, and Los Angeles were calling to see if we knew anything. How they knew about it so quickly I have no idea, but they soon knew more than I did. "We've confirmed that Christie Brinkley is aboard," they'd say. "Really? That's fantastic," I'd respond. "How did you find that out?"

Fortunately for me, Kovash showed up and started fielding the calls. Kovash was his usual unflappable self. I don't know if he had calming help from controlled substances that day, but he could've been covering another story about zoning rights for all you could tell from his cool demeanor and tone of voice. He gave live phone updates for CNN, Denver, and New York stations, and anyone else that wanted one. I wisely decided to leave that to him, and headed over to the local medical center in case they brought in any of the injured. A short time later, they did.

Here is how timid and inexperienced I was as a reporter at this point. They brought in Christie Brinkley and not only did I not get her photograph, ask her how she was, or determine how badly she was injured, I didn't even get close enough to confirm it was Christie Brinkley. I respectfully stood 75 feet away, because I didn't want to impose on the rescue team and the injured. All I could report afterward was that I had seen a blond woman being escorted into the medical center with what looked to be her arm in a sling.

I went back to the radio station with essentially no information. By this point, it was near our scheduled news time, and we still didn't know the details of what had happened. So instead of going on and reporting what we knew, we pushed back the news. I got on and reported that we thought there had been some sort of accident and would provide a newscast as soon as possible. We ended up delivering our newscast about an hour after its regularly scheduled time, after the sheriff's department finally condescended to tell us what had happened. Viewers back in New York City had quicker information about the Telluride crash than listeners in Telluride. Most news outlets go on early when there's breaking news; we went on late. I am still astounded when I think back on it that we were neither ashamed of this nor received any public criticism for it. It was the biggest story in years in Telluride, and I was unable to handle it.

Brinkley was apparently so amazed at my lack of aggressiveness that she ended up giving the KOTO news department a generous donation during our annual fund drive. Actually, I don't know why she gave the money, but I would not be surprised if my lack of paparazzi instinct contributed. It probably shocked her. After that, I knew I'd have to leave Telluride if I wanted to develop further as a reporter. It was clear that although I had learned a great deal, I wasn't learning how to cover news that didn't originate at a meeting.

What's a little strange about my move into television news is that for the entire time I was in Colorado, I didn't even own a television set. The radio station had a TV, and every now and then I would sneak in on weekends to watch a Knicks basketball game, but otherwise I didn't miss TV. I have never been a huge TV viewer, and almost never watched local TV news. What made me consider TV as a career, oddly enough, was an offer of a full-time job at the *Times-Journal* newspaper, with all the attendant status and salary, and most importantly, health benefits.

The offered wage was $15,000, hardly a king's ransom even in 1993, but about $4,000 more than I was earning working part-time at the radio and newspaper. But the newspaper offered it to me on one condition: that I stop reporting for the radio. The paper felt there were inherent conflicts in working for a competing media outlet in the same town. Faced with this condition, I realized that I preferred broadcasting to newspaper work. While I had gone into journalism with the notion of becoming a print reporter, newspaper writing didn't enthrall me. Instead of feeling like Woodward and Bernstein, I felt more like a stenographer, copying down quote after quote and fact after fact, in long "he said/she said" articles about tedious topics.

Broadcasting, on the other hand, seemed creative and challenging even when the subject matter was far from it. The narrative, the story, the "what, when, and how," was still the most important part, not the analysis afterward, as is often the case with print reporting. I could also mix in music and natural sound and let people tell their own stories. It seemed much more interesting and inventive than being a newspaper scribe.

I found myself spending hours and hours at the radio station, happily slicing and dicing in the editing booth to get the perfect mix of narrative track, sound bites, and natural sound. Sometimes I wouldn't even notice the hours go by until my deadline reared its ugly head. These days, radio editing is done with digital mixers and computers, but in Telluride I was editing with a razor blade and some splicing tape. I spent so much time at it that I developed a hard callus on my thumb from pushing down on the blade. I wore this callus like a badge of honor, even though no one else ever noticed it. When faced with the choice of print or broadcasting, I thought about it for a bit (the health insurance was tempting) and chose broadcasting.

This, in turn, made me reconsider my future, and really drove home the point that I couldn't stay in Telluride. Besides the fact that it seemed unlikely another helicopter would crash, there weren't many career prospects in broadcasting in Telluride. At best, I could wait for Kovash to leave and hope to ascend to his lofty position. There was no telling how long that could take, since unlike many in Telluride, Jon wasn't out for a year or two of fun and sun on the slopes, he was there for the duration. Even if I did eventually get his job, at most I'd be earning low to mid-twenties, not enough to live on in an expensive resort town like Telluride once you get past the life-as-a-ski-bum phase where you don't mind bunking with seven other people. Telluride was a pricey place, with homes listed as "Affordably Priced at $900,000" and "A Real Bargain at $1.3 million!" The only reason Kovash was able to live there was because he'd arrived before the big real estate boom and because, as a former construction worker, he had built his own home.

Anyway, I was ready to leave behind Telluride stories. Apart from the Christie Brinkley adventure, all my Telluride stories began to seem overly familiar. In small markets, news occurs in cycles. Each spring you do the same stories you did the spring before, and the same goes for summer, fall, and winter. It's hard to come up with a new angle on how this year's Mushroom Festival is different from the last three. All you could hope for was that listeners had forgotten what you did the previous year, which wasn't usually a problem for me, since most of my stories were eminently forgettable.

And despite my failure at covering the helicopter accident, I did want to cover important and unforgettable events. Living in Telluride, I would see a national news story about riots in Los Angeles or the fall of some Iron Curtain regime, and here I was attending architectural review hearings. Sitting in on some of these affairs, I would get so bored that I would try to amuse myself by seeing how low my heart rate could go. A long discussion about road grading standards once got my pulse down into the mid forties, near the level at which paramedics start reaching for their electric paddles.

Sometimes I lost patience and became very agitated at meetings. I'd mutter under my breath, "Let's vote now, no more questions. You there! Enough discussion already." I'm told these utterances were not always inaudible. Once, during a droning discussion about development plot size, I loudly crushed an empty Coke can, making one of the county commissioners jump out of her chair.

I got burned out on all the arguing, especially because it seemed to me that it wasn't even over real news and life-and-death issues. Telluride arguments weren't about survival, about the future of their children; they were about aesthetics and money and self-interest. Moreover, a lot of people in Telluride were there by choice. They didn't *have* to be there. They had moved to Telluride because they liked the scenery and the lifestyle. This could make it a little hard to empathize with their plight. It is one thing to do a story about someone forced to sleep in a car because of high housing costs, layoffs, or foreclosure rates. It's another thing if it's a college-educated kid from an affluent background who doesn't want to pay rent because he prefers to ski 120 days a year instead of getting a day job.

I loved living in Telluride, but I couldn't shake the feeling that I wasn't covering the real world. I wanted to interview average Joes and do stories about the downtrodden, the victims, the people who fought and struggled because they didn't have a choice. I had romantic visions of bearing witness to dramatic events and getting to experience the true grit of crime and punishment, not listen to legal wrangling over how roof setbacks might alter the aesthetics of a six-million-dollar real estate development. I wanted to see real life in America.

I found it in TV news. For good and bad, I got my wish. As the old saying goes, be careful what you wish for, you may get it.

Chapter 4

TV and Making a Tape

It would be hard for me to have chosen a vocation with a worse reputation than that of local TV news. Local TV news is often perceived as shallow and sensational, with anchors and reporters viewed as vain airheads willing to stoop to whatever means necessary to get their moment in the spotlight. If you think I am exaggerating, look at how TV news reporters are depicted in films and on TV. In the movie *Die Hard*, for instance, a smarmy TV reporter gets to shoot video of Bruce Willis's frightened children by asking the family's Spanish-speaking housekeeper about her immigration status and implying that he'll turn her in to INS. The audience cheers loudly when this reporter gets his comeuppance at the end.

In the film *To Die For*, Nicole Kidman's aspiring weathergirl is so nakedly ambitious she actually gets naked with a teenage boy and convinces him to kill her husband. Her husband's not a bad guy (why would you want to kill Matt Dillon?), but she views him as an impediment to her career. She sums up her attitude toward the work/family balance when she tells her mother-in-law that she doesn't want kids because "a woman in my field with a baby has two strikes against her … and pregnancy gives her blubber and boobs out to here. It's gross." (She's wrong, by the way, at least about her marketability in TV. In local news, lots of stations trumpet the pregnancies of their female anchors and reporters, practically going live from the delivery room to update viewers on the latest contractions. It's seen as a way of "humanizing" on-air people and making viewers like them. Lots of local anchors make on-air references to their children for the same reason.)

Even when TV news is depicted in a somewhat positive light, as in *The Mary Tyler Moore Show* or *Murphy Brown*, the on-air people are generally depicted as vacuous idiots, a la Ted Baxter. Just the fact that Will Ferrell portrays the title role in *Anchorman* really says it all.

Yet the irony is that the same audience laughing at these depictions is also watching and trusting its local news. A study by the Radio & Television News Directors Association found that eight in 10 Americans watch local news several times a week. And more than two-thirds of the public told pollster Bob Papper of Ball State University that they rate the quality of *their* local TV news as "good or excellent." Other surveys have found that viewers trust their local newscasters more than they trust network anchors and newspapers like the *New York Times* and the *Washington Post.*

All of this has no bearing on my decision to get into TV. I switched simply because I preferred broadcasting to print reporting, and because opportunities in radio news are so limited. Fewer and fewer radio stations provide their own local news, instead relying on big media outlets to send them news from a centralized source. It cuts down on staffing costs. If you want to be in radio news in the United States, you basically have to work for one of the big-city all-news stations or get a job at a public radio station that has its own news department. The other option is to work for National Public Radio, but the chances of getting a job with NPR is infinitesimally remote.

I tried all of these avenues. I sent tapes of my stories to NPR; I wrangled job interviews at two all-news stations in New York City; I called up big local public radio stations. All to no avail. There just aren't a lot of radio jobs out there. Most big cities may have one public radio station that provides news and one or two commercial radio stations that do their own local news. Which means that, all told, there may be eight or nine radio reporting jobs for a city of over a million people. And the folks that have these jobs aren't in a hurry to leave, because there's nowhere for them to go.

To make matters worse, radio pay is poor. And when I say poor, I mean atrocious. Radio reporters earn the lowest salaries in all of journalism; it's just slightly above that of inmate labor. In the 1990s, when I was trying to find another broadcasting job, the median salary for a radio reporter was about $19,000. I'm not talking starting salary, that's the *median*, and includes radio reporters who have been at it for decades.

I sincerely wish it wasn't so hard to make it in radio news, because I loved it. I wish I'd lived back in radio's heyday, when Edward R. Murrow was broadcasting from London rooftops during the blitz, and Orson Welles was scaring the daylights out of people with his *War of the Worlds* radio drama. I found radio reporting to be cozy and personal and yet creative as well. And as my friend Jon Dienst once said, in radio the words still matter. I loved everything about radio. But there just aren't a lot of openings or jobs that pay the bills.

So after trying and failing to find a radio job outside of Telluride, I took the suggestion of my father, who commented, "You're a good looking guy, why don't you try TV."

Sure, TV, what could be so hard about that? It's like radio news except with shorter stories and you have to comb your hair. Getting a job in TV news, of course, wouldn't be a whole lot easier than finding a job in radio. But there are actually more TV news jobs than radio positions. Unfortunately, there was also more competition. And even with a few years of newspaper and radio reporting under my belt, I was basically starting from scratch.

Working as a newspaper and radio reporter may train you how to write and report, but it doesn't train you how to write and report *for TV*. It also didn't provide me with much tangible proof that I could show to a TV news director, since handing them my newspaper clippings or a tape of my radio stories would require them to envision what I'd be like on TV. I have found that forcing people to imagine my future doesn't work well. Most people have a limited imagination when it comes to my future. They want to actually see what I can do right now, not envision what I might become. Besides, TV news directors need to cover themselves. Explaining, "I imagined he'd be good," to a disgruntled general manager upset over an incompetent new hire isn't going to win a lot of stars.

So aspiring TV reporters have to put together video resume tapes, or "reels," as they are sometimes called, and show these to TV news directors. Resume reels are tapes that start with a few brief shots of the reporter walking and talking, and then a few full-length stories. By full length, I'm talking a minute and a half each. Your entire reel is about 10 minutes long.

People who study broadcasting or communications in college usually make their tape in school or during a summer internship at a local TV station. But I'd never done an internship, and my college papers dissecting Dante and his circles weren't going to be of much help. So I sought help from my old flatmate, Jon Dienst, who by then had become a TV reporter with NY1, a fledgling 24-hour cable channel focused exclusively on local New York City news. I figured Dienst was partly responsible for my getting into journalism in the first place, so he should share the burden of moving me along. For better or worse, Jon agreed to help.

Unlike reporters at other New York stations, NY1 reporters operated as one-man bands, meaning they shot their own stories instead of working with a cameraman. Lugging his own video camera around was undoubtedly a huge pain for Jon, but also a great opportunity for me. It meant that Jon could help me put together a resume reel without violating some union rule about doing the same story twice. Which is what we did.

I shadowed Jon for two days and we covered two stories, with Jon doing the shooting and interviewing and me helping carry the gear. Then we shot each other standing on the street talking into the camera for 15 seconds — a vital TV story component known as a "stand-up"— before returning to his station, where Jon wrote up his version and I wrote mine. Jon edited and voiced his story, which aired that night on NY1, and then helped me edit and voice mine, which ended up on a tape that I could present to news directors. With just two stories, it was a fairly short tape, but it was a lot better than nothing.

The first story concerned an asbestos problem in New York City public schools. While the subject matter was fairly serious, the story was fairly bland. That's because the asbestos had been discovered in the summertime, when there weren't any crying students or irate parents around. To show you how ignorant I was in the ways of TV, I didn't realize this was a problem for a TV story. In radio, you can talk about students in class without needing them to actually be in class, but in TV, you need something to show. Fortunately, the school system realized that TV crews needed something to show, so they trotted out a few maintenance workers to go through the motions of searching for asbestos.

So with the TV cameras rolling, two or three union guys in overalls walked through school hallways with tape measures and acted as though they were calculating how much wall area to tear down to get at the deadly asbestos. At least I think that's what they were doing. I'm not sure they knew either. It was staged solely for the news cameras. This was my first experience with TV staging.

The second story was a bit more riveting. It involved the arrest of an alleged firebomber; a man accused of throwing a Molotov cocktail at New York City firemen during a race riot. That's a pretty dramatic story. But getting this for TV involved sitting around a police station for five hours until the NYPD was ready to parade the suspect before the cameras. Again, everything was done for TV.

"The presser's at 5:00, and the walk right after," explained the NYPD public information officer. The "presser" I understood. That meant a press conference. But the second phrase had me puzzled. "What's the walk?" I asked Jon. "That's when the detectives escort the suspect out into a car," he explained.

"So they tell everybody when they're going to do this?"

"Oh yeah," he said. "It's when the cops get their moment in the sun."

And sure enough, that's exactly what happened. All the camera crews lined up outside the precinct doors, and the police officers walked out very slowly with a tough looking guy in handcuffs. Just as they started him down the steps, one of the cameramen shouted that he wasn't ready, so the police stopped and waited. When the cameraman signaled that he was good to go, the officers started down again, and the "perp," guided by two or three of New York's finest, did a wonderfully thuggish "pimp roll" down the steps toward the waiting patrol car.

My favorite part occurred when the officers, who for all we know may have beaten the suspect up (or assaulted him with a broomstick) back in the cells, made sure to gently lower his head as they lowered him into the vehicle so he wouldn't knock his noggin on the doorframe.

"Where are they taking him?" I asked Jon after the patrol car drove off.

"I'm not sure," he replied. "They might take him to central booking. On the other hand, they might take him around the block and back into the precinct through the rear entrance."

That was my first exposure to the now infamous perp walk. At one time, these were commonplace, and police would do them at the drop of a hat whenever the media requested. Jon told me that once, while he was shooting a walk in Savannah, his videotape jammed and he couldn't get any footage. So the police were accommodating enough to walk the suspect again.

Those were the good old days. At some point suspects and their attorneys began to challenge these meaningless exhibitions, and they became much less common. In 1995, a suspect accused of robbing an apartment was being questioned by New York City police when a local TV station asked for a walk. The police drove the guy around the block for the cameras and returned him to the station for more questioning. When charges were later dropped, the man sued the detective for staging an unnecessary perp walk and won. Sort of. The court held that a perp walk done solely for the cameras is an "inherently fictional dramatization" serving no reasonable law enforcement purpose, and thus violates a suspect's Fourth Amendment rights against unreasonable search and seizure. Unfortunately for the man, the court also held that prior to its ruling, the detective wouldn't have known he was violating the Fourth Amendment, and so the detective was protected by qualified immunity and didn't owe anything for the unreasonable perp walk.

The end result of this lawsuit, and others like it, is that while "perps" are still occasionally paraded in front of the cameras, it's not supposed to be done solely for the benefit of the media. So instead, photographers now spend several hours camped outside of central booking waiting for the 15 seconds when police actually transfer the suspect somewhere for a legitimate law enforcement purpose. The end result is the same, of course — a brief shot of someone presumed innocent looking extremely guilty. You could have Mother Teresa do a walk and she would look like Tony Soprano.

For me, seeing how TV news operated was very interesting and instructive. More importantly, I went home with two TV news stories and a decent resume tape. Decent, of course, is a relative term. It was decent for a fledgling reporter with no TV experience applying to tiny TV markets. In real news terms, it was a terrible tape, and my writing and on-air performances were horrendous.

I had no idea how to do a TV story. I thought it was like a radio story but with pictures. In fact, I arrogantly assumed that I had the hard part figured out already. That is, I thought I knew how to be a reporter — how to interview people, gather facts, and put it all together — and figured all I had to learn was how to put on makeup and keep my tie on straight. Needless to say, I was wrong. Radio and print reporting didn't even begin to teach me what I needed to know to be a TV reporter, and especially didn't teach me how to be a one-man band where you shoot and edit your own material. Reality would be a rude awakening, but I only learned this after I got a job. First, I had to find one.

Chapter 5

The Great Paul Spelman Job Tour

In general, there are two ways to go about getting a job as an on-air TV reporter. Neither is particularly effective. The first approach is to do it horizontally. By that I don't mean relaxing your moral standards on the news director's couch, I mean getting a job at a station behind the scenes and then trying to work your way on the air. It is a thousand times easier to get an off-air job in TV, such as a producer or production assistant, than it is to get an on-air position. Off-air jobs often go to people straight out of college. At the station I worked at in Knoxville, the producer of our six o'clock news (our most important show, our "show of record" so to speak) had graduated from the University of Tennessee a few months earlier. I had actually visited her class of broadcasting students, and less than 12 months later, she was reading my scripts and telling me what to do. She did a good job, too, but you would think that TV stations would be hesitant to hand the reins of their most important newscast to a 22-year old with little TV experience. They're not. In local news, this isn't unusual.

That's because it's hard for stations to find enough producers. Producing a local newscast involves setting up the order of the stories and writing anchor segues from one story to another. It also involves timing the stories and making sure everything fits together and is well paced. A good producer is as important as a good reporter, often more so, but not a lot of people want to do it. It's a lot of work for not a lot of pay in order for others (the on-air people) to get the credit. If you don't hanker for the limelight, producing can be a great TV career. Producers are always in demand, so they get hired quickly and move up much faster than on-air reporters. Producers can also start out in bigger markets. There are plenty of producers who launched their careers in Chicago and Atlanta. By contrast, most on-air reporters start in places like Steubenville, Ohio.

But as for using a producing job to slide into an on-air reporting career, I'm not fond of the practice, especially if it's done to avoid working in a small market. That, of course, is why people try it. They don't want to spend the time in Steubenville, so they get jobs as producers in Miami or Philadelphia and hope to work their way on air by showing what good workers they are and by constantly asking the news director to give them a shot in the field. People who start out this way don't learn a lot of the lessons you glean from small markets. They also don't get to work out their mistakes where fewer people can see them. On the other hand, they also don't pick up some of the bad habits you get into in small markets, where understaffing makes shortcuts a matter of necessity.

Besides the issue of training, though, I   find it a bit deceptive to apply for a producing job knowing you want to be a reporter and will leave as soon as someone offers you an on-air position. It also gets really annoying working with producers who spend all of their time begging the news director to let them on the air, constantly making remarks like, "I could have done just as good a live shot as that reporter. Why won't they give me a chance?" I worked with a producer like that, and let me tell you, it gets old. Then again, she was finally allowed a few chances on air, did a good job, and ultimately became part of the permanent on-air staff. I think she's an anchor now. The squeaky wheel got the grease. But it always seemed a bit oily to me.

A lot of people try the lateral technique, though, and sometimes it works. There are network reporters who started in off-air positions and never spent a day in small markets. As far as I can tell, they do a good job. I'm sure some of my dislike for this method is based on resentment. I had to pay my dues and suffer in a small market, so they should too, right? I expect I would feel differently if the sideways slide was the strategy I selected for getting my first TV reporting job.

Instead, I tried the traditional vertical approach. That's where you get a job in a small market as an on-air reporter and work your way up through bigger and bigger markets, always as a reporter. It's not easy to get that first on-air reporting job, but an applicant with little or no TV experience at least has a shot of getting hired in Utica, New York, or Bangor, Maine. And I did have my brilliant asbestos and fire-bomber tape.

So I started sending out tapes from Colorado. I put together dozens of news director "care packages," each one complete with a videotape with my two New York stories, an audiotape with a few radio stories, and a plastic folder with 10 newspaper clippings. It was a veritable smorgasbord of Spelman stories, and each package cost about $12 to send out. It was also an enormous waste of time and money, because most news directors were only going to look at the videotape and throw the rest in the trash bin. Some probably threw the whole thing in the trash, on the theory that the thicker the package the thicker the applicant. But I didn't know that and, besides, I was prouder of my radio and newspaper work than I was of my two days pretending to be Jon Dienst, so I wanted to include that material.

I mailed these packages all over the place, and when I say all over, I mean all over. Any TV market smaller than 90 was a target. Care packages went out to Binghamton, New York (market 154), LaCrosse, Wisconsin (123), Columbus Georgia (126), Charleston, South Carolina (105), and Bluefield, West Virginia (149), just to name a few. They also went to stations

69

in Florida, Kansas, Nebraska, Massachusetts, Maryland, Maine, Missouri, Montana, Oregon, Virginia, and Washington. I was willing to go almost anywhere. All I wanted was a job; a place to cut my teeth and get some TV experience.

I also paid for a subscriber service called *Media Line*, a telephone recording system where TV stations would list on-air job openings. For $40, I got six weeks of access, updated every two days. It sounds great, except that everyone else who wanted a TV reporting job also subscribed to *Media Line*, so whenever there was a new listing, my tape arrived with a hundred others. Even in really, really small markets, stations get about 60 tapes for each reporter opening, according to one survey of news directors.

All in all, I sent out about 25 care packages and got one response. That was a brief phone message from a TV news director in Macon, Georgia, named Dodie Cantrell. I liked the musical sound of her name, but that's about all I can tell you about her because when I called back she was too busy to talk. She promised to get back to me but I guess things never quieted down enough. I still have no idea why she called, perhaps to advise me not to go into the business. Since hers was the *only* response I ever got from my mass mailings, I still think fondly of her.

After several months of this, I reached the conclusion that applying by mail wasn't getting me anywhere and was wasting a lot of money. So following the poker maxim that you should either raise or fold, I chose to up the ante and really throw money at getting a job. I decided to quit both of my jobs in Colorado and take an extended road trip in search of an on-air position. TV news or bust.

The reasoning behind this was that stations receive so many unsolicited tapes that it was exceedingly unlikely they would pick mine out of the pile. I needed some way to stand out, and the way to do that was to visit in person. I had also noticed that whenever there was an opening listed on *Media Line*, it often turned out that the station already had a candidate in mind. I'd hear of a new reporter position listed, only to call the next day and find out that it had already been filled. I decided I needed to make my mark with a news director before they had an opening so I'd be next in line.

So I crammed everything I owned into the back of my new used pickup truck and headed east from Colorado. Thus began the *Great Paul Spelman Job Tour, Summer of '94*. You may have seen the posters. The plan, first suggested to me by a Chicago reporter I talked to, was to visit as many small markets as I could in person. Face-to-face meetings give you a better chance of breaking through the clutter of tapes. I would then follow up my visit with letters, phone calls, and threats, if necessary.

I started out with cities relatively close to my family in New York. I hit stations in Utica and Binghamton, Burlington and Springfield. Later on, I moved south through Virginia, the Carolinas, Georgia, and Tennessee. If you live in a small East Coast city or town that has a TV station, I probably stopped there. It didn't matter if I had already sent a tape. I figured that since the station never responded, they probably wouldn't remember that they had already turned me down.

My method was fairly simple. First, I'd map out my route, selecting the stations and cities I wanted to target. Then, when I was a day or two's driving distance away, I'd call up a station news director, usually from a roadside gas station pay phone. It often took several tries to get through, so I'd call three times a day, at 10:00, 1:00, and 3:00. I didn't want to call too early, when they might be busy getting their day planned out. I also didn't want to call too late, because news directors tend to get antsy in the afternoon as their show approaches and are noticeably cooler toward inexperienced reporters hassling them about employment prospects.

Whenever I managed to get a news director on the line, I'd explain (shouting to be heard above the din of the roadside traffic and announcements that "pump six is not operational, please move to seven") that I was a radio and newspaper reporter from Colorado now looking for TV work. And since, by happy coincidence, I just happened to be driving through Florence South Carolina Augusta Georgia Bristol Virginia Fill-In-The-Blank Small Market this week anyway, how about if I stopped by, introduced myself, and dropped off a resume tape?

I doubt they were fooled about my presence there. After all, what would a New York City native, most recently working in Telluride, Colorado, be doing in Albany, Georgia? But despite the transparency of my motives, news directors were fairly receptive. They agreed to see me about two-thirds of the time, although I use the word "see" in its most literal sense. Often they'd meet me in the lobby, take my tape and escort me to the parking lot. Sometimes they gave me coffee and then escorted me to the parking lot. But that was okay; all I wanted was some way to break through the clutter, and this brief face-to-face visit accomplished that feat. At least this way, a news director would be able to put a face to my name the next few times I phoned. Of course, being able to describe what I looked like would also make it easier to file a restraining order against me, but sometimes you have to take your chances.

I found that I could never predict what sort of a reception I'd receive. Sometimes I handed over my tape and was quickly shown the door. Don't let it hit you on the way out, fella. Other times, news directors would chat with me for so long that I began to think they were very lonely. Sometimes my reception varied depending on what time of day it was. At WCAX in Burlington, Vermont, the news director, Marselis Parsons, was quite gruff when I phoned at 10:00, repeatedly telling me that he wouldn't have time to talk but I was welcome to drop off my tape. Maybe he hadn't had his coffee yet, because when I arrived around noon, he spent an hour and a half with me, pleasantly discussing journalism and showing me around his station.

Another news director, who I remember only as Stewart, was quite friendly over the phone, telling me to stop by as soon as I arrived in town. When I did, his secretary informed me that the news director had gone on vacation for the entire week. No wonder he was in such a good mood when I called. In a similar vein, one news director told me to drop my tape at the reception desk because he would be "tied up in meetings" all day. When I arrived, the receptionist explained that he had already "left for the beach."

Despite these occasional blow-offs, on the whole I'd say most news directors were encouraging, if not overly enthusiastic about my chances. Most said they would consider me should anything open up, but they had no idea when that would be. It also seemed that many demanded higher standards from job applicants than they tolerated on their newscasts, although that may just have been sour grapes on my part.

I also tried to utilize every connection I could think of. I learned a lot about connections. Before this experience, I had always thought "connections" meant having a congressman for an uncle or living next door to Cokie Roberts. Those are good kinds of connections. I didn't have those. But I quickly learned that you don't need a "real" connection to create a workable one. For instance, I had my friend Jon ask around his NY1 newsroom to find out where other reporters had gotten their first TV job. One reporter said Fort Myers, Florida, at a small station called WINK. Jon's colleague told me the name of a producer there, so I called the producer and dropped the NY1 reporter's name. After the producer talked with me for a bit, he suggested I contact his news director and said I could use *his* name. Essentially, I created a connection where there wasn't one. It wasn't as good as knowing Cokie Roberts, but the WINK news director was more likely to give consideration to my tape than to an unsolicited one tossed over the transom simply because it had the implied recommendation of someone he knew and worked with. On the other hand, I didn't get a job at WINK, so take all of this for what it's worth.

But unless you are a Kennedy or a Bush, or actually do live next to Cokie Roberts, you have to rely on these tenuous connections. Beware, though, it can lead to some awkward moments if the interviewer asks pointed questions about the person whose name you just dropped. "Oh, you know Mary. That's swell. Has she had her baby yet?" Hmm. "Last time I heard, everything was well," may be your best response.

I quickly grew accustomed to calling people I'd never met and pitching myself. This is a skill that is essential if you actually do land a job as a reporter, since you have to overcome initial resistance from strangers you want to interview. You may only have a few seconds to convince them that you are not a maniac. For my job tour, it was like being a salesman or telemarketer, except that I was selling myself as opposed to some miracle hair-loss remedy. It was similar, however, in that I was offering something they usually didn't want.

I couldn't let that deter me, though, and I developed a routine, both for the words I spoke, and for what I did before and after my trip to the station. Beforehand, I'd always drive to the city and scope out the exact location of the station so I wouldn't be late. Then I'd scout out a place to change clothes. This was vitally important because it was the middle of a brutally hot summer and my pickup truck didn't have air-conditioning. Living in the mountains of Colorado, I hadn't even realized I had purchased a vehicle without air-conditioning until I left to go east. I hit Kansas and started to sweat. Uh, oh. Where's that air-conditioner button?

For my TV tour, the lack of AC was exacerbated by the fact that the majority of small East Coast TV markets are in the South. There's nothing like driving through Augusta, Georgia, in August in a suit and tie and a non-air-conditioned pickup truck. I couldn't even roll down the windows very far, because if I did I'd arrive looking a bit too windblown for a job where you are supposed to have stationary hair.

To deal with this problem, I came up with a quick-change routine I called my Reverse Clark Kent. I'd locate a fast-food restaurant or shopping mall not far from the station, then change into my suit and tie in a public restroom. Then I'd drive to the interview, tell them I was good enough, smart enough, and doggone it, people liked me, and immediately return to the public restroom and change back, hopefully before my suit was soaked through with sweat. I'm sure I sparked some curiosity among restaurant workers. At one city, where I had two interviews on the same day and both were near the same Hardees, the workers there must have wondered if I was casing the place.

Other times I would use a public library for the quick change. One time I made the mistake of glancing at one of those career advice books they have in the self-help section. Finding out there are fewer than 10,000 working TV reporters in the whole country when you know there are six or seven times that number who graduate every year with journalism and broadcasting degrees doesn't make you feel cheerful about your chances.

After my interview and quick-change routine, I'd plot out the next small-market city and start making calls from the nearest pay phone. Thus began the whole process all over again.

All in all, it was an experience. I spent a little over six weeks on the road, with two brief pit stops back in New York to rest up and plan my next voyage. I had to learn to always think a couple of days ahead. I rarely knew precisely what I'd be doing on any given day, but I might know that the news director in Savannah had agreed to see me on Thursday, that I could get more resume tapes duplicated in Atlanta on Friday, get my shirt and jacket cleaned over the weekend, and meet with another news director in Columbus on Monday. Then it was on to Johnson City, Tennessee.

Johnson City was particularly memorable because the news director at WJHL, the local CBS affiliate, gave me a writing test and then proceeded to grill me with a pop quiz on current events. At first, he didn't reveal what he was doing; he just innocently asked a question or two about my home state.

"Oh, you're from New York, what's the name of that governor up there? I can't remember."

"You mean Governor Cuomo?"

"That's right, and you guys have that senator, what's his name again?"

"Moynihan? Or do you mean D'Amato?"

"D'amato. Yeah ...."

Soon he dropped all pretense that he was just inordinately curious about New York politics and started hitting me with all sorts of questions.

"Name the three branches of government. Is murder a state crime or a federal crime? Explain what GATT is in three sentences or less ..."

Amazingly, I got almost everything right, although I struggled with the GATT question. This was long before the General Agreement on Tariffs and Trade made any sort of splash in the media, but from somewhere in the deep recesses of my memory I recalled hearing that French farmers were upset over something called GATT. That can't be it, I thought, that's so obscure. Besides, French farmers are always upset. But I couldn't come up with anything else, so I hesitatingly offered, "Is GATT a treaty we have with France?"

"That's right. Among other countries," he replied, seeming moderately impressed.

He later apologized for putting me through this examination, but explained that he felt he had to test my knowledge or at some point I would embarrass his station. I asked him how I was doing. "Pretty good," he said, "Better than most people." Apparently not good enough to get a job, though.

Despite experiences like that, or perhaps because of them, that summer was exhilarating but also exhausting. It's tempting to look back nostalgically at this young reporter's rite of passage, but whenever I start to do so, my family reminds me that at the time, I swore I would never look back fondly on this period. To be honest, it wasn't a lot of fun. It was lonely and frustrating and hard.

It was also tremendously expensive. To do this sort of thing, you have to either have some money saved or be prepared to go heavily into debt. I had some money saved and was headed into debt by the time I finally landed a job. I tried to cut costs every way I could, mainly by mapping out where all my old college friends were living and then staying with them if they were within driving distance of a small-market station. I got to see a lot of people I hadn't seen in years.

I stayed with friends of my parents in Portland, Maine (driving distance of Bangor TV stations); friends of friends near Burlington, Vermont (Burlington and Plattsburgh stations); a fraternity buddy in Washington D.C. (driving distance of Harrisonburg and Charlottesville, Virginia markets); and other college friends in Wilmington, North Carolina (Wilmington and Myrtle Beach markets), Savannah, Georgia (Savannah market); and last but not least, Atlanta, the true mother lode of small-market proximity (driving distance from the Macon, Columbus, Augusta, and Albany markets).

But even with relatively few motel bills, I still had to shell out for gas, food and a constant supply of videotapes. I was also ringing up hefty long-distance phone charges since I had to keep calling the stations every few weeks to remind them that I was still interested in a job. I would be in South Carolina calling stations in New Hampshire and Maine to check in. I developed an index card system whereby I'd call a station and then place that station's card at the back of the pack. I generally called about four or five stations a day. When a card worked its way to the front again, it was time to give that station another call. It was a relatively efficient method but did nothing to lower my expenses. I figured that by the time I got a job, I'd be filling out my W-2 and filing for Chapter 7 at the same time.

In the end, I didn't have to file for bankruptcy, but it was close. I probably wouldn't have made it if I'd had any costly truck troubles. My trusty truck was nine years old when I started and seemed about 25 by the time I finished. In two months, I put over 8,000 miles on her. I ended up naming the truck "Proud Mary," a name that just popped into my head one day when I took the truck to an auto repair shop in

Wilmington, North Carolina after meeting with a news director. By that point, the truck was showing some signs of exhaustion. Nothing devastating, but it did require some maintenance. The truck was propped up on the lifts, but seemed to endure the indignity without complaint, sitting there proud and unbowed while far more glamorous and expensive vehicles — vehicles with AC — got much more attention.

I'm not normally a fan of giving names to inanimate objects. I don't call my bicycle "Steve" or have a pet name for my refrigerator. But when you've driven thousands of miles without any other company, you do develop something of a bond with your vehicle. By the end, I knew every noise and nuance of that truck by heart. I was also far too familiar with every musical tape I owned. When one song finished, I'd find myself humming the next one before the song even started.

I don't know how long-haul truckers do it. After all that time on the road by myself, I was starting to hallucinate. I began to see ominous portents all around me, foretelling whether my quest would succeed. Road signs declaring "Be Prepared to Stop" and "Rough Pavement Ahead" seemed like bad omens.

I was nearly ready to quit when I finally got a job offer from a station in Wilmington, North Carolina. By that point, I'd applied to some 53 stations and visited more than 25 in person. Several stations I'd applied to more than once. For WWAY, the station that offered me the job, I had sent three resume tapes and driven down twice in person. I was fortunate in that I was able to stay in Wilmington with a college friend, Jeff Goldblatt, who worked as a reporter/anchor for WECT, the other local station in the area. Despite my connection to Jeff (or maybe because of it), WECT and its news director expressed little interest in me. But the competitor, WWAY, was more encouraging. The WWAY news director, Jon Evans, didn't know Jeff personally, but knew of him, of course, so by mentioning Jeff's name I was able to appear more "TV worthy" by association. I interviewed with Jon a couple of times and even spent several hours with him visiting his station's bureau in Whiteville, about an hour's drive west of Wilmington.

Two weeks after my second visit to WWAY, I was back in New York trying to get my mind off my job search. I went to see a movie with my Dad. It was the film "Forrest Gump," and as the movie started and the camera swept out above what appeared to be a picturesque Southern city, I joked, "I probably interviewed there." I had. It was Savannah, not one of my more inspiring stops. In Savannah, one news director refused to see me, another talked with me but wasn't encouraging, and another told me over the phone that he'd see me but then walked past me in the station lobby without saying a word, leaving the receptionist to explain that he'd "left the station for the day to attend to some personal business." Maybe looking at me in the lobby was what he meant when he agreed to "see" me.

Back in New York, as I left the theater, I decided to check in with WWAY from a corner pay phone. I got through to Jon Evans, and when a taxi honked he asked where I was calling from. When I told him it was a New York City street corner, he replied, "Well, if you've got the guts to call from a New York City street corner, you've got the guts for the job. It's yours if you want it." Geez, if I had known that was all it took, I would have set up shop in a phone booth at 75th and Lexington long before then. I said yes.

Jon asked me when I could start, and I told him one week. I was actually afraid that if I asked for longer, he might give the job to someone else. I was also elated and eager to start.

And scared. A week later, I began the longest and loneliest year of my life.

Chapter 6

Whiteville

If you could "do over" part of your past, would you? I mean, really, who wouldn't want a chance to set the clock back and relive those carefree days of youth; revisit your college years, or get a romantic second chance with that high school classmate that got away or, more likely, never gave you the time of day?

But there are some experiences in life that are so difficult or unpleasant that nothing could entice you to go back to an earlier time if you then had to re-live that later experience. For me, that point of no return is Whiteville. There is nothing you could offer me, no rejuvenated physique, no increased hairline or decreased waistline, no second chance to reconsider an important decision or relive a great experience, that would make me want to return to a period pre-Whiteville if I then had to relive the year that I endured there.

The reason I spent a year in Whiteville, North Carolina, is that that's where my new employer, WWAY-TV, had an on-air reporter opening. WWAY is a small ABC affiliate based in Wilmington, North Carolina, a picturesque city on the Cape Fear River about 20 minutes from the Atlantic Ocean. The Wilmington area has beautiful beaches and a historic downtown section with old Southern mansions and a scenic riverfront.

Whiteville, on the other hand, has none of these things. Whiteville is located about an hour west of Wilmington in the flat swamplands of Southeastern North Carolina. Whiteville has hog farms and tobacco warehouses and a Wal-Mart. But Whiteville did have a small WWAY news bureau so that the Wilmington station could stay abreast of events farther afield.

The Whiteville bureau covered three counties, Columbus, Bladen, and Robeson, which included the communities of Elizabethtown, Bladenboro, Lumberton, Tabor City, and, of course, Whiteville. It was the job of "Whiteville Bureau Chief" that I was offered and gratefully accepted. Bureau Chief. It sounded quite lofty until I saw the town and the bureau and realized that I could have left the word "chief" off of my business cards and they would not have been any less accurate. I *was* the bureau, and wasn't chief of anybody.

Whiteville is really not a bad place, and I don't want to come down too hard on it. It is a small Southern community of about 5,000 people, mostly farmers, former farmers, and people who are friends of farmers. There's something cozy and traditional about the town, with a pleasant tree-lined main street and a small three- or four-block downtown section where teenagers still cruise in their cars on Friday and Saturday nights. The downtown on a Friday night looked like a scene straight out of *American Graffiti*, and it would take 20 minutes to travel four blocks. Especially during the fall football season, because Whiteville's biggest social activity every week was the Friday night high school game. Whiteville's second biggest social event every week was the Sunday church service.

Despite the Friday night cruising ritual, businesses in Whiteville's downtown were struggling, as they are in so many small towns, after the downtown was bypassed by a road leading straight to the Wal-Mart outside of town. What remained downtown were a number of shuttered department stores; a classic old drugstore still in possession of an ice cream counter; a small greasy spoon specializing in hot dogs topped with chili and coleslaw; a decrepit movie theater; and an abandoned train depot. As the county seat, Whiteville also had a few government buildings, including a police department and a courthouse. The courthouse was classic Southern style, with traditional white columns and steps leading up to the door. It looked as though it could have been featured in *In the Heat of the Night*, the film and TV series about small-town law enforcement in the 1960s. It wasn't, but it was used as a set for the peculiarly named TV movie, *Bastard out of Carolina*. I never saw this, though, so I have no idea how the courthouse was featured.

Whiteville also had one modern building, a hospital, by far the biggest structure within a 50-mile radius. It was four or five stories tall, and may well have been the only building in Whiteville with an elevator.

As for the area outside of town, that was swampland and farmland, the latter mostly tobacco, cotton, and wheat, with a few other fruits and vegetables here and there. There were also a rapidly growing number of hog farms, often operated by former tobacco growers looking for a more promising and less controversial product. They didn't get it, unfortunately, as hog farming became just as controversial as tobacco, but for different reasons. With tobacco, it is the product that's the problem; with hog farming, it's the by-product. Hog waste has a tendency to smell bad and damage the environment. As one resident complained to me, "Them hogs is more dangerous than tobacca."

All in all, there's nothing wrong with Whiteville and that part of North Carolina except that it was a hard place for me to live at that stage of my life. Raised as a city kid in New York and educated at a Northeastern liberal arts university, I was unaccustomed to the small Southern town way of doing things. I felt about as out of place as you can get.

I had lived in a small community before, since Telluride actually had fewer residents than Whiteville. But Telluride had a certain cosmopolitan sensibility about it. Most people in ski towns are college educated and relatively affluent. Or at least they were affluent until they voluntarily abandoned their privileged upbringings in order to live in their car and ski all the time. Whiteville, on the other hand, had a small number of well-educated, well-off white families, and a far larger number of uneducated farmers and poor African-Americans. I say uneducated only in the classically trained manner. Many Whiteville residents knew an enormous amount about farming and faith and life in general. But they weren't as conversant in art and literature and traditional rules of grammar. It was the kind of town where the most high-brow beer you could find was a Miller Genuine Draft, and where, if covering an armed robbery, I learned it was vitally important to ask if the victim returned fire.

Here I was, a native New Yorker dropped into this town without any friends, contacts, or even co-workers. I worked alone, lived alone, and slept alone. Admittedly, some of this isolation was my own choosing. I did not make a great effort to fit in, because I secretly hoped that I wouldn't be sticking around. Jon Evans had told me to expect to remain in Whiteville for at least a year, but I was hoping it would be shorter. My dream was that I would get a few stories under my belt and show the station how much potential I had, and the station would then decide to immediately move me to Wilmington. It would be a battlefield promotion of sorts. This was arrogant and presumptuous of me, and I'm sure I came across as a snobby city slicker, looking down upon these Whiteville "country rubes."

On the other hand, there really wasn't much of a social scene available for me in Whiteville anyway, since there were very few unmarried professionals, or unmarried anyone over the age of 17. Whiteville also had just two "nightspots" where I could meet other people. These weren't genuine taverns or clubs, but rather a couple of local restaurants that also happened to serve beer. When one of these restaurants burned down a few months into my stay, it cut my social opportunities in half.

The real social life in Whiteville centered around the (at last count) 86 local churches, the majority of them Southern Baptist. When a new person arrived in town, Whiteville residents usually took it upon themselves to get the newcomer settled into the appropriate devotional facility. This was partly for the newcomer's benefit, and partly so that residents had a way of identifying you. "Who's that?" you would ask about some new arrival. "That's John Smith," they'd reply, "he attends First Methodist."

Once settled in, social activity revolved around the church. Parties, get-togethers, social functions — it all involved the members of the congregation. That doesn't mean Whiteville residents didn't like to carouse and have fun. It's just that they had fun with people from their church. Once, when I was complaining about my lack of social opportunities — in other words, eligible women to date — a Whiteville man explained, "Son, if you want to get laid in this town, you've got to go to church." This may also have explained a sign situated outside one Whiteville church imploring passersby to "Let Jesus Fix Your Achy Breaky Heart."

All of this was disheartening for me, a half-Irish, half-Jewish New Yorker whose only religious experiences came from attending classmates' bar mitzvahs. My mother had been raised Catholic but stopped attending church after marrying my father, a Jew by ancestry but under the mistaken impression that he is Norwegian. (Legend has it I escaped being named Sven Olaf only by a firm stand by my mother.) It's safe to say that my Dad did not put a lot of emphasis on instilling me with religious fervor.

While this sort of background was certainly unremarkable in New York City, it definitely was in Whiteville. I was regarded as something of a curiosity, if not an outright heathen. Whiteville and Columbus County did not have the most admirable track record for tolerance and diversity. Back in the 1950s, the Ku Klux Klan was fairly popular in the area, and more than 100 local residents were arrested for Klan activities. I should note that two Columbus County newspapers won Pulitzer Prizes for taking courageous public stands against the Klan, but the fact that they had to take such stands says something.

By the time I got there, nobody was wearing white hoods around, at least not in public. There were, however, some less than progressive views lingering just below the surface. The "N" word could be heard with unsettling frequency, even from local leaders, and I once heard a Columbus County Commissioner ask, in the middle of a public meeting, if it wouldn't be possible to "Jew down" a building contractor who was demanding a more reasonable wage. Oddly enough, I don't think the commissioner actually meant anything nasty or derogatory toward my family tribe when he said this, the term was just part of his vernacular as a way to describe hard bargaining. Nobody else at the meeting batted an eye.

To make me feel even more isolated in Whiteville, I was also completely alone at work. For most of my time in Whiteville, I did not have a single colleague at the bureau.

The bureau itself was a small three-room office in a dingy strip mall across the street from the county courthouse. The bureau's front two rooms had at one point been occupied by a small dress shop, but when I arrived they were vacant. These empty rooms served as my lobby and reception area. A third, inner room was a combination office, editing room, and TV studio rolled into one. It was a windowless rectangle about 20 feet long and 15 feet wide, with a desk, a fax machine, a couch, a TV, and a video camera that looked as though it dated back to the days of Jack Benny. There was also an editing desk, complete with two antiquated ¾-inch professional videotape recorders, a microphone, and a small sound mixer. The walls were blank except for two framed publicity stills of Peter Jennings and Hugh Downs, apparently taken sometime in the 1970s, judging by the width of their ties. Since I can assure you that neither one had ever set foot inside the Whiteville bureau, I can only guess that these photos were meant to either impress visitors or inspire the current inhabitant of the bureau. Off to the side of the room, there was a small bathroom of about equal inspirational value.

The room also had two high-intensity lights focused on a chair which doubled as the news set. So I would edit a story, feed it back to the main station via a microwave transmitter, then sit in the chair and perform a live introduction into the camera. The camera itself was unmanned and on a tripod, so I had pieces of tape marked on the floor designating precisely where to sit. Once in position, I couldn't move more than an inch or two or else I'd slide out of the shot. Another problem was that the editing desks were positioned right behind the news set. This provided a newsy looking backdrop but meant that I couldn't use the editing machines if someone else had to go live from the bureau and sit in the chair. This wasn't ordinarily a problem since, as I've mentioned, I worked by myself, but on rare occasions the station sports anchors would schedule live interviews with area high school football coaches, who would invariably show up just as I was trying to finish a story by my deadline.

The sports anchors would almost always neglect to warn me ahead of time, so I'd be frantically trying to finish my piece, thinking I had another fifteen minutes, and in would walk some high school coach ready for his 60 seconds of TV glory. I'd set him up in the chair facing the camera, then kneel down behind him and keep editing, right up until the last second before he went live. Then I'd jump to the side, let him talk about his big victory over East Columbus High, and then jump back in and finish editing while he disentangled himself from the microphone and found his way out the door.

That was pretty much the way everything was at the bureau — rudimentary but workable. If you are wondering where my computer was, keep wondering. I wondered the same thing. There wasn't one, at least when I first arrived. I was eventually given a computer, but for my first four or five months I had to rely on my own means to get stories written. The previous bureau chief had written her stories in longhand and then faxed them to the station for editorial approval. This wasn't an option for me because my longhand is so illegible it's often mistaken for shorthand. I can't decipher it out myself if it's been more than an hour or two since I wrote it down. So I brought in an old electric typewriter I had lugged to college nine years earlier. The typewriter couldn't edit or erase so I had to type my stories perfectly in one shot.

Quite frankly, I don't understand how people used to write books before computers made it possible to delete and rewrite. My first drafts were and are invariably pathetic, and I concur with the maxim that "there is no such thing as writing, there's only rewriting." I usually get things presentable by the fourth or fifth edit. This book is closer to four or five hundred. In Whiteville, my lack of a computer meant that I didn't have a chance to re-write, so before typing a single sentence, I'd have to sit and ponder and deliberate and try to make sure that what I wrote was precisely what I wanted to say. Usually I'd end up throwing away four or five pages with just one or two sentences on them. By the time I finished, the bureau floor was covered with crumpled up paper. My task got even more interesting when I ran out of typing ribbon. I had to type my story on a piece of carbon paper, and couldn't see what I had written until I finished and lifted the carbon sheet.

Working like this in a small, windowless office is how I spent the better part of eleven months. The only time I wasn't at the bureau was when I was out on a story. This was fairly often, though, because I had a lot of driving to do. I had to monitor three large counties, Bladen, Columbus, and Robeson, and cover every newsworthy story by myself.

The counties consisted mostly of rural farmland with nearly every crop you can imagine. There was tobacco, corn, cotton, wheat, potatoes, watermelons, strawberries, blueberries, yams, soybeans, you name it. If it grows, they grew it. There were also hog, chicken, and turkey farms, not to mention an ostrich ranch or two. Although the three counties had pretty much the same crops, each county had its own distinct feel to it. Columbus County was the least cosmopolitan. Parts of the southeastern region of the county, a densely forested and swampy area near the South Carolina border, brought to mind the movie *Deliverance*. There was one community in particular, in the heart of something called the Green Swamp, which had been relatively isolated for centuries and remained so when I got there despite a paved road that now made the area more accessible. The community was called Crusoe Island, and although technically not an island, it had only one way in and out. Residents there spoke with a peculiar sing-song delivery that some believe dates back to Olde English. There's even some speculation that Crusoe residents are descendants of Roanoke's Lost Colony. Others suggest that their ancestors were likely French settlers fleeing Haiti during the slave insurrections of the late 1700s. No one knows for sure, and everything about that area was a bit murky. It was also said that people there didn't take kindly to strangers, and I was strongly warned not to go there by myself.

Other parts of Columbus County were more welcoming but still seemed foreign to me. In some areas, everybody seemed to have the same last name. I got so I could tell where someone lived by their surname. Anyone named Gore, for instance, hailed from the southwestern part of Columbus County, near a town called Tabor City. I recall a story there about one Gore charged with vandalizing a business owned by another Gore, while the trial was presided over by a judge named Gore. None of these folks were related, and yet nobody thought it the slightest bit unusual that they all had the same last name.

Whiteville, to the north, was the county's "metropolis," and something of a tobacco hub. Whiteville had several old tobacco warehouses where you could hear the prattle of auctioneers winding their way through bales of leafy tobacco with big 'bacca company buyers right behind them. These warehouses fascinated me, with rows upon rows of golden leaves and a wonderful aroma of raw tobacco. As a reluctantly reformed ex-smoker, I would sometimes go inside these warehouses just to see if I could get a nicotine buzz without lighting up. Once I actually took a nibble of some raw tobacco and felt nauseous for hours.

The leadership in Columbus County was very good-old-boyish, with a bunch of white middle-aged men making most of the decisions from their perch on the County Commission. A lot of power also lay with the sheriff, a sort of old-style "High Sheriff" with influence extending far beyond normal law enforcement matters. The sheriff's department in Columbus County had been under Democratic control since the Civil War, but these kind of Southern Democrats made Northern Republicans look like knee-jerk liberals.

Apart from Columbus County, my other main coverage area was Bladen County, about 25 minutes north of Whiteville and centered on the county seat of Elizabethtown. Bladen was a much like Columbus County but less dependent on tobacco. Bladen had a few other big industries including a textile plant, a peanut-processing firm (which supplied nuts to major league baseball teams), and a huge Smithfield hog processing facility in the town of Tar Heel. It was the biggest hog slaughtering facility in the United States. Perhaps due to these plants, Bladen County seemed a bit more prosperous and cosmopolitan than Columbus County and more accepting of a Yankee-in-exile such as myself.

The third and final county in my coverage area was Robeson County. It was the farthest from Wilmington, with Lumberton, the county seat, about 40 minutes farther west and north of Whiteville, a full hour and 40 minutes from Wilmington. Robeson was considered a fringe county, meaning some of it was actually outside of the Wilmington TV market. The Wilmington TV market shared Robeson County with the Florence/Myrtle Beach TV market, and Lumberton residents had their choice of watching Wilmington TV news, Myrtle Beach TV news and Raleigh/Durham TV news. Because of this, and because of the distance, I didn't do as many stories in Robeson County as I did in Bladen and Columbus counties. Which was probably a good thing, because Robeson County was a very odd place.

It is probably best known, unfortunately, as the place where Michael Jordan's father was killed. James Jordan pulled off the road to get some sleep at a rest stop outside of Lumberton and was murdered in his car by two local youths looking for someone to rob. Much of my time in Robeson County was spent covering pretrial hearings for the two young men accused in that case.

You shouldn't judge a community by one incident, but Robeson could be a rough place. While Lumberton was the most populous of my three county seats, in many ways it was the least sophisticated. The population was very poor, and more than once I did stories about Lumberton residents whose homes flooded every single year but couldn't afford to move. They had actually come to accept four inches of water in their living rooms as a ritual occurrence, something you dealt with every year much like cleaning out your gutters.

Robeson County also had some racial issues. The county was an unusual mix of almost exactly one-third white, one-third black, and one-third Lumbee Indian. If you walked into any store, restaurant, or government facility in Lumberton, you were as likely to be greeted by a Lumbee as by anyone else.

The Lumbees are an unusual tribe. There are about 40,000 members, and it is the largest tribe east of the Mississippi River. Yet they still don't have full recognition from the federal government, and their name isn't of Native American origin — it comes from the Lumber River, which winds its way through Robeson County. Just as residents of Columbus County often had the same name, the Lumbees have practically just four: Oxendine, Chavis, Britt, and Locklear. Where they got these I have no idea, but these names were everywhere, especially the name Locklear. You cannot turn around in Lumberton without bumping into a Locklear, and while I imagine Heather Locklear might be surprised to hear this, many Lumberton residents claim the fair-haired Hollywood beauty as one of their own because of her name.

The three ethnic groups pretty much kept to themselves in Robeson County, but I guess relations could get testy. One of our sports anchors once went to do a feature on a Robeson county football team and asked the coach if he could interview "a couple" of his players. "You can't do that," the coach replied. "You can interview three. You can interview six. You can interview nine. But whatever it is, there will be equal numbers of white, black, and Indian, and you'll put them all on the air or you'll never do a story here again."

*　　*　　*

Whether I was covering a story in Robeson, Bladen, or Columbus county, my workday was long and challenging, made much more so by the fact that I didn't have the foggiest idea what I was doing. Despite my two-day stint shadowing Dienst in New York, I really had no idea how to do a TV story and how to operate the equipment. And in Whiteville, I was a one-man band. While Jon had done his best to give me a crash course in the basics, I had only the vaguest notion of which buttons to push and how to adjust a camera's sound, color, and focus.

In this, I must admit I misled the WWAY news director during my job interview, professing a proficiency I did not possess. A one-man band in TV lingo means you do all your own filming and editing as well as reporting. It's become increasingly common in smaller markets, and even sometimes in bigger markets, because it allows the stations to hire fewer photographers and editors. Jon Evans wanted a one-man band reporter, so that's what I told him I was. I found out later that Jon actually told another applicant she lost out to me because I had "more video expertise." This made me feel a tad guilty but my guilt was assuaged considerably by the fact that the other applicant somehow ended up getting her first on-air job soon after in Raleigh, North Carolina, market 29, 115 spots ahead of me. The fact that she was a very attractive blonde with a winsome personality probably didn't hurt.

Naturally, I was concerned that my inability to operate the equipment would be a problem, but Dienst assured me that it wasn't difficult and I would pick it up quickly. In some ways that's true; shooting and editing is not rocket science. But like so many aspects of TV news, there are an enormous number of things that can go wrong. Photographers are rarely noticed or credited if everything turns out right, but one mistake and the video is unusable. Which means your story is unviewable. Which is a problem. I had to learn everything in a hurry and there was a lot to learn.

First off, I had to make sure the lens had the correct filter, since a professional camera uses different filters depending on whether you are inside, outside, outside on a cloudy day, or outside in bright sunshine. Then I had to "white balance," which involves aiming the lens at something white, such as a piece of paper, until the camera determines the "color" of the white. White balancing is sort of like telling the camera, "Hey, this is what white looks like in this light," and the camera says, "Oh, if that's what white looks like, now I know what everything else should look like." When I forgot to white balance, my video came out blue, which is sometimes referred to as "Smurfing," and isn't recommended if you want to stay employed. It happens, though. Even in big markets, Smurfed video occasionally makes it on air. In Whiteville, it was more than occasional.

In addition to figuring out the filter and white balance, I also had to figure out how to focus and "back-focus." The way you focus a professional video camera is by zooming in as close as you can, focusing until everything looks sharp, and then pulling back out again. If the camera's back-focus is accurate, everything should stay sharp when you zoom back out. If the back focus is out of whack, everything goes blurry and you have a problem. Finally, I had to make sure that the camera was level when I shot or else viewers would get vertigo looking at a slanted picture.

95

These are just the rudimentary basics you have to get right before you even start shooting. Then I had to learn to properly frame the shot, which is extremely important since, unlike with a still photograph, I couldn't crop the picture afterward. In framing, you want to make sure the shot has everything you want — such as the crime scene tape and the flashing patrol car lights — and doesn't have anything you don't want — such as your news car or a gleeful group of teenagers waving "Hi Mom."

When conducting an interview, you also have to learn to place the interviewee slightly off-center, so that it appears as if they're talking to someone and not doing a reality TV confessional. There's an art to framing a shot, and it's something I can't fully explain since I never fully mastered it. It is especially tough as a one-man band to frame yourself for your stand-up, since you can't look through the viewfinder and stand in front of the camera at the same time. Different reporters have different techniques for shooting their own stand-up. I knew one reporter who tied a six-foot long string to his camera, then set his camera's focus at six feet and walked out in front holding the string. When the string got tight, he turned around.

That string isn't going to help you, though, if the camera is focused too high, too low, or off to the side. I would usually focus on a portable light stand I had and then walk around and push the stand out of the way. I can't tell you how many times I shot numerous stand-ups only to discover later that they were all unusable, with part of my face out of focus or out of the picture or with my head in the shot but no neck, making it appear as though I was a peeping Tom trying to peer in through a high window.

My problems were exacerbated by the fact that I often messed up the words to my stand-up, which meant that sometimes it took me 15 or 20 tries to get it right. This was okay if I had the time, but I rarely had that luxury. Repeated mess-ups also caused problems in other ways. One time I was doing a story about a town garbage collection problem and had this brilliant idea to do a stand-up in which I'd toss a garbage bag into a dumpster while talking to the camera, thereby *demonstrating* what residents would have to do for themselves if the trash problem continued. This wasn't a bad idea. It is good if you can demonstrate things in your stand-up. It almost makes it seem as if there is a point to your being there. The problem was that I flubbed my lines the first time I tried it, and my flub occurred after I had tossed the garbage bag into the dumpster. And I only had one bag. Which meant that to try a second take, I had to climb into the dumpster in my suit to retrieve my prop. I smelled a bit sharp the rest of the day. It was one of the few times I was glad to be by myself all day.

Sometimes I'd ask bystanders to look through the viewfinder and tell me if everything looked okay. The problem here was that most people who don't work in TV don't know what to look for. One time I was assured I looked fine only to return to the bureau and find, when I looked at the tape, that my head completely cut off and the rest of my body off-center. Evidently the bystander thought I worked for the Ichabod Crane Network. Or perhaps she felt I looked better that way.

As for interviewing people as a one-man band, it's easier than shooting your own stand-up, but still challenging. There are two ways to do it. One is called "off the shoulder," in which I'd hold the camera with my right arm and the microphone with my left. I'd ask the person a question, then move my head slightly while they responded so I could glance through the viewfinder and make sure they were in the frame. At the same time, you want to keep eye contact with the person so they keep talking. Which means I had to learn to be like one of those military helicopter pilots who has each eye looking at a different thing at the same time. Another drawback to interviewing off the shoulder is that the interviewee has to be very close to you because your arm holding the microphone can reach only so far. By being so close, the interviewee tends to look large and distorted in the lens. Sometimes I'd end up putting moon people on TV.

The other way to do a one-man band interview is to put the camera on a tripod, push "record," and walk around in front with the microphone. This requires less physical dexterity and actually looks better when you get it right, but it also requires faith that the person you are speaking to won't move or shift during the entire interview. If they move, they stray out of the shot, a fact that you are blissfully unaware of because you're out in front with the microphone asking questions. I got in the habit of telling people that they could sway all they wanted but "please, please, just don't move your feet." I repeated this mantra so often that some people saw me coming and yelled out, "I won't move my feet! I promise. I won't move my feet!"

No matter which method I tried, I could also mess up by hitting the record button at the wrong time. Pushing record when you want to record sounds fairly straightforward, but with some cameras, like the one I had in Whiteville, there was no way I could tell if it was actually recording because the recording indicator was broken. This led to the dreaded "double-click," where I would accidentally hit the record button twice, thus turning the camera on *and then off*.

It usually happened when I accidentally knocked the button while unloading the gear from the car. I'd then carry all the equipment in for the interview, set everything up, interview the person for 20 minutes, pack up and drive back to the bureau, only to find I had some riveting "Blair Witch"-type footage of the ground as I unloaded the gear, the hallway as I carried everything in, and the chair as I set up for the interview. Then, just as the council member or police chief sat down and I pushed the record button a second time, (believing I was doing so for the first time), the camera would shut off, leaving me with nothing I could put on the air.

Even if I got all the video stuff right, I had to worry about the audio, too, of course. A professional camera generally has two microphones, one for doing interviews, another for picking up ambient, or natural sound, such as the sound of a bird, or, more often, a large semi going by at full speed while you're trying to interview someone by the side of the road. If I had my sound level too high on either of the mikes, the recorded sound became distorted. If it was too low, I'd have to crank it back up in the studio, and again — distorted.

All in all, being a one-man band gives you an awful lot to think about. All I needed to do was mishandle or forget about one thing and I could waste an interview and perhaps ruin my whole story. And with some items, there was no way I could tell I'd messed up until I got back to the bureau hours later.

That was just dealing with the basics. When you get more sophisticated as a TV photographer, you start thinking about cutaways and shot sequencing and how to comply with the "180-degree rule" so you can edit without jarring jump cuts. I actually came to understand some of this stuff eventually, but for a long time I was lost. I had my hands full trying to remember to white balance and check the sound level. I actually wrote out a detailed checklist of things to do every time before shooting, and would studiously consult it before heading out on a story. I also wrote out a list of necessary equipment to take whenever I left the bureau; things like the microphone, tripod, videotape, and batteries. I taped this list to my car's rearview mirror so I'd see it every time I left the parking lot. You'd be amazed how easy it is to leave vital gear behind when you're in a hurry to get to breaking news. I once drove 45 minutes into Robeson County to cover some news event only to find that I'd forgotten to bring any videotapes along. It took me almost an hour to track down a bureau reporter from the Florence/Myrtle Beach market and beg her to lend me one. I was lucky to find her. And lucky she was nice.

There's actually a fair amount of cooperation among one-man band reporters, even ones theoretically competing against each other, simply because you need all the help you can get. Sometimes I'd make deals with other one-man band reporters: you go for the DA, I'll try and interview the victim's mother. Then we'd swap tapes and end up with identical footage on both of our stations.

Of course, even after mastering all the technical aspects of one-man banding, you still have to worry about the story itself. When a reporter and photographer work together, the reporter can focus on the facts and the script and the stand-up while the photographer worries about video and sound. Many TV photographers don't even listen to what the interview subject is saying, they're so focused on monitoring voice levels and making sure the video looks right. As a one-man band, I had to pay so much attention to making sure the camera and sound were working properly that sometimes I'd forget to ask the right questions or forget to ask the name of the person I was interviewing. One time I had to return to a neighborhood and go house-to-house knocking on doors in an effort to learn the name of someone I'd interviewed three hours earlier.

Another time, I was so intent on making sure I got the right shots that I failed to grasp what was really going on. I was on my way to cover a different story when I spotted an overturned tractor with a man trapped underneath and an emergency services crew working frantically to get him out. I slammed on the brakes and grabbed my gear as fast as I could. My urgency was intensified by the fact that there was already a TV crew from a competing station on the scene and shooting video. I was afraid the paramedics would whisk the injured guy away before I could get any footage.

I ran over and started filming, jostling aggressively with the other photographer for space. I practically shoved him aside in order to get into prime position, right where the rescue crew was setting up to pull out the injured farmer. The firemen strained mightily to lift the tractor a few inches while others worked to free the man's legs.

I was in perfect position to get it all as they pulled the injured man clear, and I waited until the very last second to move aside, like a matador sweeping his cape. To my horror, I saw that the man's legs had been crushed completely flat. And they seemed to be bursting with … straw. Straw? Wait a minute, his arms were also filled with straw. And his body. And he didn't have a face. It was at this point that I realized the entire drama was a drill, and I had acted like a complete jerk for nothing. The rescue crew did the whole thing over again a few minutes later.

I stood off to the side muttering to myself and wondering if anyone had recognized my mistake. The other cameraman came over and made some friendly comment about how these drills were a pain to shoot, and how he had spent an hour waiting around before the rescue guys got their act together. "You did the smart thing not getting here when they said they were starting," he said approvingly, "I rushed out here without my morning coffee."

"Yeah," I responded, "I don't like to wait around."

Once I almost did miss a big story because I was by myself, simply because I went to the bathroom. That happened during a court hearing for the James Jordan murder case, and there were about 15 TV crews milling about in the Robeson County courthouse parking lot during a break in the proceedings. I went inside to use the facilities, and I guess I was in there a bit, because when I came out, every last crew had disappeared. I asked a police officer where everyone had gone, and he said, "Oh, they all went to the plane crash."

Plane crash? What plane crash? It turned out a small aircraft had made an unscheduled landing in a local resident's backyard. I raced out there in a panic, sure I was going to arrive and find I'd missed it. Indeed, the ambulance had departed by the time I got there, but fortunately for me, it's unwieldy to remove plane wreckage. What was left of the plane was still there, along with the police and fire departments, and several news crews who had surrounded the guy who lived there. He and his home had escaped obliteration by about 15 feet.

When a bunch of TV crews surround someone and everyone tries to do an interview at the same time it's called a "gang bang," and it's really hard to get a good sound bite, especially as a one-man band. Half the time, you can't even get a good angle to film the person, and have to hold your camera up over your head and hope the guy talks really loud. Here I tried forcing myself into the mix, thrusting my microphone in as close as I could, but couldn't get a clean shot. The man wasn't saying much, anyway, just answering the usual "How do you feel to have escaped certain death?" queries with a shrug and an "Okay, I guess."

After about five minutes of two- and three-word answers, the rest of the crews gave up and went looking for other survivors. This meant I could finally move close enough to ask a question myself. I tried a different tack. Instead of asking a direct question, I merely said, "Strange day, huh?" To which

102

he replied, "It's been a really strange day. I sure am lucky. I tell you, God was watching my footsteps today." It was a great sound bite. Maybe it's a good thing I spent so long in the bathroom.

* * *

Another thing I had to learn as a one-man band was where I could and couldn't shoot. This can cause a lot of headaches, because TV cameras are prohibited in a vast array of places where normal people are permitted to go. Courtrooms, for instance: you have to get the judge's permission to bring a camera into a courtroom, and despite what you might think after watching the O.J. trial, judges don't always say yes.

I may be biased, of course, but I believe cameras ought to be allowed in court at all times unless the security of a witness or defendant is at stake. By law, the U.S. judicial system is supposed to be open to the public. As long as there's an open seat, anyone is supposed to be able to walk in off the street and watch (with the exception of a few cases involving children or sexual abuse). A TV camera is simply a surrogate for people who aren't able to take time off from work to come watch in person. A TV photographer isn't any different than a sketch artist or a court reporter.

In fact, a TV camera can do a more accurate job of showing what a trial is really like. After all, which looks more lifelike, a charcoal sketch or a video? You don't see a lot of pastel driver's license shots, do you? Nevertheless, as a TV reporter, I was always at the mercy of the judge as to whether I could do my job. Sometimes I wondered if there was a powerful sketch artists' union somewhere. Either that or lobbyists working hard for Crayola.

It's not just courtrooms that make life difficult for a TV journalist; cameras are forbidden in all sorts of places. I needed permission to film in shopping malls, schools,

103

amusement parks, jails, airports, and even on some sidewalks and public parks. I once made the mistake of neglecting to ask the school principal for permission before getting a couple of comments from some students standing on the street outside the Whiteville High School. The principal never let me forget it. I had to grovel before him for months before he would return my phone calls, and all stories related to that high school were out of bounds for a while.

I also couldn't interview hospital patients until they signed a release form; I couldn't step on a private driveway if the owner forbade me; and even if a judge did let me in the courtroom, I was barred from showing jurors' faces. In fact, I know one reporter who was fired for inadvertently showing a juror's face on TV.

Believe it or not, you can't even show prison inmates on TV without their say-so. Meanwhile, there are few such restrictions on someone merely *accused* of a crime. You are allowed to take all the shots you want during the glorious perp walk, but as soon as the person is convicted and becomes an official ward of the state, TV reporters need the inmate's permission to get pictures or video of the person in jail.

For a TV reporter, there's certainly self-interest in wanting cameras allowed everywhere, but the only reason I can honestly see to limit their use is that, at least initially, cameras do magnify the Observer's Paradox, the principle that you cannot observe something without affecting it. People do act differently when a TV camera arrives on the scene. Lawyers may grandstand, protesters may make more noise, and crime scene witnesses may flee, or more likely, start waving into the camera. TV reporters don't have the luxury of being anonymous observers, as you can when you are a print reporter. Your very presence has an impact. In fact, some events would not occur at all were it not for TV cameras. A lot of protests, for example, aren't very eventful until the TV cameras show up. Many are done solely for TV's sake. This gives the TV crew power over the protestors, and I knew one impatient photographer who was sent to cover a protest and, when it was a bit slow to get going, went up to the organizer and said, "If this doesn't start within five minutes, me and my camera are outta here." They started immediately. There wouldn't be much point in doing it without the camera there.

All that said, I found that after TV cameras have been around for a bit, most people forget about them. Their effect is *initially*, when the crews first arrive. The overall concern about TV's impact is wildly exaggerated. In court, for instance, my experience was that people got used to the cameras by the end of the first day and then didn't pay them much attention.

Still, I had to learn all the rules about where I could and couldn't shoot, and I got yelled at a lot. One time a man actually picked up my tripod and threw it into the street, breaking it. I couldn't do much about it because I had placed the tripod a few feet into his property. By law, you are allowed to shoot from public thoroughfares, but private property is a different story. You can actually get sued for trespassing if you go onto private property while shooting a story.

Even on public property, not everyone is willing to recognize your right to be there. Once, later on when I was working in Tennessee, I had a guy go for his gun because he didn't want me shooting video of him or his property. Believe it or not, he was a former county judge who had been arrested for allegedly growing marijuana on his farm. I wanted video of this farm, so along with a photographer, Dan Hellie, I headed out to the farm, which was located about an hour north west of Knoxville in a remote rural area of Tennessee. Unfortunately, Dan and I got lost on the back roads, and by the time we arrived, the judge had had enough time to bond out of jail and beat us back. I assume he knew the way.

When Dan and I pulled up in our news car, with its bold station logo on the side, the guy understood why we were there and started yelling at us to leave. I tried to explain our legal rights about shooting from a public roadway, but despite his legal background, he was unreceptive to my argument. He said something to the effect of "I'll show you your rights," and moved in a deliberate manner toward his pickup truck, from whence he retrieved a long black rifle case. At this point, Dan and I decided not to press the rights issue and got back in our car in a bit of a hurry.

We drove off, but unfortunately, we drove in the wrong direction, heading farther down a windy back road that didn't seem to lead anywhere. So with a sinking feeling, we realized we'd have to turn around and head back by the farm. We decided that if we were going to get shot, we should try to get it on video, so I drove and Dan got in the back seat with the camera. I generously allowed that if the guy started shooting Dan was permitted to duck. "But keep rolling," I said, "if we survive it'll be good footage."

Fortunately for us, the judge seemed to have calmed down by the time we rolled back past and kept his rifle pointed towards the ground. Unfortunately, I hadn't calmed down quite as much, and drove too fast for Dan to get any usable video. We decided against going back for a second try.

Even encounters like this aside, the demands of shooting and lugging around TV gear can wear you down, particularly if you are a one-man band. In Whiteville, I was using heavy, ¾-inch tape equipment, also known as *U-matic*. U-matic was one of the first professional videotape technologies, and one of the weightiest. Unlike most modern video cameras, the ¾-inch camera and tape deck are separate entities, both large and both several pounds, connected by a thick cable. The ¾-inch format had long been abandoned by most stations by the time I arrived in Whiteville, and whenever I ran into a crew from a bigger market, they would crowd around and gaze at my equipment like IT guys reminiscing about old Commodore computers and the Apple IIe. But WWAY still used ¾-inch, which meant so did I.

Along with my heavy camera and tape deck, I also carried a tripod, a microphone, and a heavy battery belt that encircled my waist and attached by a cable to a clunky metal light that screwed on to the top of the camera. When I had everything strapped on, I was so loaded down someone told me I looked like a Ghostbuster. It was hard work. One time I had to carry all the equipment up six flights of stairs to shoot video from a firetower, and I was so weary I stumbled and nearly fell all the way down. Another time, I lost my balance and almost tumbled off a moving tractor while shooting video for a story about tobacco planting. Fortunately, I was able to grab onto a metal rail, or else there would have been a tractor accident that was more than just a drill. Someone else would have had to cover it, though.

Once, when my arms were full of equipment, I tried to kick open the door to the Bladen County Courthouse and missed the door lever. My foot went right through the glass, and large shards rained down, slicing my pants in several places and leaving me with a shallow but bloody cut on my leg. When I went in and reported this, I was bleeding so profusely that they were more concerned that I might not make it than about the fact that I had just demolished their glass door.

Even when I didn't fall down or break anything, I'd usually return to the bureau exhausted and disheveled. It wasn't long before I started having back problems.

After a while, you do get the hang of one-man banding, but it is *always* challenging. I found that even when I'd become competent at shooting and editing, something always suffered, whether it was the video, in that I didn't have time to shoot creative footage; or the audio, in that I wasn't monitoring it carefully and the person spoke too softly; or the facts themselves that got jumbled while I was trying to keep the gear from malfunctioning. The quality was never as good as it would have been for a two- or three-person news team.

These days, one-man banding is probably less physically demanding than when I did it because TV cameras and tape decks have gotten considerably smaller in the past few years. But there are still an overwhelming number of things to worry about when you are by yourself. I have nothing but respect (and sympathy) for reporters that one-man band. It is thousands of times easier to work with a photographer. But in Whiteville, I didn't have that option, and I had to sink or swim.

And admittedly, there are some benefits to one-man banding. As a one-man band reporter, you develop a much better understanding of what you need in terms of video and sound to tell a story. You also learn which shots are a waste of time and which are worth spending an extra 10 minutes on. Later on, when I got to work with photographers, many said they could tell the difference between reporters who had or hadn't one-man banded. They told me that reporters who had never one-man banded often didn't think as much about what kind of video they would need to tell the story, leaving them in a jam when they had to find pictures to cover the script and nothing matched. Photographers also told me that reporters who had never one-man banded were more likely to order them to shoot all sorts of material and then never use any of it.

After having to shoot my own video in Whiteville, I felt guilty just asking them to shoot anything.

So while I certainly wouldn't want to one-man band forever, I do think it helped me develop a better visual sense for my stories and taught me to be more economical about what video I needed and what I didn't. It also gave me a much better appreciation for the job photographers do. Some reporters treat photographers as pack horses; mules carrying equipment under their command. Whereas if I had to choose between a good reporter and a good photographer, I'd take the photographer every time. TV news is all about the pictures, and if those are good, you don't need a Pulitzer prize winner to tell a good story. But if the pictures are horrendous, you do need a genuine genius to make it seem interesting to viewers.

My first few months in Whiteville, I wasn't even trying to make the stories seem interesting; I was ecstatic if they were in the right color. I made so many mistakes it boggles my mind just to think about it. Fortunately, I was helped immeasurably by two things. The first was that because I was in a bureau, my station couldn't see my mistakes. If I had to climb in a dumpster seven or eight times, or reshoot an interview because I forgot to plug in the microphone, my station was none the wiser. So long as my story got done, the news director and general manager had no idea how many times I had messed it up.

They had no idea, for instance, that one day I left behind thousands of dollars in camera equipment at a local public school where I was doing a story, only remembering this at 11:00 p.m. while watching my story on TV. I drove out to the school in the dark and peered in windows until I spotted my gear sitting safely in the principal's office. I'm lucky I wasn't arrested.

My station was also unaware of the fact that I once locked myself out of my car, with the engine running, while covering a police officer's funeral. I had to go around asking all the cops in attendance if any had a slim-jim. Fortunately one did, and helped me pry open the door before I missed my deadline. The station remained blissfully ignorant. I also never told the station about that courthouse door mishap. What happens in Bladen County stays in Bladen County.

The second, and equally important factor in my favor was that for two weeks at the start I had help. The former Whiteville bureau chief, Leigh Powell, convinced the station to let her stay on in Whiteville for two weeks in order to show me the ropes before she moved to the main station in Wilmington. In theory, Leigh stayed to introduce me to local contacts I would need to know. I suspect, however, that she really just wanted to hang around without doing too much work. She did help with some stories, but much of the day we just drove around, visited friends, and picked up her dry cleaning.

Leigh was a pretty Southern Belle type who favored flowery dresses and nice shoes and never appeared outdoors without plenty of makeup and hairspray. She loved to gossip and socialize, chatting away in a syrupy Southern drawl while lunching on sweet tea, Carolina barbecue, and hush puppies. Later on, when I got to know her well enough to joke around, I used to call her Scarlett O'Powell. But beneath the demure exterior, Leigh was also pretty tough. She had studied journalism at the University of North Carolina and could buckle down and do a great job when she felt like it. By the time I arrived, however, she readily admitted that she didn't feel like it all that often. She had been the Whiteville bureau chief for several years, was tired of Whiteville stories, and really tired of lugging around the camera equipment all by herself. I don't know how she managed as long as she did. If I was having back problems after a few months, I was surprised Leigh wasn't in a wheelchair.

So when I took over, Leigh was more than willing to let me handle the gear and practice as much as I wanted. For two weeks she accompanied me and taught me all the intricacies I had failed to fully grasp during Dienst's brief tutelage in New York. And even more important, Leigh never let the station know the full extent of my incompetence.

Leigh was only with me for two weeks, but she was the one who really taught me how to edit. Editing involves mixing a reporter's voice track, sound bites, and video (called b-roll), onto a studio tape, creating a finished pretaped story (the term b-roll derives from when stations used film and had two reels going during editing, one, the a-roll, with the reporter's voice track, and the other, the b-roll, with the background pictures). The end product is referred to in news jargon as a "package," probably because it's a nice gift all wrapped up for the station to broadcast. All they have to do is pop it into a tape player and they've got a minute and a half of airtime they don't have to worry about.

Editing is another of those TV things that isn't all that difficult to do but is difficult to do well. My main difficulty was that I was very slow. Part of this was because it was all new to me, and part because the bureau's ¾-inch equipment was from the stone age. Even if I made all the right edits the first time and didn't have to redo anything, the fastest I could edit a full story was 50 minutes. Most editing jobs took me an hour and a half. That meant I had to have my story completely shot and written by 4:30 in order to get it on the six o'clock news. The machines were so slow, and I was so stressed right before deadline, that I would push the edit button and then pace around the room while the tape machines took their time getting to the actual edit.

I was usually so frazzled by this point that I wouldn't even look up if anyone entered the bureau to pitch a story or ask a question or tell me that my car was on fire. "Can't talk right now. I'm near deadline," I would yell without a sideways glance. "Please take a seat. I'll be with you at 6:03." Sometimes they stayed, and sometimes they left and I had no idea who had come and gone. It could have been the town mayor or someone looking to steal my wallet for all I knew.

When I finished editing, I'd phone the station and feed them my story via a microwave transmitter stationed outside the bureau. I was supposed to have everything done at least five minutes before air time, but I often missed my slot. Sometimes I'd end up feeding the story during the first commercial break in the newscast, well after my story was supposed to have aired. I didn't care; I was just relieved it was done. Then I'd collapse.

Chapter 7

The Daily Grind

While the rigors of shooting and editing were a challenge for me, the greatest difficulty I encountered in Whiteville was simply coming up with enough stories. It was my responsibility to fill between two and a half to three minutes of WWAY's airtime, turning in at least one "package" and one VOSOT on different topics every day. VOSOT stands for "voice over — sound on tape," and it's generally shorter than a package, but unlike a package, it requires assistance from the folks in the station control room. When a VOSOT airs, the reporter or anchor speaks while the station control room plays video in the background (hence the voice over video), then the reporter stops talking while the station plays the sound on tape, commonly referred to as a sound bite.

Packages are usually between a minute and a minute, 45 seconds, in length, and may have four or five sound bites, sometimes more. VOSOTs tend to be about 30–40 seconds, and have just one or two sound bites. VOSOTs are a lot faster to write, but they don't match the video to the reporter's voice track as closely as a package, can't be nearly as complex or creative, and require coordination between the person speaking and the station control room since someone has to roll the video and sound bite at just the right moments. VOSOTs are used when there's a shortage of either video or sound or when a story isn't that interesting and only merits a shorter mention in the newscast. Stations usually like to mix packages and VOSOTS in the newscast to keep the show moving along at a good pace.

Eventually, I could do more than a package plus a VOSOT in a day, but for my first few months I struggled to come up with even one package a day and would often provide the station with three short VOSOTs instead. It didn't look as good and was not as valuable to the station, but it did fill up almost the same amount of airtime, so the station took pity on me and let me get away with it.

Even so, my days were long and stressful. I'd start around 7:30, listening to the local radio news and checking all the newspapers in my coverage area. There were about four or five small-town papers, most just eight or twelve pages in length. Unfortunately, most of these reached my bureau a few days after their issue date, so they were useless for me as far as hard news was concerned. A three-day old car crash isn't hard news anymore. But I used these papers to generate features and future story ideas, so I read them cover to cover, searching for anything that might be the slightest bit interesting.

After checking the papers, I'd make my daily "beat checks." Beat checks involve calling up every law enforcement and emergency agency you can think of to see if nuclear war has broken out and you just haven't heard about it yet. In Whiteville, I had 10 or fifteen calls on my daily list, including the police departments of Whiteville, Bladenboro, Tabor City, and Elizabethtown; the sheriff's departments of Columbus, Bladen, and Robeson counties; the state highway patrol; a couple of county 911 emergency centers; a few fire departments; and Margie down at the Dairy Twist.

"Good mornin', this is Paul Spelman from WWAY," I'd say, giving it my best imitation Southern drawl in an awkward attempt to disarm them. "Just checkin' in to see if there's anything going on." Nine times out of ten, the dispatchers would say, "Nope, nothing today" and hang up. It could get frustrating, and I often felt like I was wasting my time, but I had to check every day because every now and then they would concede that a fire had destroyed 24 barns or that the mayor had run off with the police chief's secretary. And, of course, the day I didn't do a beat check would be the day I was sure to miss the triple homicide and 14-car train derailment. Sometimes I was sure that just by checking, I was saving hundreds of lives.

I also kind of liked doing beat checks, although it wasn't that way at first. When I first started I dreaded beat checks. I am not a natural extrovert and also have something of a phone phobia. I don't always answer my phone when people call, and I can empathize with golfer Fred Couples, who once famously said, "I don't like answering the phone because there might be somebody on the other end." Quite frankly, I don't mind walking into the lion's den, but I hate calling to set up the appointment. This, of course, meant that I also had a poor phone demeanor, sounding a bit like an undertaker calling to inquire as to your progress. Phone phobia is a peculiar attribute for a news reporter, I know, but I've had it since I was a kid. In high school I once dated a girl who made me call her every night, and it ruined the relationship for me. Why did I have to call, I'd complain, we just saw each other at school a few hours ago. It's a little darker than the last time I saw you, what else has changed?

On beat checks, meanwhile, it is extremely important to be friendly because dispatchers aren't legally required to tell you anything. The only reason they'll tell you something is if they like you and think you like them. And after a while, I did like them. In fact, I found that I would come to the bureau in a somber mood, fearing the numerous opportunities for failure that awaited me during the course of the day; but after forcing myself to act jovial with various dispatchers and detectives, I'd actually *feel* a bit more cheerful and optimistic. I ended up getting friendly and on a first-name basis with several dispatchers, and the sentiment was completely genuine. At least on my part.

Though most of the beat checks didn't bear fruit, every now and then I would get lucky. I learned that the best question, after inquiring whether anything was going on in their particular locality, was to ask whether they'd heard of anything interesting going on anywhere else. The Bladenboro dispatcher might neglect to tell me about the bizarre murder-suicide involving a farmer and his twelve sheep but had few qualms describing in graphic detail the race riot over in Tabor City. Sometimes dispatchers would even phone to let me know about something juicy going on in another municipality. I encouraged this rat-on-thy-neighbor mentality.

I also carried a police scanner with me at all times and got to where, for the most part, I could filter out the unimportant chatter yet tune in when there was a big accident or a shooting. To get good at this, you have to develop a proficiency in 10-code, the language dispatchers and police use to talk to each other. There isn't a universal 10-code system, so it can vary from one municipality to another. In one place, "10-52" might mean armed robbery, whereas in another city or state, it might mean escaped seven-year-old. But all law enforcement agencies seem to have an abundance of 10-codes. I'm not sure how many they had in Whiteville, but later on in Knoxville I counted 90 different 10-codes for the sheriff's office alone, from 10-1, receiving (radio) poorly, to 10-99, bomb investigation. For some reason I could never figure out, some numbers were missing. There was no 10-92 for instance, so if you were counting up you went from 10-91 to 10-93 and kept going.

Ten-codes undoubtedly serve a valuable purpose in improving the speed and clarity of communications, but people in law enforcement also have an exaggerated fondness for them, like kids talking to each other in a secret lingo. "Okay, after this 10-24, I'm going to be 10-11 for a while, and then I'll 10-19 at 13-hundred." In layman's terms, that means that after the officer deals with a minor traffic accident, he'll head to lunch and then return to police headquarters around 1:00 p.m. As if he couldn't say this in plain English because spies might be listening in.

I've known reporters to get inordinately fond of the codes as well, and once heard two reporters trading insults in 10-code, with one referring to the other as a 10-87 (mental person) and the other responding by calling him a 10-58 (public drunk).

In Whiteville, I was never fluent in 10-codes, but I did get to where I could tell if there was something big going on. It often had less to do with deciphering the actual code than picking up on the dispatcher's tone of voice. There was often a sense of urgency to it if it was something important. Then I'd check my 10-code decoder list and see what all the fuss was about. There was also a specific 10-code that meant "Contact Coroner," and I made sure to memorize that one.

Some stations actually hire civilian scanner listeners. A reporter for WECT, my competitor in Whiteville, told me that his station had arrangements with some stay-at-home moms to keep their ears peeled while taking care of the toddlers. Every time a scanner mom alerted the station to something worthwhile, they got paid $10 or $15.

You have to be careful about scanners, though, because not everything you hear is accurate. In fact, a lot of it is completely erroneous. I would often hear the dispatcher say something like, "The robber is a tall male wearing a blue shirt," and later learn it was a short female wearing a yellow bikini. In Knoxville, my station had a rule that you weren't allowed to go on the air with any information you heard over the scanner unless you confirmed it somewhere else. It's a good rule, because scanners can amount to wireless rumor mills.

Even with all my newspapers and beat checks and scanner monitoring, I was often left to my own devices to come up with a story in Whiteville. In other words, I'd have to again resort to that craft I had honed so well in Telluride, how to make something out of nothing. I took this to a whole new level in Whiteville. In news parlance, I became a master chef at making chicken salad out of chicken shit.

The best example of this was probably the time I did a news story about an elementary school field day. Field days, in case you don't remember, are days where kids get out of class and go to a field and play capture the flag, or run three-legged races and such. The winning side gets bragging rights and an extra scoop of ice cream or something. They don't ordinarily merit front-page headlines and broadcast news coverage. But I was desperate for something to cover one day when I got a call from a principal at a local elementary school tipping me off to the fact that his students were having a field day. For some reason, this principal was an extremely aggressive promoter and was always determined to get his kids on TV. He was constantly calling me up and letting me know about some *must-cover* event, such as the fifth grade talent show, or the opening of his school's new cafeteria. He actually got upset if I didn't cover these events, and would call me afterward to chastise me and let me know that my deadly tornado story hadn't been the only important news event of the day, thank you.

Most of his school events were of little interest to 99.99 percent of my audience, but when you don't have anything else to report about, you don't look proffered gifts in the mouth. So sometimes I'd take his handouts and try to peg them to something else to make them appear more "newsworthy."

With the field day, I turned it into a story about the disturbing trend in child health and fitness; how computers and video games were resulting in flabby out-of-shape youth. I tracked down a local health official to weigh in on the issue and then interviewed the principal and a few third graders about how schools need to work harder to make kids active again. It actually turned into a decent story and led one of our newscasts. And I wasn't making it up; kids *are* in worse shape these days. Would I have done a story on it that day if I hadn't needed to fill a few minutes of airtime? That is a question you could apply to thousands of TV news pieces.

I'm not sure if this technique always serves the best interests of the viewing public, but in small markets like Whiteville and Wilmington, there's not much else you can do when you have to fill a certain amount of airtime every day. Having a school principal eager to help served my purposes as well as his.

I learned never to be dismissive of anyone suggesting a story idea. Frankly, you do not get a lot of good news tips from call-ins and people you run into on the street, but you never know when someone may actually have valuable information. One of my best sources approached me out of the blue one night in a small-town convenience store. He had stopped in to get a soda on his way back from exercising at a gym and was still quite sweaty and disheveled. But he said he knew of a couple of good stories and wanted to talk to me. At the time, I was working on a story about people passing counterfeit currency at convenience stores and didn't have a lot of time to chat, but I couldn't figure out a way to avoid it without being rude. So I listened as this sweaty fellow told me

119

some crazy story about local officials protecting a murderer and about a high-ranking official under investigation for harassing a female subordinate At first glance, the guy seemed paranoid and a bit unstable, but it later turned out that most of what he told me was true. Some county officials *had* acted quite strangely in investigating a shooting, ignoring the findings of their own medical examiner, who told them that the victim had been ambushed. It also turned out that the Equal Employment Opportunity Council *was* looking into charges of sexual harassment against a top county official.

This source was not always the calmest individual, and would sometimes call me at home late at night to rant and rave about conspiracies I couldn't even understand. But I was able to verify a lot of what I was told, and what I couldn't verify was never really disproven, making me think that it might actually be true. Sometimes valuable information comes from very unlikely sources.

Besides that fact, listening to people who call or come forward to suggest stories is the polite thing to do, even when you know that they are not going to give you a good story. Usually I could tell within 15 seconds if someone's idea was going to bear fruit, but in Whiteville, I'd talk with them for five or 10 minutes anyway as a courtesy. This sometimes took a lot of patience on my part. Most of these Whiteville "tipsters" were calling with such impossible-to-resist scoops as, "Hey, jus' wanted to let you know that O.J. Simpson is guilty," or, "It's a crime that your weather guy says it's going to rain. It ain't rainin' and he ain't been right for months."

Others would call me to correct errors made by my station's sports department. "Your guy Motley got it wrong. It weren't Virginia Tech versus Georgia, it was Virginia versus Georgia Tech." One person called to let me know she was having trouble with her TV reception.

Even after I explained that I had little control over these matters, it usually did little to dampen their fervor. Sometimes they'd get mad if I declined to act on their concern. One man, who walked into my bureau and identified himself as a "local preacher," was quite friendly at first, telling me he had a good story idea. In exchange for revealing this idea, however, he wanted me to put him on TV so he could spread the word of God. I had to explain that TV news didn't usually work on such an explicit quid pro quo basis. When I said this, however, his demeanor took a dramatic turn for the worse.

"Well, in that case I'll see you later," he said with a harsh spiteful look. "I don't believe you know the Lord anyway." As a parting shot on his way out the door he added, "You're probably in favor of a communist government too." I never did learn what his story idea was, but I don't stay up late worrying that I let a great scoop get away.

What did keep me awake in Whiteville was worrying about coming up with enough stories. By nine every morning, I had to have two story ideas I could pitch to the assignment editor in Wilmington, and they both had to be stories I was almost 100% positive I could get done by six o'clock that night. That's one of the problems with local TV news; stations get by with so few reporters that there is no room for failure. So reporters end up covering things they know they can do by the evening newscast. At newspapers, where there are usually many more reporters in a newsroom, reporters may be given time to work on a story that will take a few days to complete, or work on a story that may fall through altogether. Not so in local TV, especially at the small-market level. In over six years in local TV news, I doubt I had more than five or 10 days in which I didn't have at least one story on the nightly newscast. And most of the time, I had to come up with the ideas.

On rare occasions in Whiteville, the Wilmington news director or assignment manager would suggest a story, but most of the time they just approved my ideas. Once approved, I'd start making calls to set up interviews and get the b-roll I would need. Setting this up usually took an hour or two, but in general, I wanted to have a story set up and be out the door by 10:30. I also had to have pretty much the entire story set up by the time I left the bureau, because WWAY didn't provide me with a cell phone, so once I hit the road I couldn't make any calls except from pay phones.

It sounds bizarre now not to have a cell phone, but this was 1994 and cell phones were more of a rarity. My station had one cell phone for the entire newsroom. The phone was kept in Wilmington under lock and key, reserved for special occasions. Instead of cell phones, the station relied on two-way radios to keep in touch with crews in the field. The only problem with this was that our competitors also had two-way radios and could hear all of our transmissions. Since we didn't want them to know what we were doing, conversations between the desk and field crews became masterpieces of vague innuendo.

"This is the desk. We wanted to see if you've finished at your current location and are ready to move on the other site we discussed earlier."

"No, this thing is taking longer than we thought because of a delay getting what was supposed to be here. Is the second thing more important than the first? If so, we may want to give up here and head there, because we can only get that while the person we need to talk to is there and he may have to leave because of that other thing later on."

"Yeah, why don't you do that. We'll see if we can get another crew to pick up your current thing when they come back from where they are."

The irony, of course, is that most of the time the other station was able to figure out exactly what was being discussed since they were covering the same "things." Occasionally, though, we could fool them, either by omitting information or including misleading information. Every now and then I'd try something like, "Base, this is Paul. I'm wrapped up at that fire and headed to the hospital to talk to the survivors. I'll report in again in an hour." The idea was to make the other station waste an hour or two trying to track down some story that didn't exist. It didn't work very often. More often I fooled my own station into thinking I had a great story when I didn't. They would pencil me in to lead the broadcast when I was actually doing a story about crafters making doormats out of recycled old tires.

If the assignment desk had something really important to discuss that required going into more detail than possible via the radio, they'd tell me to "find a landline." While we didn't have cell phones, WWAY provided its reporters with a 1-800 number I could use to call the station for free from any pay phone. So I'd hear my station ask for a landline and have to immediately locate the nearest gas station with a working pay phone. I got to know the location of almost every pay phone in the three-county area. I had to; I was always on the road.

Several hours of my day were spent driving from one story to another. A light day involved an hour or two in the car; a long day, four or five. These drives weren't on well-maintained highways either, some roads I traveled on had no markings and weeds growing up through cracks in the pavement. In North Carolina, the smaller the road, the bigger the number. Forget I-95, I was driving on NC1004b.

Sometimes I'd also have to drive all the way to Wilmington, an hour away, if the bureau microwave transmitter was malfunctioning and it was necessary to hand-deliver the tape of my story. Other times we'd arrange a mid-way handoff. I'd finish my story, put it on tape, drive 30 miles toward Wilmington and pull into the median of the highway. The station would send someone 30 miles out from Wilmington, and I'd pass them my tape through the car window. I felt like I was making some sort of covert exchange and we ought to have secret code words like James Bond. "Excuse me, do you have a match?" "I use a lighter." "Better still ...."

I generally enjoyed my drives in the morning, when the deadline was still far enough away that I could breathe and enjoy the scenery. I dreaded the drives in the afternoon, when deadline pressure made the narrow roads and slow-moving tractors frustrating to deal with. In the late afternoon I became something of a road hazard. To this day, I'm amazed I didn't get into any serious accidents in Whiteville, although I did have a few close calls.

Once, I had drivers call my station to complain after I nearly ran them off the road coming back from a story in Lumberton. It was late in the day and I was stressed and worried that I might not make my deadline, and I tried to pass a car on a very busy two-lane road. Unfortunately, it turned out there was another car in front of the one I tried to pass, and that car's driver was reluctant to cede his position. He sped up and wouldn't let me in, despite a stream of cars which suddenly appeared heading toward me from the other direction. I floored the station's Ford Escort and made it in, just barely, but two cars had to swerve onto the shoulder and the car I passed had to slam on the brakes. Immediately afterward, I saw the driver pull right up behind me so he could read the station logo on the back of my car. I was not surprised when I got a call from my news director telling me that my conduct was inappropriate.

I just always felt under extreme time pressure, especially during my first few months at the bureau when I didn't know how long it took to do things and what I could and couldn't accomplish. The pressure was always there, from the moment I got up to the moment I finished my stories seconds before air. It would get worse and worse as the day went on. Every day around one o'clock, I'd feel tension building in my neck and shoulders. I'd start squinting more and smiling less. This pressure would get heavier and heavier until my whole mood turned dark by late afternoon, and every new delay felt like a body blow. After two or three o'clock I was usually too nervous to eat anything, so if I hadn't had lunch by then, I went hungry.

Eventually, you get used to daily news deadlines and they become less of a burden, but the pressure never completely goes away. I learned to keep an eagle-eye on the clock and mark out the time needed for everything in my mind. Let's see, I'd think, I can do my last interview in 12 minutes, then swing by the crime scene and shoot video and a stand-up in 17 minutes. I should be back at the bureau by 3:41, then 24 minutes to review the tape and interviews, another 47 minutes to write the story. Three minutes for the bathroom. 50 minutes to edit the story. Five minutes to call the station and feed it to them over the microwave. Two minutes for a last check with the police to see if anything's changed since I last spoke to them. Three minutes to get the camera and lights set up, another two minutes for the microphone. I should be ready for my broadcast with three minutes to spare. Super.

As a general rule, I tried to have everything shot and be back at the bureau by 3:30. That gave me just enough time to write and edit the story for the 5:30 and 6:00 broadcasts. Sometimes I'd try to write stories before they occurred, especially if they involved government meetings that wouldn't

125

conclude until just before deadline. I'd write something like, "City council may have *invited/averted/delayed* a lawsuit from angry citizens tonight over the controversial cell-phone tower. The council *approved/denied/postponed* the tower, planned for the nearby residential community." Then, when the council finally made its decision, I'd simply circle the words that fit.

Sometimes I'd even get sound bites beforehand, knowing I wouldn't have time to interview someone after a late vote. I'd interview a council member before the meeting, asking, "What kind of an impact do you think the cell tower might have if the board votes to approve it? Really, but how will you feel if it goes the other way?" Then I'd use whichever sound bite fit the eventual outcome. It's not the ideal way to cover the news, but when you've got a hard and fast deadline, sometimes it's the only way.

I'm certainly not the first to prewrite stories, of course. It is a time-honored tradition in journalism, especially in sports and politics. Who can forget Dewey defeating Truman, and Gore taking Florida? On a far smaller scale, I remember one night in Telluride watching two photographers shoot a group of city council candidates on election night before the results were in and positioning the "sure thing" candidates in the middle and the "question mark" candidates on the outside, where they could crop them out of the picture if they didn't win.

But even using every trick in the book, I was always terrified of what might happen tomorrow. Would I be able to come up with another story? Would I be able to handle a really big story — a Christie Brinkley-in-a-helicopter-crash story — if it came my way? What would happen if I failed?   I constantly feared that I'd encounter some story I just couldn't handle, no matter how hard I tried. I came to dread all phone calls from my station, because each call meant something big was going on, another opportunity to expose myself as a TV news fraud. Sitting in my apartment at night watching the hit new show *E.R.*. was nerve wracking because whenever a doctor's pager went off my heart skipped a beat, thinking it was my pager and I was being called out to cover some tough story.

Every Friday, I couldn't believe I had made it through another week. Friday night was the only time I really relaxed. I'd get a big Frisco burger from Hardees and sit in my apartment drinking beer and watching TV. By Saturday afternoon, I could feel the tension begin to build again as I'd start worrying about Monday's story and the coming week. Sometimes I'd get so worked up worrying about what I was going to cover, I'd have to pace around the streets of Whiteville in the dark just to calm down.

Other times, I'd go over to the bureau at night, or on Sundays, and sift through my notes and newspaper back issues, looking for something, anything, I could use for a story during the next week. I also hoarded and stockpiled stories for "rainy days" when nothing was going on. I attended city and county meetings late into the night after working the whole day, looking for stories I could hold and then use during the next two or three days. If I got something that would hold, I wouldn't mention it to my station until I had used up everything else.

The truth is, I was scared that I would flub this chance. I may not have grown up dreaming of becoming a big TV star, but I had worked so hard to get into TV news, I didn't want to fail. TV was all I could think about. I wanted to succeed, make it to the major leagues, prove all those news director doubters wrong. Sometimes, when walking across a small street in Whiteville, I would imagine that my life was a movie and this was the part where the scene would dissolve into a shot of me

127

crossing a busy intersection in Chicago, Boston, or New York. The words "Eight Years Later" would flash on the bottom of the screen and the audience would know I had fulfilled my quest. I thought how nice it would be if I could fast-forward to that part, since I really didn't care to endure the eight years it was going to take me to get there. And that was if I made it. There was no guarantee of that, especially if I failed here. If I flopped in Whiteville, I might never get another shot.

Chapter 8

Help and the Human Boomerang

Fortunately for me, people in Whiteville were extremely kind. They seemed to take pity on this floundering fish out of water and tried to help me as much as possible. They rarely complained when I had to reshoot an interview three times because I couldn't get the camera to work, or got impatient when I was 45 minutes late because I got lost on my way there, or got upset when I mispronounced their names or the names of their towns. They didn't even take offense when I pointed to a brightly colored flag flying over someone's house and said, "That's pretty. What is it?" only to be told it was the state flag of North Carolina.

The people in the area often went to such lengths to help me that it was almost embarrassing. One night, for instance, a convenience-store clerk shut down his store so he could lead me down a warren of back county roads to an ongoing law enforcement stand-off. I'd still be looking for it otherwise. Other times people would drive 20 minutes out of their way to show me where to go. I got so where if I heard something was going on, I would head in the general direction and then put my faith in the hands of the first person I saw. "Hey, I heard there's a big fire, can you point me in the right direction?" I found that if I didn't act as though I already knew everything (which really wasn't a problem), they would give me more help than I ever would have asked for.

The hospital administrator would bend over backwards to escort me around his facility for a story about a flu shots. The sheriff would let me accompany his officers on a nighttime gin joint raid (yes, they still had gin joints around Whiteville). The farmers and agricultural extension agents would stop what they were doing at a moment's notice and help me do a story about the potato harvest or blue mold infiltrating the tobacco crop.

The farming community, in general, was the friendliest and most accommodating group of people I have ever met. Whenever I was desperate for a story, I'd call up the local agricultural extension agents and see if they had any ideas. They rarely failed me and could always find some farmer willing show me around his farm and talk about his crop. Obviously, some of my stories probably helped the farmers or the sheriff or the hospital, so their cooperation was not devoid of self-interest. But their patience and warmth went far beyond anything they could have expected to gain from my story. I still feel deeply grateful for all the assistance I received.

I'm also greatly indebted to a Whiteville radio news reporter who seemed intent on making sure I didn't get fired. Why, I have no idea, other than that he was a nice guy and perhaps rightly realized I was little competition for him. His name was Mitch, and he was in his early twenties, younger than I was, but much wiser in the ways of the business. He had studied journalism and broadcasting at the University of North Carolina, and he lived and breathed the business.

Luckily for me, he did not feel threatened by my presence. For one thing, at that stage in my career, I wasn't in the same league. He could also have his stories on the air in seconds since he was in radio, while mine didn't air on TV until five or six that evening. And because his radio signal only reached the immediate vicinity, whereas my station reached something like eight counties, we weren't really competing for the same audience, since the majority of my viewers were outside of his listening area.

Because of this, and because he was a nice guy, he provided invaluable help to me in my first few months in Whiteville. I'd hear one of his stories on the radio and immediately call him up to find out who I should talk to and where to go to do the same piece. Sometimes he'd call me first to make sure I was aware of what was going on. I'd be working on my fascinating story about the upcoming yam festival when he'd phone to let me know about the runaway freight train. "I was just checking into that right now," I'd reply. "Thanks for calling."

Later on, when Mitch moved on to a better radio job in Raleigh and was replaced by a novice, I helped out the new guy in much the same manner. Radio and TV reporters often have these mutually beneficial relationships, perhaps because both are undermanned and overworked and have to cover so many different things in a short period of time.

Newspaper journalists, on the other hand, are less likely to share with their broadcasting brethren. I think that's probably because many print reporters don't view TV reporters as true news colleagues. In fact, many look a bit askance at TV folk and don't hide this fact. No doubt some print reporters would say the same thing about people in TV, but my experience is that most TV reporters are genuinely impressed by print journalists, even if they don't always like them. Most people in TV are impressed by all the stories that newspaper reporters break, what with all their Deep Throat contacts and unnamed sources. TV reporters are also aware that print articles are far more detailed and thorough than TV pieces.

If newspaper journalists are ever impressed by TV people, they hide it well. More often, they don't bother to hide their disdain, and relations can get a bit testy.

In Knoxville, there was one newspaper photographer who would deliberately get in the way of TV crews just to amuse himself. I once nearly got into a brawl with the guy while covering a Thanksgiving Day dinner at a homeless shelter. The newspaper photographer kept jumping in front of me and my photographer as we tried to shoot video, and we ended up chest-to-chest, mano-a-mano, shoving each other in front of a hundred homeless people. I think they were cheering us on.

It was archetypal embarrassing reporter behavior, and I felt so ashamed afterward I wrote a letter of apology to the shelter for causing a scene. But I didn't apologize to the newspaper photographer. He was known for doing stuff like that. The truly ironic thing is that a minute or two before he started disrupting my story, I had been praising him for a photograph of his that I liked in a recent paper. Apparently I wasn't effusive enough.

While that guy represented the extreme, I suspect the general dim view of TV news held by print journalists derives from the fact that many believe, as I did before I got into TV, that print is the purest form of journalism. I recall that when I was a newspaper reporter interviewing for a job at WWAY and was asked if I thought I was "ready for TV," I almost snorted with contempt. What a ridiculous question. Don't you know I've been a *newspaper* reporter for three years? I write articles that are three times the length of your little TV stories. How hard can it be to string together 10 sentences and smile for the camera? I ought to be asking if TV is ready for me.

A lot of print reporters also resent the fact that sometimes they do the legwork while TV types get the credit. A Whiteville newspaper reporter once told me that if it weren't for his paper, nobody in TV or radio news would have any stories.

There is something to that, since, as I did in Whiteville, it's common for TV and radio reporters to borrow ideas from the papers. Many small-market radio stations don't even have news departments and tend to just rip and read what's in print without crediting the source. Station owners see no problem with this and use it as an efficient way to keep salaried staff to a minimum.

In Whiteville, Mitch's station was the only radio station that did its own local news, and Mitch was the entire department. His station as a whole only had two on-air employees — Mitch, and a morning DJ. The rest of the day the station relied on a satellite feed using DJs based in Colorado. Anyone tuning in to "Whiteville's Local Oldies Station" after 11:00 a.m. heard a DJ in Denver. The Denver DJ was careful never to refer to local events, weather, or time (other than to say things like, "It's five minutes before the hour"), and if Whiteville listeners had a song request, they dialed a 1-800 number, so they didn't know where they were calling.

It was quite clever and I'm sure most listeners had no idea that their local DJ was the same "local" DJ heard on dozens of other "local oldies" stations across the country. I'm not sure it mattered much anyway. Jerry Lee Lewis and Ricky Nelson sound pretty much the same no matter where the DJ is located.

This remote–local technique is the coming wave in broadcasting because it saves stations so much money. Why pay for a DJ in every city if one in Denver can do the job for all of them? They have even tried the same thing in TV news. One company, Sinclair Broadcast Group, tried using a TV studio and news team in suburban Maryland to handle national news, sports, and weather for dozens of Sinclair-owned local stations around the country. They called it "News Central," and it meant that viewers of Sinclair-owned stations in Oklahoma, North Carolina, and Michigan were all watching the same meteorologist in Maryland and perhaps thinking it was their local weatherman.

Or perhaps they weren't thinking that, since ratings for all those stations declined precipitously and Sinclair ended up dumping the News Central format. The technique is still used for some D.C. news bureaus, though, so a "local" reporter you see on your station in Boston going live from the White House may be the same reporter viewers see on their local station in Philadelphia a few minutes later. Which also explains why you never run into that reporter at your local mall.

But TV will always need some local reporters and photographers, because unlike in radio, in TV you can't just rip and read from the papers or the newswires. You have to have people at the location where the news actually occurred because you need video and on-camera sound bites. This forces TV stations to go out and cover stories for themselves.

What often happened with me in Whiteville was that I would learn of a story from a newspaper report and then go and delve into it myself as if starting from scratch. And in the process of interviewing people and sorting through the facts, I would often end up with very different conclusions about what really happened than what the newspaper had reported. A story idea is really just the beginning in TV. You have to track down video and find people who will talk on camera. In radio and print, I could do almost all of my research over the phone, but in TV, that doesn't work. I had to actually go places, film the scene, and show the people I talked to.

I also think that the idea that TV, radio, and newspapers are direct competitors reflects a misunderstanding of their respective roles. TV isn't well suited for the same kinds of stories that print and radio reporters do, and doesn't do them in the same way. TV's best attribute is that it can show pictures and emotions, not list detailed facts and figures. If the story is big enough, what happens is that TV and print each whet the public's appetite for the other. The pictures make people yearn for more details, and the details make people want to see the video.

Try convincing print reporters that TV is not a direct competitor, however, and all you'll get is a lot of derisive looks. This is what I got much of the time anyway, even though I encountered more than a few print reporters who got a little help on their stories from watching my TV news coverage. I can't tell you how many times I'd broadcast an interview with someone only to have the exact same quote, word for word, show up in the newspaper the next day without any attribution to my newscast. Either the interview subjects had memorized their lines and repeated them verbatim for the newspaper reporter or the newspaper writer had watched my interviews on TV. (You see this even with so-called "high quality" publications. I've seen articles in Pulitzer prize-winning newspapers where I'm pretty sure the quotes were pulled from interviews that aired on *Sportscenter*.)

But as someone who looked askance at TV when I was in print, I guess I deserved to have print reporters look down at me. Particularly when they saw me putting on makeup for a live shot. It's just hard to respect a man wearing blush and foundation.

The irony of TV reporting is that the better you are, the easier it looks. But trust me, it isn't that easy. Even apart from the intricacies of shooting and editing and worrying about the stand-up, stories have to be written quite differently for TV. You could take a radio story, throw in a few more details, and have a short but tolerable newspaper article. Likewise you could take a newspaper story, cut it in half and voice it into a microphone and you would have a boring but airable radio piece. But you couldn't take either a radio story or a newspaper article and run it on TV because the words would clash with the video.

I had to learn to let the pictures dictate the structure and order of the story. A good example of *not* doing this would be a story I tried to write about a North Carolina street fair, named in honor of a slave who became a free man and went on to great things. I started my script talking about what a wonderful guy he was. Then Leigh Powell kindly explained that this didn't work because we didn't have any video or pictures of the guy. There weren't a lot of video cameras back when he was around, and what still cameras there were weren't usually trained on slaves. So here I was, writing about a great man and all I had was video of people dancing at the fair.

If we had aired the story written like that, it would have looked as though the station put in the wrong tape. I had to completely rewrite the story, and start out by talking about people celebrating at the fair, and then proceed to explain who the fair was named after.

For another example of the challenge of writing for TV, take the time I did a story about a jet plane that had to make an emergency landing after depressurizing at 30,000 feet. Nobody was hurt, but it was a frightening incident for the passengers nonetheless. I went out to the airport and found dozens of shaken travelers.

In print, I would've started my story describing the panic at 30,000 feet. But I didn't have any footage of the plane at 30,000 feet, or of oxygen masks coming down, or even of the successful landing. All the video I could get were shots of the plane sitting at the gate and the passengers milling around in the luggage area. So I had to start the story at the end, talking about the passengers' relief at being back on the ground. Then I let the passengers tell the story of what had happened through sound bites. I asked everyone I interviewed to describe for me what had happened, from start to finish, even after I had heard it several times. I then used snippets from different people, cutting back and forth from one to another, each describing a small part of the narrative.

One person would say, "We heard this loud noise and the oxygen masks dropped down." Then I cut to another person saying, "The flight attendant came over the loudspeaker and told us to remain in our seats." Then cut to a third person saying, "I thought we were going to die ...." It was a way to present the story without showing any video of what had happened.

Learning these sorts of techniques was a challenge for me, but I was aided immeasurably by a complete stranger — a Florida TV reporter named Stephen Stock. Stock happened to notice an article I wrote about the Great Paul Spelman Job Tour, and he called to let me know he liked it and was pulling for me. Stock had undertaken a similar road trip when he started out in the business, although I believe he landed a job a bit faster than I did. By the time he called me, he had become a fairly prominent reporter with a station in Orlando (market 23!), and he offered to aid my career development.

I'm not sure why he did this, but I am eternally grateful. I only met him a couple of times, and only for an hour or two each time, but for years I would send him a tape of my stories every few months and receive back lengthy suggestions and critiques. His advice was invaluable.

His best suggestion was to concentrate on people — who is affected by the story; who is really impacted by a news event? Focusing on people does two important things. The first is that it humanizes a TV story, making it seem real to viewers because you're talking about a genuine person instead of a theoretical concept. News doesn't happen in a vacuum; it's generally not news unless someone is affected. Equally as important from my point of view, focusing on people also helped out immeasurably in terms of providing video to show and write about. Coming from print and radio, I had no idea what to use for b-roll. If I was doing a story about an outbreak of scarlet fever, what should I show for pictures? Hospitals? Thermometers? Helen Keller?

Trying to cover stories, I often found myself with 45 seconds of script and not a single second of video to cover it with. But if I could find someone with the illness and focus my story on that person, all I had to get were a few shots of him or her lying around and I could report about it to my heart's content.

I became very adept at a technique I nicknamed the "human boomerang." I didn't invent it (other than the name), but I probably became its most ardent practitioner. I would start with an affected person, move on to the bigger issue, and then boomerang back to the real person at the end. So if the story was about a bad drought affecting the region, I'd find some Columbus County farmer and start with him. "Frank the Farmer lost a third of his crops last week ...." Then, because the big picture was about all farmers and not just Frank, I'd move on to the details of how many farms were impacted, how bad it was compared to previous droughts, and why consumers would soon see produce prices go through the roof. Then, in order to bring closure to my story and remind viewers of the human toll, I'd close the piece with something on the order of, "And if it doesn't rain soon, Frank could see 200 years of his family legacy dry into dust. In the farmland, I'm Paul Spelman."

This technique is a bit hackneyed and you can overdo it (I know I did), but for a reporter in need of video to show, it was a godsend. And I really needed it because in Whiteville I was always short of b-roll. Being in a bureau, I didn't have access to the station's video archives, so any video I needed I had to shoot myself the very same day.

About the only stories for which I didn't struggle to find video were the rare spot-news pieces. Spot news is breaking news, something happening at that instant, allowing the reporter to be "on the spot." Car accidents, fires, explosions, shootings, and tornadoes are examples of spot news. Spot news is local TV's forte, nobody does it better. By the time a spot-news story gets written about and published in a newspaper, it's old news, since people have already seen the tanker explosion 27 times on TV. They don't need a newspaper writer to provide a picturesque description of the carnage.

In big cities, there's often so much spot news that TV reporters can pick and choose, or sit around waiting for something to happen. In Whiteville, I did not have that luxury. If I waited for spot news to happen, at six o'clock there was a good chance I would still be waiting. So I had to plan my day as if there wasn't going to be any spot news, and then if spot news broke, I'd drop whatever story I was doing and go cover the exciting stuff. This was great if spot news happened early in the day, but exasperating when it happened after I'd already spent five hours working on some less riveting story and had to throw it away because a car wreck was more newsworthy.

No matter what I was covering, I came to rely heavily on another sage piece of Stephen Stock advice: always put the best pictures first. That meant starting with the most arresting video I had and developing the story from there. It works like a visual version of a newspaper lead. In print, the first line is supposed to grab your attention and make you want to read the rest of the article. In TV, the first pictures you see should do the same.

So if I was doing a story on a snowstorm, and had a great shot of a school bus sliding down a hill (this actually happened later on when I was in Knoxville; the bus nearly ran over my photographer Jason Grant), I'd make that the first shot viewers saw. After all, who wouldn't pay attention to a shot of a school bus sliding down a hill? Then I'd write about all the snow on the roads and what the city was doing to handle it, show trucks dumping salt, and interview kids building a snowman. Then, at the very end, I'd let viewers know what happened to the bus. The idea was that if you were walking by your TV and saw a school bus sliding down a hill, you would stop and watch, if only to find out what happened. And if I could say, "Frank the Farmer's son was on this school bus …," well, even better.

Starting a story with the most visually arresting video is a technique I never stopped using, and I am not the only one. Many many TV news stories begin with the most arresting video and end with the second- or third-best shot. That way, you grab the viewer's attention at the start and leave them with a lasting impression at the finish. It's not much for subtle storytelling, but when you've only got 90 seconds to tell a tale, subtlety goes out the window. If TV news had made the film *The Titanic*, we would have started with the boat going down. That, or Kate Winslet with her shirt off.

Chapter 9

Creative Fabrication and Fair Play

Another big challenge I faced was that despite the helpfulness of people in Whiteville, a lot of them still did not want to be on TV. This is true of people everywhere. Despite the seemingly endless supply of folks willing to make fools of themselves on reality shows and the like, there are an equal number of people with a deep fear of TV cameras.

People I encountered would often refuse to go on camera even after I promised that I would show them in a favorable light. "What do you mean you don't want to do an interview," I'd complain, "I'm going to make you look good."

This again, was a huge change from my previous experience. People are quite willing to say things to a newspaper or radio reporter that they wouldn't dream of uttering on TV. I've heard people practically confess to being on the grassy knoll and then refuse to divulge their last name when a TV photographer ambled over. The fact that several newspaper reporters were clearly scribbling down their confession didn't bother them, but have something they say air on TV? Oh no. This always makes me wonder what people think print reporters do with their comments. If someone says something stupid, that person looks just as stupid in print as they would on TV. Well maybe not just as stupid, but stupid, nonetheless.

Yet when I switched into TV, I was very surprised to encounter all sorts of people who would agree to do an interview when I called, but then change their minds when I showed up with my TV camera.

"Oh, you mean do the interview for TV?"

"Yes. I work for a TV station. That's the way we do interviews."

"I'm sorry, I didn't realize that's what you meant when you said you worked for Channel 3 Eyewitness News. I'm sorry, but my house is a mess and I haven't washed my hair."

So, just as in Telluride I had had to learn how to get people to return my calls, in Whiteville I had to learn how to get people to go on tape. There are a variety of ways to do this, some more devious than others.

There's always the hidden camera, of course, often called "lipstick cams" because the first ones were about the size and shape of a tube of lipstick. While once the sole province of well-funded network news magazines, they are now much cheaper and more widely available, even in small-market news. I've never been a big fan of hidden cameras because I feel they are deceptive, but apparently I'm one of the few who feel this way, since you see hidden camera stories all over the place and they're often big ratings getters.

On the other hand, more than one of these stories has led to a lawsuit, and some TV crews have been held liable for invasion of privacy. But these are hard cases for plaintiffs to win, and they don't seem to have put a damper on the number of hidden camera stories.

I think that there are times to use hidden cameras —when the end *is* worth the means. Using a hidden camera is justifiable when infiltrating the Mafia or running an expose on deceptive tactics used by used-car sellers. But some reporters use hidden cameras because they don't feel like asking permission to shoot video. One reporter I worked with liked to put a hidden microphone on himself, hide his photographer across the street, and then knock on the door of the person he wanted to interview. This seems excessively sneaky when you are just trying to get a councilman's comment about new parking restrictions.

That said, I understand the impulse, because many people have a stubborn reluctance to talk on camera. I've never used a lipstick cam, and in Whiteville, I didn't have one, but I can't deny that I've participated in a few schemes to get people to do an on-camera interview.

Once, when covering the James Jordan murder case, I encountered a defense lawyer who liked to expound at great length and on the record for any reporter with a pen and pad, but refused to do any interviews on camera. He did this despite the fact that the court proceedings themselves were being videotaped and aired on TV. His favoritism toward the print media made life difficult for all the TV reporters, so one sharp reporter (not me) came up with the idea of using the official courtroom camera to conduct an interview. We told the courtroom camera operator to keep rolling during a court recess, while the reporter and myself subtly maneuvered the defense attorney close to one of the table microphones, set up to record the hearing. The camera in the back of the courtroom filmed from a distance while we asked questions and pretended to scribble down his comments like print reporters. The nearby microphones picked up all the sound, and the attorney ended up doing a splendid TV interview without realizing it.

The funny thing is that he probably saw it on TV later and was pleased. That's a really odd thing about TV – a lot of people are initially reluctant to talk to you but then are quite happy when they see themselves on the air. Often, to get someone to talk on camera, I would say, "Let's do the interview, and if you think it went badly, I promise I won't use it." I always kept my promise. But after using this tactic more than a hundred times, I had only one person ever ask me not to

143

run the interview (and I reluctantly complied). It was much more common for them to ask for a copy of the tape.

I am sympathetic to the fact that people have a right to be camera shy, but I also believe that much of the reluctance is misguided. Not just because people end up liking the way they look, but because people are often better off with an interview on tape since they can't be misquoted. Print journalists misquote people all the time. I know I did when I was a newspaper reporter. It's not that I intentionally fabricated quotes, it's just that it is impossible to copy everything down verbatim, and different people tend to hear the same comments differently.

I learned this early on when I compared my notes and those of other print reporters with an actual audiotape of an event we had all just witnessed. Our accounts were all over the map. Everyone must have his or her own subconscious editing filter, because no one had heard the same sentence the same way unless it was extremely short, of the "I shall return" variety. When it comes to jotted-down quotes, not only don't I believe everything I read, I don't believe everything I wrote.

If you told a roomful of reporters, "I think, perhaps, I'll head down to the store and get a new sweater for the winter," you would end up with several different quotes in the papers the next day. The differences might be small — things like "go down" instead of "head down," or "buy" instead of "get" a new sweater — and might not alter the meaning of the sentence, but the differences would be there. And sometimes they do affect the meaning. For instance, if someone reported that you said, "I think, perhaps, I'll head down to a whore and be a cheater this winter." On TV, though, you don't have to worry about being misquoted; it's all on tape.

Of course, there are drawbacks to taped accuracy. A lot of print reporters, whether consciously or unconsciously, clean up the grammar and syntax of whomever they're interviewing. That's why many athletes sound more intelligent in print than they do on TV. It's also why, a few years back, there was some controversy when then-D.C. Mayor Marion Barry complained that a reporter *hadn't* cleaned up his comments in the same manner that reporters cleaned up everyone else's. Barry was quoted as saying that he was not worried that he could face Jesse Jackson as a mayoral candidate because Jackson "didn't want to be no mayor." Barry did not deny that he used that expression, but said the reporter acted in a racist fashion in not cleaning it up.

Believe it or not, radio reporters sometimes clean up people's speech too. Radio reporters often edit out the "uhs" and "ums" and other less coherent utterances of an interviewee, mostly for brevity purposes. As a radio reporter, I was taught how to cut and paste sentences to make them shorter and to the point, so if someone said, "I think I'll go down to the store, and, I don't know, maybe buy a new sweater this winter," I might snip out the "I don't know" part. I was also taught to turn on the tape recorder and remain silent for a few seconds before beginning an interview in order to record ambient noise *of the silence*, also known as "white noise." That way if I needed to insert a slight pause, say, between the words "and" and "maybe," I'd have a piece of silence with just the right background hum.

Some radio editors get so good at slicing and dicing they can even take consonants and move them around. So if a person slurs his words together so that it sounds as if he said, "I think I'll go down to the storean'Idunno, maybe buy a new sweater this winter," the editor can find somewhere else on the tape where the guy said "in this land," and take the hard "nd" from "land" and tack it onto "storean'" to make the quote come to a full stop for a second so they can then cut out the

"Idunno." I was once told by a national radio reporter that he was allowed to do this for everyone but the president, George W. Bush. I'm not sure why Bush was excluded, perhaps because every presidential utterance is considered a part of history. Or maybe the radio management just found Bush's tortured syntax entertaining.

In TV, I couldn't do much to clean up a person's speech because I usually *showed* the person while they were speaking, and it would have resembled a badly dubbed martial arts film if their mouth wasn't synched with their words. TV reporters do occasionally snip out sentences to shorten a sound bite, but you have to cover the speaker with video of something else to do this, and the process often isn't worth the effort.

A much bigger dilemma in TV is staging, where the photographer specifically asks someone to do something so they can get video of it. If, for instance, a TV photographer asks a police officer to wallop a protester over the head so he can get some exciting footage, that's considered staging. The most infamous example of TV staging occurred when an NBC news crew supposedly rigged a car to explode for a story about exploding gas tanks.

While that level of egregious behavior is uncommon, casual staging is done all the time, despite the fact that most TV crews claim they don't do it. When you are watching *60 Minutes* and see someone walking down the hall before moving past the camera and out of the frame, that was staged. The photographer told the person to walk down the hall and not acknowledge the camera. How else would someone fail to notice a TV cameraman crouched down at the end of their hallway? If you see someone on TV walking down a hall, or sitting at a desk, or driving down the road, all the while apparently never noticing that there is a camera crew filming them from just a few feet away, it is probably because they

146

have been told to act that way. On the other hand, if you see someone staring straight into the lens, or fleeing as fast as their legs will carry them, well that probably wasn't staged.

Staging is not necessarily unethical and verboten. In that hallway shot, for instance, the reporter and photographer need some video to show while they are introducing the person in the story, something like, "John Messerschmidt is a nuclear arms expert who's single, a Virgo, and loves long walks on the beach ...." For that sort of a passage, it is considered acceptable to stage a hallway walk or something similar as long as the reporter doesn't pretend that whatever he is describing occurred at the same time the video was shot. In other words, if you write, "John Messerschmidt was walking down the hallway Thursday when he realized he loved long walks on the beach...," that might be a no-no.

It's a very fuzzy line, I know. If I'm doing a story about forensic detectives tracking down a serial killer, is it staging if I got shots of them looking up fingerprints on a computer database? It probably is if I write it like a reenactment. "It was a dark and stormy night, and Detective Kowalski was at his desk checking the fingerprint files when he suddenly found a match for the much-feared mustachioed killer." Whereas it probably wouldn't be considered improper if I write, "Detective Kowalski runs fingerprints through an FBI database. That's how he found a match one day ...."

While it can be hard to tell what is "permissible" staging and what isn't, a far clearer no-no is to physically alter the scene to make it look better. But this is pretty common, too. TV reporters and photographers are always moving things around to get them in or out of the picture. I even knew one photographer who claimed he brought along his own props, such as a Teddy Bear, to throw onto crime scenes and thus invest them with emotional impact. "A broken guitar is good too, but they're a pain to lug around," he used to joke. At least I think he was joking. I never actually saw him do any of this, so maybe he was pulling my leg. But some photographers I worked with said they knew a photographer who was fired for placing a mannequin in a fire scene so it looked as though burned legs were lying in the ashes. This sounds so ridiculous and far-fetched I find it hard to believe, but they swore it was true.

Even if TV photographers and reporters *don't* do this sort of thing, they still have an immense power to decide whether something is "newsworthy" just by what gets left in or out of a story. If I'm covering a Ku Klux Klan rally, for instance, and there are only 9 Klansmen, do I show an intimidating and impressive close-up of bright white hoods and menacing torches (which looks great on TV), or do I show a wide shot that reveals their miniscule numbers and the fact that the marchers are outnumbered by bemused hecklers? The difference in terms of impact can be tremendous..

In addition to reporters' and photographers' decisions about what to show, you also have to make judgment calls about what people say, since you can only include short sound bites in a 90-second story, and only so many. I once covered a speech by George W. Bush, for instance, in which he referred to himself as the president. The problem with this was that at the time he wasn't; he was running for it. And it wasn't a line like, "As president, I would ...," it was more like, "Being president has been great ...." It seemed presumptuous for him to be speaking as if the election was over long before the voters went to the polls. Then again, maybe he'd been talking to some Supreme Court justices and knew something we didn't. In any event, I didn't think it was worth making a big issue out of it in my news story, so I didn't mention it.

148

Some people might say I made a judgment call that should have been left to the viewers. But I only had 90 seconds for my story, and had I focused on Bush's verbal blunders, I couldn't have reported on anything else. It also seemed like a minor slip of the tongue by a campaign-bleary candidate. Now if Bush had said, "Being president of Canada has been great," I might have given it more play.

As for actually fabricating quotes and information out of whole cloth, this is a hot topic these days following revelations that reporters at nationally renowned publications such as the New York Times and USA Today invented stories and sources.

At the Times, the reporter Jayson Blair displayed remarkable creativity, using a cell phone and laptop computer to make his editors think he was covering stories in Maryland, Ohio, and Texas, among other locations, while he was, in fact, relaxing in his New York apartment. He also invented several quotes and plagiarized others from other newspapers.

Meanwhile, at USA Today, its star reporter Jack Kelley fabricated substantial parts of eight major stories and lifted dozens of quotes from other newspapers. According to USA Today's own investigation, Kelley even conspired with a translator to impersonate a "source" so that his editors wouldn't find out that his stories were fake. Kelley's "sins were sweeping and substantial," according to the USA Today report on the matter. I'll say.

Another reporter, Stephen Glass of the New Republic, invented so many stories that they made a movie about it, Shattered Glass. And even the Washington Post, one of the Times' loudest critics on the Blair episode, ought to be careful about throwing stones, since it had to return a Pulitzer Prize after admitting that one of its reporters invented an eight-year-old heroin addict named "Jimmy" and then fabricated all sorts of interesting material about him. When confronted, the

149

reporter, Janet Cooke, said that Jimmy was a "composite" of several people but conceded that he didn't actually exist. It turned out Cooke's resume was something of a composite as well, and included a degree or two she didn't earn.

I have never done anything like that, and I honestly don't think the practice is widespread. While mistakes are common, and reporters may fudge small details at times, most journalists simply don't do large-scale fabrication. But I can see how it might be tempting, especially with quotes. I say that because a lot of the time, you know exactly what someone is going to say before you interview them and almost feel as though you should just pencil in their comments ahead of time.

Are the concerned parents going to say, "You can't put a price tag on a child's education," when asked their thoughts about school budget cuts? Is the neighbor going to say she is "shocked to see something like that happen around here" after being informed of a gruesome slaying in her quiet residential neighborhood? I knew a photographer who heard this so often that when he was out getting public reaction to something that he would knock on doors and say, "Could you come out and tell us that you're stunned to hear this and that your neighbor seemed like a regular guy, but kept to himself a lot?" You air these sorts of comments so often, people must feel they are *supposed* to say them.

The same goes for the word "hero," invariably used to describe anyone who has done anything mildly courageous. The word has become cheapened by overuse. In my book, heroes are people who, at great risk to their own safety or well-being, voluntarily put someone else's interest above their own without any expectation of personal gain. In other words, a passerby who jumps into an icy river to save someone from drowning. Or someone who, while still living, donates an organ to a complete stranger. A hero is not someone who returns a lost wallet, or someone with $20 million dollars who gives $10 million of it to charity. Those actions are admirable, but it's not like they were risking life and limb, or even financial security, in order to help someone else.

Even firefighters and police and astronauts do not automatically merit the term "hero" in my opinion just for having a dangerous occupation. First off, it's their job; they know the risks when they sign up for it and they get paid to accept them. Moreover, they may derive a lot of personal benefit from their job. Maybe from the job status, or from the opportunity to play with cool equipment, or from the fact that it's just more interesting than sitting at a desk all day.

For an astronaut, they get to go up in space. This is something wealthy "space tourists" are willing to pay $20 million to do. If somebody is willing to pay $20 million to do something, I'm thinking you don't need to be a hero to do it. Whereas you don't see people lining up to throw their bodies on hand grenades.

Now if someone with a risky job voluntarily accepts risks way beyond what would normally be expected (like a police officer putting down his gun and trading himself for a hostage, or those firefighters who continued to battle the blaze at the Chernobyl nuclear plant even when they must have known they were getting dosed with deadly radiation), that may well qualify as a genuinely heroic act. But otherwise, I feel that people with risky occupations deserve our admiration and respect as courageous individuals, but not necessarily the designation "hero."

There is a difference between courage and heroism. On the morning of 9/11, I agreed to go to New York City and cover the terrorist attack. No one knew how bad it was going to be, and I was, in essence, "running toward danger," as some have called it, while most people were headed in the other direction.

This required a moderate degree of nerve on my part, but there was nothing heroic about my actions. I was a journalist and accepted the fact that I had to cover the news even when it might be personally dangerous to do so. I also knew that I might get a lot of good exposure and experience and it could help my career. Yet you hear people described on TV as heroes for doing far less. The word has been devalued to such an extent that these days you can get labeled a hero for recycling your garbage.

Similarly, the line, "Our thoughts and prayers are with the families" gets repeated with aggravating regularity by a lot of people whose thoughts and prayers couldn't be farther from whatever calamity is at issue. I once had a defense lawyer give me that "thoughts and prayers" line five or six times in a row in response to my questions. I was covering a case where a crime victim, a young boy, had been killed in an unrelated accident just before he was to testify against a man charged with assaulting him. The boy's death made it likely that all charges would be dropped against the alleged assailant because he was now unable to confront his accuser as required under the Constitution.

The defendant's attorney maintained a grave expression for the camera while repeating over and over again, "We're really not thinking about how this will affect our case. Our thoughts and prayers are with the family of the boy." He said this so many times that I finally joked, "So, would you say your thoughts and prayers are with the family?" We both laughed, but afterward I felt ashamed, as though I'd been complicit. Shortly thereafter I declared a personal moratorium on including that thoughts-and-prayers line in any of my stories.

Other clichés you hear all too often as a TV reporter include the old "she always made you smile" and "he would've done anything for you," invariably said about the recently departed. Just once, I'd like to hear someone say, "Well I wouldn't say good riddance, but I never liked the guy." At least then I'd know they were being honest, and not just saying something because they felt they were supposed to. When I die, I sincerely hope someone says, "Yeah, Paul could be an ass sometimes, but on the whole, he did more good than harm." That would be honest praise.

The fact that reporters hear the same old clichés over and over again does not justify inventing quotes. I say it merely to suggest one reason why creative fabrication may be tempting. I think that what little fabrication occurs is probably done more out of laziness or cynicism than a deliberate attempt to mislead. Heroin is a genuine problem, and there may be an eight-year-old heroin addict somewhere; Janet Cooke just didn't work hard enough to find him.

Personally, I've never invented a fact or a quote for one of my stories. Observant readers may notice that I said "one of *my* stories." Parse that a little bit and some might ask, "What about someone else's story?" To that, I must plead guilty. I did once help a friend make up a few quotes for a story.

It happened when I was a newspaper reporter in Telluride, and another reporter (who shall remain nameless) was assigned a feature story about a well-known local extreme skier. An extreme skier is someone who skis off cliffs and jumps over cars and things like that. Unfortunately, my friend waited until the very last minute to contact the skier and was unable to reach him. So late at night on the day before the story was due, the two of us sat around concocting quotes for the article. We had the skier say stuff like, "The only way to ski is to ski on the edge," and, "If I'm not close to losin' it, I really don't feel like I'm alive." Those are the sorts of comments that extreme skiers tend to make anyway, and we

153

figured if the quotes made the guy look cool to his buddies, he wouldn't complain. He never did.

We borrowed this technique from a guy I knew in college who used it for a variety of tall tales, mostly about his exploits with the opposite sex. In order to ensure that no one challenged the veracity of his stories, he would invariably make all available witnesses appear suave and debonair in the retelling. Had I been with him when he made a play for some attractive coed, and I was there when he recounted the story, he would include me by saying, "So while I'm chatting up this beautiful babe, Paul lays a hundred on the bar and tells the bartender, 'Keep 'em comin'....'" All the while you're thinking, "I never did that. When was the last time I had a hundred dollar bill?" But with awed listeners now gazing at you with respect and admiration, you'd just nod and stay silent.

This technique is not fail-safe, by the way. There is a famous court case in which Baseball Hall of Famer Warren Spahn sued a journalist who wrote that Spahn had been a great war hero who had "raced into the teeth of the enemy barrage" during the Battle of the Bulge, going "from man to man, urging them on." Spahn had been at the Battle of the Bulge but apparently had done none of these things and did not appreciate this exaggeration of his service. He sued and won. But then again, Warren Spahn had a lot of other things to brag about, so he didn't need a writer making stuff up. Extreme skiers, on the other hand, generally welcome all the favorable publicity they can get.

In addition to helping my friend come up with extreme skier quotes, I should also confess that once or twice I did not object to being named as the speaker of fictitious quotes in someone else's story. This happened when a reporter friend (not the same one as above, but one who shared some of the same traits) was writing articles about extreme sports for a small newspaper. He asked if I minded being included in his stories and I said he could write whatever he wanted. Or rather, he could write that I said whatever he wanted. As a result, I became featured as a mountain unicyclist who had been "one wheelin' for about 15 years." I was quoted extolling the joys of riding up and down hills and through the woods on my one knobby tire, a lone pinky raised in the "universal unicycling salute." This was all made up. At the time there wasn't any such thing as mountain unicycling. There is now, affirming once again that life imitates art.

In another article, I was described as "Paul Spelman, back-country enthusiast." This for a native New Yorker who rarely went hiking. I have to admit I kind of enjoyed these moments in the limelight but was also a tad relieved when my friend got serious and stopped inventing his sources. As for me, I always left that part of my reporting ability unexplored. Maybe I just don't have a vivid enough imagination.

I have, however, included true things in stories that I never intended for publication. For instance, in some stories I wrote as a newspaper reporter in Telluride, I used to refer to a local real estate agent I didn't much care for as "Mark the Shark," figuring the editors would delete that line. I stopped doing this after spotting it still in the paper just moments before it went to the printer.

You have to be very careful about these sorts of things, because they get you in a lot of trouble when they make their way into the newspaper or on the air. A prank or joke making it past unwary editors is not uncommon. I once noticed a photo caption declaring "Ding Dong the Witch is Dead" below a picture of the town manager announcing her resignation. I noticed this just in time for the editors to change it. I didn't write that one, I swear, but I probably saved someone's job by catching it.

Quite frankly, the media makes enough mistakes without intentionally shooting itself in the foot. Every year you'll see glorious headlines such as "Air Head Fired," "Stud Tires Out," and "War Dims Hope for Peace." Those are genuine headlines, by the way, along with "Police Begin Campaign to Run Down Jaywalkers" and "Typhoon Rips Through Cemetery; Hundreds Dead." You can find a whole book full of examples of media blunders in a compilation called *Red Tape Holds Up New Bridge*. In Telluride, one of the papers once ran a headline referring to the "Pubic Library." I'm still on the lookout for that institution. Maybe it just means there's a lot of Internet access.

TV also has its fair share of blunders, of course. I've heard of an anchor who, when introducing a story about Valentine's Day, announced, "Let's go to Don with his big red heart on …." In a similar vein, a female anchor, wondering aloud why it didn't snow as forecast, once asked the weatherman, "So Bob, where were those six inches you promised me last night?"

I never made a mistake like that, but I did have my moments. In addition to mistaking emollients for accelerants, I once misread a Teleprompter and kept reading after my story was over. The result was that I started to introduce the next story, which had nothing to do with the one I was reporting on. That was a minor mistake. The bigger mistake was that when I realized what I had done, I grimaced and silently mouthed the word "fuck," believing that my camera was off. It wasn't, and it's a good thing I didn't say it out loud because my microphone was still on too.

I was very fortunate that nobody noticed and called in to complain. Actually, I shouldn't say nobody because one photographer noticed and saved the tape for the station's Christmas party blooper reel, to go along with a couple of other classic Spelman moments, such as the time I jokingly told the news photographer not to show me from the waist down because I was concerned about my physical endowment. He really should not have been rolling at the time.

Apart from these small blunders, I've never done anything as a reporter that I'm truly ashamed of. And besides, while you can make lots of mistakes in TV, it is actually a lot harder to invent material like those now legendary newspaper reporters. In TV, not only is it hard to make up quotes, it is hard to misquote someone, because it's all on tape. There's something about a TV clip that's just hard to refute. Maybe that's the *real* reason people don't like giving TV interviews – it eliminates what Oliver North so artfully referred to as plausible deniability. TV cameras can mislead, but they usually can't lie. The tape speaks for itself.

You can lead the witness, of course. Some reporters practically tell the person they're interviewing what to say. I knew of a reporter who once asked, "Would you say that this is an important issue?" When the person said yes, the reporter said, "No. Could you say that? And say it slowly." It's also possible to edit comments out of context. If you are artful enough, you can take someone saying, "No, not yet," and make it appear as if the person is confessing to all sorts of heinous crimes and misdeeds.

Reporter: *"It appears that Johnson has not stopped wetting his bed.*

Cut to sound bite of Johnson: *"No, not yet."*

But I really don't think this happens very often. TV sound bites, while quite short, may be a more accurate reflection of what a person said than what you read in the newspaper, especially in smaller markets where print reporters don't all

157

carry tape recorders. In big cities where print reporters are more likely to record their interviews, there aren't as many mistakes. The invention of recording equipment has made incorrect quotes a lot less common than they once were. The days are mostly past when, according to the New York Public Library's historical records, a reporter could take Nathan Hale's comment, "It is the duty of every good officer to obey any orders given him by his commander in chief," and transcribe it as, "I only regret I have but one life to lose for my country." You may not find it in the history books, but MacArthur may have said, "I'll be back later" instead of "I shall return." As I noted earlier, if a reporter isn't using a tape recorder, the quote is probably not 100% verbatim. To borrow a line from the film *Memento*, memory is just an interpretation.

That said, newspaper reports are much more detailed than TV stories and may provide a more accurate picture in their entirety. Newspaper stories may also *appear* more balanced because the need for sound bites in TV presents a genuine equity problem. A TV story (and radio, to a lesser degree) can appear unbalanced without sound bites from both sides. If one side speaks on tape, and the other side doesn't, viewers almost always side with the person they heard. Most people instinctively feel that that person has less to hide. This can be a big problem if one side either can't or won't talk on camera.

I first noticed this when I did a TV story about kids getting burned by Volvo automobiles. On some Volvo station wagons, the tailpipes were flush against the rear bumper (I'm told the problem has been corrected), and kids climbing out the back could inadvertently press their legs onto a scalding hot tailpipe. I called Volvo to get its side and its representative seemed genuinely concerned about it. I would too, if a TV reporter called telling me he was doing a story about kids getting burned on my vehicles. The Volvo spokesperson promptly said they would conduct a thorough investigation, and gave me all sorts of good quotes for my story.

Unfortunately, I was doing the story from Tennessee, and Volvo's American headquarters were in New Jersey, which was a bit far for me to go to get an on-camera sound bite and make it back for the six o'clock news.

Since the local Volvo dealers all deferred to Volvo headquarters for comment, I wasn't able to get an on-air sound bite representing Volvo's side. So although I prominently included the company's comments in my story, no one from Volvo appeared on screen expressing concern. Meanwhile, I had plenty of emotional video and sound bites from a distraught mother and her scarred child. It simply wasn't a fair fight. While I had tried to be as fair as possible, and my script was fairly balanced in its written form and in terms of how much space I afforded each side, the version that viewers saw made it look as if Volvo was hiding something.

That's not to say TV reporters are always fair-minded individuals who want perfectly balanced stories, but sometimes you try and can't.

And no matter what news medium the story appears in, it is an undeniable fact that people who cooperate with the media get better coverage than those who don't. It is just impossible to be as fair to someone who won't talk to you, or as critical of someone who will.

Take the time I covered an accused embezzler charged with stealing money from his Knoxville nightclub, the *Cotton-Eyed Joe*. The defendant was a large Middle Eastern immigrant named Nazif "Gingi" Bakri, whose accent was closer to West Palestine than West Texas, but he dressed in cowboy boots and jeans, and his country and western saloon was a genuine all-American success. It was one of those clubs

159

the size of a football field with sawdust on the floor and lines of hat-wearing boot-clad men and women dancing around the floor. People in Tennessee would literally drive for hours to come to the *Cotton-Eyed Joe*, and the place raked in the cash. Unfortunately, all that cash may have been a temptation for Mr. Bakri, because the government charged him with pocketing $800,000 of it instead of divvying it up among his investors. Prosecutors said he was skimming from the till and funneling it to his family in Jordan. He was now facing mail fraud and international money laundering charges that could send him to prison for 181 years.

I had met and interviewed Bakri once before about an unrelated matter, and found him an engaging character. But sitting behind him at his arraignment, I figured he wouldn't be as accommodating this time around. I was wrong. He immediately turned and greeted me and the other reporters with a big smile and said he would talk to us right after the hearing. He also noted, "Don't forget to mention that we're still open for business. Dollar-fifty long-neck Budweisers tonight."

How can you rake a guy like that over the coals? I have no idea whether he was crooked (he ended up pleading guilty to tax evasion) but in my news report that night I made sure to stress that these were "just allegations" and that Bakri denied them. I even mentioned the beer special. Bakri and his club got much more favorable coverage, from me and the other reporters, than they would have had he shunned the media like so many defendants. There's no way around it, people who cooperate get better coverage. My advice to someone accused of something would be: lie, cheat, deceive, fool, spin, mislead, twist, or slant your story however you want, but don't just refuse to say anything.

160

Besides, if you talk, the media will generally feel obligated to include whatever it is you have to say. News reporting would actually be a lot easier if you could ignore one side. News stories are simpler to write that way and often more compelling. It makes for a more sensational story if one side's wild allegations go unchallenged. I've even known reporters who deliberately waited until it was late in the day to phone one side for comment, just so they could keep their story onesided and gleefully state, "Joe Smith did not return our calls." This is completely unfair and I didn't do it. But if one side won't talk, it is hard to be fair and balanced no matter how much opportunity you provide.

That, of course, is why so many corporations and organizations hire public relations firms and public information officers, known as PIOs. Besides promoting the interests of the organization, PIOs are supposed to be available at a moment's notice to respond to whatever situation offers the slightest possibility of tarnishing the organization's image. Reporters and PIOs thus have a symbiotic and yet mutually distrustful relationship.

As a reporter in local news, you deal with PIOs of one sort or another almost daily, especially law enforcement ones. They set up interviews with police officers, provide news briefings about crimes and arrests, and occasionally even let you know if there's something worth doing a story on. Of course, their idea of what's worthwhile (a lot of D.A.R.E. anti-drug stories and pieces about the effectiveness of "community policing") don't always mesh with yours, but you deal with them so often you get pretty friendly nonetheless. In fact, most PIOs are former journalists, so they understand what the media needs.

Whiteville was too small for most agencies and organizations to have PIOs, but when I worked in Knoxville, the police and sheriff's department each had their own, and even had automated PIO systems called Code-A-Phones. These were basically answering machines with numbered message boxes. The PIOs would update the boxes during the day and reporters could call in, punch in a code, and learn the latest on whatever story they were covering. The messages often didn't provide enough information for a complete story, but they were great for checking to see if anything had changed since you last spoke to a real officer (if the police had named a suspect, for instance) and for letting you know if there was something worth exploring further. And best of all, the Code-A-Phones were always accessible. Believe me, it's a lot easier to reach an automated answering machine than a civil servant at 4:30 on a Friday afternoon.

While law enforcement PIOs can be quite helpful, I can't say the same about PIOs working for large corporations. Although in theory it is the corporate PR person's job to talk to the media, it is also his or her job to talk to you without actually saying anything. PR people take classes in this and specifically learn how to avoid giving attention-getting sound bites. I once spent 25 minutes interviewing a spokesman for a North Carolina community hospital who answered every question with, "Paul, we're just concerned about maintaining the quality of care for local residents and we want what's best for the community."

"I see. But how do you think your sale to a private for-profit entity will affect care for the indigent?"

"Well, we're in the process of evaluating all possible options because we want to make sure quality health care is maintained for local residents, and we want what's in the best interest of the community."

"Yes, but are you concerned about losing control to an out-of-state organization that may have profit requirements?"

"What we're concerned about is making sure that whatever happens will be what's best for the community, so the community will have the best possible care …"

He reiterated the same sentence so many times, with just slight variations, that I finally finished one of his sentences for him.

"We just want…" he began to say, and I cut in, "What's best for the community. Yes, I got that. I'm tired of that line, you need a new one."

He wasn't very friendly after that. His thoughts and prayers were not with me.

Some people would no doubt say he was just good at his job. That's what it's all about in public relations, staying on message. Many in PR view the media with suspicion, as if reporters have an agenda and are always out for blood. A friend in PR once lent me a company handbook, created by a prominent national public relations firm, describing how to handle press interviews. The guide instructed interview subjects to address reporters by their first names, as if the two of you are pals (a mistake by the way, it sounds condescending and messes up TV sound bites), and make sure to "listen, answer, bridge" so that the subject always returns to whatever topic it is the company wants to talk about. Whatever's in the best interests of the community, undoubtedly. To help the interviewee accomplish this, the handbook provided no less than 23 useful transition lines, such as, "Before I forget, I want to tell your audience …" and, "That's an important point because …"

The guide also warned interview subjects to beware of four interviewer types: the "machine gunner," who barrages the interviewee with questions; the "interrupter" (fairly self-explanatory); the "paraphraser," who tries to put words in your mouth; and the "dart thrower," described as "a contentious reporter [who] uses negativity to dislodge interesting negative quotes from you and, in a sense, break down your story." Dart throwers, warned the guide, should be treated "as if they are kind and caring individuals, despite any evidence to the contrary." I'm not making that up. This guide covered everything; it even provided fashion suggestions on what to wear for a TV interview. Red ties and no vests.

Chapter 10

Don't Go Back to Whiteville

After about six months in Whiteville, I started to get the hang of things, and became much more comfortable shooting, editing, and handling the equipment. Working in a bureau by yourself, you become so familiar with your gear and its quirks that ultimately you are the only one who can get it to work. Sometimes the station sports guys would come out to Whiteville to shoot a game and borrow my camera instead of bringing one from Wilmington. They'd usually end up calling me at home when they couldn't get the tape to roll or the back-focus to work properly.

"You've got to hit it three times right below the viewfinder and then spin the focus ring once," I'd explain. "That's what works for me."

As my proficiency improved, I stopped making as many mistakes, and even earned the occasional compliment on my videography or use of natural sound. I also became more resourceful at digging up stories and staying on top of the news in my coverage area. Occasionally, I even had my pick of stories to choose from. I was still stressed out much of the time, but at least I had reached the point where I knew what I could and couldn't do, and how to take shortcuts in a hurry to get things done. Instead of viewing every single day with trepidation as a do-or-die challenge, I started to evaluate my coverage in terms of weeks, and gauge whether I'd had a good week or a bad week. My reporting certainly wasn't winning any awards, but I saw victory in continued survival. I had made nearly every mistake you could make and I was still standing. I wasn't home free, but I had gained some breathing room and had a footing in the TV business. I felt I was on my way and started to actually believe that becoming a big-time TV reporter was attainable.

Despite this, I was miserable. That's because I was almost always alone. I'd wake up in an empty apartment, go to an empty office, work by myself all day, and return to an empty apartment at night. My only human contact came from people I met in the field while on a story. And they weren't always happy to see me.

I lived in an apartment about two blocks from the bureau. It was actually part of a garage that had been converted into a two-room living area. It was very small, but the rent was low and, most importantly, it came fully furnished. Aside from a small TV, I didn't own any furniture, so I needed a place with something already there to sit on. The former Whiteville bureau chief, Leigh Powell, knew the family living in the main house and heard they had a vacancy in their garage apartment. I took it immediately so I would have one less thing to worry about while I was floundering around at my new job.

The apartment resembled a small hunting cabin, much like the type you'd find up in the mountains. It had dark wooden walls, small windows that were difficult to pry open, and a very low, stained ceiling. The main room was about fifteen feet square and contained a two-seat sofa, a table made from the sort of rough wood you would find in a boardwalk, and a kitchen area with an old stove, a sink, and a refrigerator with one of those metal handles that sounds like you are releasing an airlock when you pull it open. Adjacent to my kitchen/living/dining room was a smaller room with a bed, a dresser, and a closet formed by angling shelves into a corner. The apartment also had a tiny bathroom with a rusty shower, sink, and toilet, all within a foot or two of each other. To use the toilet, it helped if you kept one leg at an angle.

It wasn't a terrible place, but it was very dark and damp. After a few months, my books developed a strange green mold on the outside. The apartment also had lots of bugs, some of alarming size, which I was constantly swatting during the night. It was also poorly insulated and quite cold. At times I felt colder in Whiteville than I ever had in Colorado.

Still, the place was my sanctuary; my respite from the daily stress of the bureau. I spent most of my nights and weekends there; reading, watching TV, and drinking beer by myself. A festive night for me was to rent a movie and get Chinese food. I guess you could say I was a bit of a recluse. I didn't start muttering to myself or building mail bombs, but I did spend so much time alone I got in the habit of saying "gesundheit" whenever I sneezed because saying "God bless me" sounded ridiculous, and no one else was going to bless me.

Sometimes, for company, I'd play an audio tape I had of an old family dinner. The tape had been recorded by my aunt in order to preserve some of my grandfather's stories. My grandfather was a major league baseball player and told wonderful tales of playing alongside greats such as Hank Greenberg, Ralph Kiner, and Bob Feller. I enjoyed listening to the stories, but just as important for me was simply the sound of other people on the tape; the sound of plates clinking and phones ringing and people washing dishes in the background. It was comforting. This all sounds very pathetic, I'm sure, but it made me feel better. At least for a little while.

At work at the bureau I was usually alone too, although near the very end of my tenure in Whiteville, a one-man photo restoration shop rented one of the outer rooms. But that was just for the last month or two. My only other company at work, apart from the people I met in the field, was a college-age intern the station gave me for a few months. I was terrifically excited when my news director first told me I was getting an intern. Interns amount to free labor in the TV news business. Great, I thought, someone to help carry my equipment, shoot my stand-ups and help me make beat checks. More importantly, someone to talk to. I had visions of me and this intern developing into a real team as I took him under my wing and taught him all that I'd learned. I would be his mentor, and someday we'd look back fondly on these formative early days when we were both big shots at CNN.

It didn't work out that way. He was a very nice kid, but he wasn't quite all there. He was about 20 years old, short and pudgy with big glasses and some type of a developmental disability. It wasn't Down syndrome, but as he explained to me quite readily at our first meeting, he was "missing a chromosome." I have no idea which chromosome it was, but the lack of it evidently made him sweat profusely and prevented him from closing his hands all the way. So much for help carrying the gear. In fact, it turned out he really couldn't help much at all. He couldn't shoot or edit without a lot of assistance, he couldn't drive, and he tended to fall asleep an inordinate amount. Sometimes he would be snoring away while we drove to and from our story locations.

I later learned that his father was a judge, which may explain how he landed the position. But all I could think was that this must be another test from God. To give me a helper who needed more help than he could provide. I felt like I was the Job of journalism.

I did, however, come to truly appreciate his company. When you are by yourself all the time, even someone who doesn't say anything can be remarkably good company. And as I said, he was a nice kid who meant well. So I made sure to include him as much as possible in whatever story I was working on, and always introduced him as my "news

168

assistant." He may not have fulfilled my craving for help and human companionship, but I enjoyed having him around.

I also ultimately had one genuine friend in Whiteville — the radio reporter who replaced Mitch when Mitch moved on to bigger and better things in Raleigh. The new guy was named Mike Helm, and he had been an engineer before deciding he wanted to try radio. Mike was from upstate New York, so we felt a certain kinship as Yankees-in-exile. We'd play racquetball at a local health club, have lunch together sometimes, and even took a trip one weekend to explore the Outer Banks. But unlike me, Mike was married, so we couldn't exactly go cruising for girls together. Plus, Mike normally had to get up at three or four in the morning for his radio shift, so we really didn't see each other all that often.

Which meant that for the most part, I was alone for a year. It was easily the longest year of my life, and to this day, I still dislike doing some things by myself, because it reminds me of how lonely and displaced I felt in Whiteville. Before Whiteville, I used to enjoy going to movies or museums alone. I used to like sitting at a bar by myself having a beer and watching a ball game, or traveling solo and visiting new places. Being by myself gave me time to think, to listen to music, or to enjoy the scenery. But in Whiteville, I had too much time to think, listen to music, and enjoy the scenery. I guess I just wore out my welcome; I got tired of my own company. It seemed like I had been sentenced to an indefinite solitary confinement, and I prayed daily for my release.

After eleven months, I got it. Another WWAY reporter landed a job at a station in Asheville, market 35. This was a good career move for her, and more importantly, opened up a reporting spot in Wilmington. Amazingly enough, the news director bothered to ask me if I wanted to move from

Whiteville. You've got to be kidding, I thought. I'd wanted to move since the day I got there.

Chapter 11

Life Is a Festival

Moving to Wilmington, North Carolina, was beautiful in almost every possible way after my year in Whiteville. It felt like getting out of prison.

There were many reasons for this. First off, Wilmington is a very nice city. The hometown of Michael Jordan (yes, that Michael Jordan), it is located along the Atlantic coast about 45 minutes north of the South Carolina border and an hour or so south of the Marine base at Camp Lejeune. Wilmington is near a couple of nice beaches — Wrightsville Beach and Carolina Beach — and has picturesque marshlands along the Cape Fear River. It also has a historic downtown area with brick and cobblestone streets and several statuesque antebellum houses. The heart of the city is a waterfront commercial section reminiscent of Savannah and Charleston, albeit on a somewhat smaller scale. There are several interesting restaurants and coffee houses downtown and a thriving nighttime scene with numerous taverns and nightclubs.

The city also has a medium-sized university, the University of North Carolina at Wilmington, or UNCW, as it is invariably called. UNCW specializes in oceanography and sea-related pursuits, but it also has plenty of students taking the typical undergraduate curriculum. Rounding out the Wilmington area, there's a large Coast Guard presence and a growing TV and film industry. Dino De Laurentis built a movie studio in Wilmington a while back, and although the studio went through various owners and varying levels of prosperity, it is now the biggest studio on the East Coast. It even has an outdoor back lot with a fake Main Street that can

171

be dressed up to resemble New York, Chicago, Hong Kong, and nearly everything in between. A number of major motion pictures have been shot in Wilmington, although when I arrived the studio was in a bit of a lull. Most of the films made while I lived there were of the smaller made-for-TV variety. Of these, there were dozens and dozens.

Sometimes it seemed you couldn't go anywhere without running into a film crew shooting some production you had never heard of and would never hear of again. The stars of these productions were either up-and-comers, such as Anthony LaPaglia (pre-*Without a Trace*) or came-and-wenters like Cheryl Ladd (post post-*Charlie's Angels*), who I nearly knocked over one night when she was filming a TV movie a block or so from my apartment. I was coming home from a downtown tavern and stumbled onto the set. Perhaps I got a film credit as "drunken reveler #1," but since I never heard what it was they were shooting, I never got a chance to review my performance.

The Wilmington studio also filmed a lot of TV series episodes. Again, though, my timing was poor. Before I arrived, *Matlock* was shot there, and Andy Griffith made regular appearances around town. After I left Wilmington, *Dawson's Creek* and *One Tree Hill* were produced there. During my tenure, the only series of note was the short-lived *American Gothic*, notable mainly for fact that former Hardy Boy Shaun Cassidy was its producer.

Despite this film industry presence, Wilmington was actually a very down-to-earth city, and as a TV reporter, I had very little interaction with the glamour and glitz of the movie industry. At one point I did a few stories about local actors trying to break into the business, but that was about it. What I covered instead were festivals. Quite simply, I became Paul Spelman, Festival Guy.

The reason for this focus on festivals was that as low man on the totem pole, I was placed on the station's weekends-and-nights shift. That's where you work during the day on Saturdays and Sundays and at night (2:30 p.m. to 11:30 p.m.) Mondays through Wednesdays. Although I was often teamed with a photographer on the night shift, I was again a one-man band on the weekends. And with little else going on on weekends, I was often left to cover a festival.

And does that area have festivals. I did stories about the Azalea Festival, the Shrimp Festival, the Oyster Festival, the Grape Festival, the Mullet Festival (the fish, not the hairstyle, although that was not an uncommon feature among attendees), the Spot Festival (another form of fish), the Spring Fling, the 4th of July parade, the Fall Festival, the Christmas-By-The-Sea Festival, Winterfest, Riverfest, the Festival of Trees, and the Herb Fair. Those are just the ones I remember off the top of my head. I did so many festivals they all blurred together into one big festival.

That's really what they were anyway, one big festival. Because besides the featured item of the week (fish, flowers, fruit, etc.) the festivals were almost exactly the same. They all had the same vendors selling the same kitschy crafts; the same amusement rides, amusing mainly for people under age 6; and the same Rolaids ready menu of funnel cakes, Italian sausages, and deep-fried onion bloomers. I put on more than a few pounds covering these things and became fairly proficient at winning stuffed animals.

The festivals were so similar to each other that I might as well have just replayed the same news report each week. But that was frowned upon, so instead I had to come up with a different angle each time. This required some creativity. I'd wrack my brains each weekend for some way to make the oyster festival different from the clam festival I had covered the week before. When I ran out of ideas, I even made the lack of differentiation the focus of the story.

"What makes this festival better than the others?" I asked in my story. "Is it the food? No, that's no better than at the _____ festival. Was it the music? Quite enjoyable, but so was the band at the _____ festival." Etc., etc. Finally, I wrapped up my story by declaring that what made this particular week's festival so special wasn't one particular item, but that it had a little bit of everything. This was a long-winded way of saying that I didn't have anything new to say, which is a skill that really cannot be overemphasized in local TV journalism and comes in especially handy on live shots, a practice I'll discuss later. I don't know if my festival forays served the time-honored journalistic credo that reporters should "comfort the afflicted and afflict the comfortable," but they did fill my required weekend airtime, which was all I could hope for when there wasn't any "real" news to report on.

The main reason local news is so monotonous on weekends is that the usual suspects you turn to for sound bites and information just aren't available, which means you can't do "serious" stories if you need an expert to weigh in on a topic. If I wanted to do a story about coastline erosion — a genuine issue in North Carolina — I could get plenty of video of crowded beaches on a Saturday or Sunday, but good luck getting a scientist from the Army Corps of Engineers to talk about it on his day off. Instead of stories that relied on the usual expert opinions, I needed stories that were all-inclusive in and of themselves, so-called "story-on-a-stick" pieces. Festivals fit the bill.

The only times I was spared the weekend festival formula were days when there had been some sort of fatal shooting or tragic accident. In those instances, I'd perform my ritual interviewing of neighbors to see how shocked and dismayed they were. As my colleague Steve McGhehee once put it, all of my weekend stories fell into two categories: "A good time was had by all" or "A really bad time was had by a few." But unlike in Whiteville, at least in Wilmington I wasn't doing stories involving loads of fertilizer. Other than the spoken kind, of course.

On my weeknight shifts I had more options and flexibility, although working nights is a lot tougher than the day shift. The big problem with the night shift is that if there has been a big news story that day, it has probably been covered by one of the day reporters by the time the night reporter gets out of bed. Which meant that I was stuck with leftovers.

So once again I had to resort to lots of creative fabrication. Not out-and-out lying, of course, just coming up with issues on my own. Enterprising, as it is sometimes called in the business. That's where I'd look at a town playground and think, "Hmm. There must be a story there ... How come there aren't any swings? I wonder if the rise in liability insurance is making towns get rid of their swings ...." You can always come up with some question and turn it into a news story. As I've noted, it is often not something anyone was wondering about before you raised it, but it's still a news story.

The best example of this was a series of stories I did in Wilmington called "Could You Be A Witness?" My WWAY news director, Jon Evans, suggested the idea. I don't know if he came up with it on his own or saw it on a station in another market. Stealing an idea from another market is a common practice in local news, where anything that hasn't been done (or just done for a while) in your market is considered new. It's like that promo the networks run when they air repeats — it may not be original, but hey, it's "new to you."

In this case, the idea behind "Could You Be A Witness" was to demonstrate the inherent unreliability of eyewitness accounts. Quite simply, they are tremendously fallible. As I noted earlier, you could ask 10 people what they saw and get 10 different accounts. So that's basically what I did, after staging a robbery.

I did it at UNCW. I had a professor purposely leave his wallet on a chair not far from the classroom door and then had a plainclothes police officer run in, take the wallet, and run out. It was quite convincing. So convincing, in fact, that three students jumped up and started chasing the officer down the hall before we intervened and stopped them from, literally, taking the law into their own hands. I then explained to the class what my story was about, and we interviewed them one at a time about what they had seen and what the "thief" had looked like.

Their descriptions were all over the place. One insisted that the thief had a mustache, while another recalled a beard (the officer was cleanshaven). He was further described as somewhere between 5'6" and 6'2," which was accurate, but covers about 90 percent of men in America. His age was described as 20–25 years old, when, in fact, he was 32. One student even pointed the finger at my cameraman as the culprit.

Then, in the next part of our "special series," I took a photo of our longtime station weatherman, Kim Downing, the most readily recognizable person on our air (probably aided in this by the fact that he bore more than a passing resemblance to Grandpa from *The Munsters*), and stopped random pedestrians and had them describe the picture. I wrote down their descriptions and presented these descriptions to other people to see if they could figure out who we were talking about. Nobody got it. Nobody was even close. Yet when we then showed them the photograph of Kim Downing, everyone immediately recognized him as our venerable weatherman.

"Oh sure, I know that guy. His forecast ain't been right in weeks, but I know who he is."

The object wasn't to make people look silly but to show how difficult it is both to describe someone accurately and to recognize someone from someone else's description. Perspectives and preconceived notions color even our most routine observations. Just as people listening to the same conversation may hear different words and take away different meanings, witnesses see different things and remember things differently.

I expect other people's memories of the incidents in this book are different than mine (although I'd like to think mine may be more accurate, since I was taking notes). It is the whole *Rashoman* thing: there is no single definitive truth; it is all based on the perspective of the viewer. There is also, unfortunately, a big discrepancy between the accuracy of eyewitness accounts and the weight juries give these accounts in court proceedings, a fact becoming all too clear by the number of death-row inmates since exonerated by DNA evidence.

The "Could You Be A Witness" story sounds somewhat contrived and trite, but it turned out to be fairly interesting and actually ended up winning an award from the North Carolina Associated Press for "Enterprise Reporting." Which shows that even when you create the news, you can do an okay job at it.

And whether I was enterprising stories or following festivals, I was much, much happier in Wilmington than I had been in Whiteville. I started to feel comfortable enough to enjoy the work, and certainly enjoyed not living in Whiteville. I moved into an apartment in a restored old house a few blocks from the Cape Fear River and relatively close to the downtown nightlife. It was also just three or four blocks from the station.

I couldn't afford to buy new furniture, but I was able to pick up a few castoffs at the local Salvation Army and Goodwill stores.

I was also fortunate in that some friends of my family lived in Wilmington. Len and Vivian Landsman had literally known me since the day I was born. They had been guests at a dinner party hosted by my expectant mother when I unexpectedly arrived, several weeks before my due date.

Years later, the Landsmans retired and moved to Wilmington. When I moved there, they became a surrogate family for me, treating me to dinner or taking me to a local play or a Sunday brunch. Vivian was also a master yard-sale scavenger, and all I had to do was provide her with a list of my apartment needs and a few weeks later she'd show up lugging a desk or dresser she and Len had found for only a dollar. Or so they claimed.

All in all, moving to Wilmington was like emerging into the sunshine after a year spent underwater. On my days off, I could visit the Landsmans, go out to the beach, or wander around downtown. There were restaurants and taverns I could to go, and even a few museums. And best of all, I was now part of the station newsroom and was no longer constantly alone.

Chapter 12

Newsrooms

Moving to the main station in Wilmington meant working in a newsroom. For me, this provided one of the great joys of being a TV reporter. A local TV newsroom is a very fun and entertaining place. I think a good deal of that derives from the fact that everyone sits out in the open in the same room. In all my years as a reporter, I never once had my own office (unless you count the bureau in Whiteville), and never worked with any reporters who had their own offices. Instead, everyone had the same small desk with a computer and a phone, and faced several other people with similarly extravagant décor. This is not so hot from a privacy perspective, but it also creates a lively and egalitarian atmosphere, where everyone feels free to listen in on other people's conversations.

Physically, all the newsrooms I've seen (and I've seen about 40 or 50) look pretty much the same. They're crowded rooms with small desks bunched back-to-back amid an atmosphere of controlled chaos. In Wilmington, the room was about sixty feet long and perhaps 15 or 20 feet wide. In that space were crammed about 15 desks housing four or five producers, four or five reporters, three or four anchors, and an intern or three. Later on, when I worked in Knoxville, we probably had 20–25 desks, with about the same ratio of personnel.

In Wilmington, as in most newsrooms, there was an elevated platform at one end of the room consisting of the assignment desk, which oversaw the daily news coverage. On the wall behind the desk was a big white board listing the names of the reporters and photographers and the stories to which they were assigned that day. There was also a police scanner, loudly broadcasting the latest emergency radio traffic, and a two-way radio for communicating with news crews in the field. Mounted higher on the wall were several clocks and TV sets, each tuned to a different station, usually the local news competitors, although occasionally non-news shows would slip in there. In Wilmington, *Baywatch* reruns somehow popped up on the screens every day at 4:00 p.m., which could make it difficult to finish a story by deadline.

The only one with his own office in Wilmington was our main anchor, Jon Evans, who was also the news director. This double duty is rare but not unheard of in small markets. Jon would spend the early part of his day dealing with news-director functions, and then in the afternoon he'd pick up his anchoring duties, anchoring both the five-thirty and six o'clock shows. For variety's sake, the shows were produced in different studios, one right next to the other. So Jon and the female anchor, Jill Callaham, would do the five-thirty show and then get up and walk 30 feet to the six o'clock set for the next show. I guess the idea was that with different backdrops, viewers would think it was a completely different show, despite the remarkable resemblance of the people doing the talking.

Anchors are the stars of the local TV newsroom and receive the lion's share of public recognition, but there is an inverse ratio in local news between the amount of credit people receive and the amount of control they usually have over the newscast. In TV news, the people that get the most recognition often have the least control, and vice-versa.

Jon was an exception to this rule in that, as news director, he also exercised ultimate dominion over the newscast. Most local anchors have little control over anything. They don't decide what stories the station will cover, they rarely go out on stories or interviews themselves, and they often don't write what they read on the air. Sometimes they don't even read their scripts beforehand and end up voicing them "cold" on the air. Even when you see local anchors out in the field reporting on something firsthand, they may not actually have worked on that story and may be merely parroting information provided to them by a producer. Some anchors are even told what to wear and have to check with station management before they can get a haircut.

It is not that anchors don't know how to cover news. Most anchors used to be field reporters, and many were quite good at it. When I worked in Knoxville, for instance, our main male anchor, Clay Thomas, was an excellent journalist who had been a statehouse reporter for several Florida stations in large news markets. The other main anchor, Lori Tucker, had covered news in Houston and San Antonio. But once you become a full-time anchor, your job just doesn't entail a lot of news gathering anymore, no matter how much the station promos depict you out in the field breaking the news (and the promos always show this). Instead, an anchor's job is to be a presence and station symbol, a conveyor of information rather than a gatherer of it. In TV news, the higher up you go, the less you do.

Life as a main anchor is not arduous. The main evening anchors generally come in around 2:30 to attend the afternoon meeting and learn what the station is covering that day, and thus what it is that they'll end up talking about that night. After the meeting, the anchors have a couple of hours to look over the scripts they'll be voicing, and perhaps write a short story or an introduction to someone else's story. Much of the time, even these introductions are written by a producer or by the reporter in the field, the one the anchor will be tossing to with a "Now let's go live to reporter Paul Spelman for the latest ..."

It always felt odd for me to write my own introduction for someone else to read, and sometimes I couldn't help but slip in superlatives such as "let's go live to legendary newsman Paul Spelman" or "now here's our intrepid Johnny-on-the-spot Paul Spelman," but I don't recall these ever making it on the air. The anchors had too much time to review scripts to let something like that get through.

Most anchors will rewrite the intros and stories a bit to better fit their individual speaking styles. This requires some skill, but doesn't take all that long. Anchors do, however, spend a fair amount of time applying makeup and making sure their hair is properly coiffed and their clothing looks good. In Knoxville, our two morning anchors used to coordinate their wardrobes to make sure they didn't clash.

Although being a local news anchor may not require a lot of heavy lifting, the job does require talent. Anchors have to possess a charismatic on-camera presence and have the ability to convey information in a friendly and convincing manner. You have to speak well and be extraordinarily comfortable in the limelight. Anchors need to come across as confident and assured even when they're not. It helps to be good looking, of course, and these days it is sometimes awfully hard to tell the difference between anchors and soap opera stars (particularly the women). But in general, it is less important for an anchor to look like a model than it is to come across as friendly and trustworthy, and thus connect with the viewers.

In Wilmington, our anchor Jon Evans was a good-looking guy and a sharp dresser, but the most popular anchor in town was the anchor at the rival station, a dowdy middle-aged man who wore thick glasses and a toupee. Actually, it was rumored that he wore three toupees, one short, one medium, and one long. That way he could look as though he got a haircut every now and then. None of the toupees made him look like Brad Pitt, but viewers had come to trust him.

Likewise in Knoxville, the most popular female anchor in the market was Lori Tucker, who was quite pretty, but not in the glamorous Catherine Zeta-Jones style. Lori was more the quintessential good-looking soccer mom, attractive to men but not overly threatening for women. She was also extremely friendly and natural at public appearances, something that is very important for an anchor because a huge part of the job involves representing the station at public events.

This may be why a lot of former beauty pageant contestants are now anchors. I know of several. One of the anchors in Knoxville, Moira Kay, had been Miss Tennessee and had competed in the Miss America pageant. On the national level, NBC *Today Show* weekend anchor Amy Robach tried out for Miss Georgia, and a pageant photographer found her so alluring he nicknamed her the "Goddess of Love." Deborah Norville was also a pageant participant, as was Diane Sawyer. It must be a pretty natural transition from pageant contestant to TV anchor.

All that said, anchors are rarely dopes. The stereotype of the TV news anchor as a vacuous shell is usually inaccurate, because it requires a lot more skill than it looks like to always appear knowledgeable, friendly, and reassuring, even amid chaotic events. You also have to be extremely fast on your feet in terms of interviewing people live on the air. Quite honestly, being an anchor requires skills I was never able to master. It is not easy, and as I've said before, it's one of those things where the better you are, the easier it looks. Still, anchoring involves more presentation and vocal-delivery skills than it does adroitness at digging up stories or tracking down facts and figures. Anchors rarely get dirty. Even their desks are clean.

I've seen a lot of anchors' desks, and most of them are remarkably free of clutter.

The mess in the newsroom is instead in the center, where reporters and producers make phone calls, scribble down notes, and hammer away at computer keyboards. There's also a lot of hubbub over by the assignment desk, as the police scanner loudly blares emergency calls and the assignment editor shouts for a photographer to go cover the latest trailer fire. Every now and then the news director will appear and demand to know why the live shot went down.

This contributes to the unusual atmosphere of a TV newsroom. It can be bipolar; some times frenzied and serious, at other times calm or even absurd. There's a random quality to it, with multiple conversations taking place at the same time as different people interject random comments from across the room. Where else would you hear, "Who's got the lawnmower accident?" followed shortly by someone else hanging up the phone and commenting, "I really get tired of people calling in about the skinny horses." All the while one producer is yelling to another, "I don't know if I'm going to use the Memphis explosion but the Florida shark attack is mine."

The word "do," used to mean working on a story, can also provoke some exchanges that might perplex an outsider. How else to explain, "Did you redo the kiddie porn?" or the query, "Are you doing the Congressman?" which begs the response, "No, we're just friends."

Meanwhile, peculiar radio transmissions are broadcast over the newsroom police scanner. Besides genuine emergency calls, I've heard, "I just got the eight-year-old to confess," "fallen leaves down on Kingston Pike," and "caller says she popped a large boil and is now worried about blood coming from her forehead."

In Knoxville, the newsroom scanner would also occasionally intercept cellular calls and private conversations made over police radiophones. I once listened to a heated argument between an officer and his spouse about their basement flooding again. It was far more interesting than the story I was covering.

The atmosphere can seem disjointed and chaotic to an outside observer, but after you've worked in a newsroom for a while, you get accustomed to this cacophony and develop an ability to pick out what's important and what isn't. I expect it's similar to the way some soldiers are able to sleep through artillery bombardments yet awake immediately to the slightest rustling in nearby trees. In a newsroom, you get a knack for focusing on your own project while keeping your ears open to the sounds going on around you.

Sometimes Wanda Williams, a reporter I sat next to in Knoxville, would chatter away at me for 10 or fifteen minutes about some issue that was bothering her, only to finally ask me, "Paul, are you paying attention to me?"

"Not really. But I did hear what you said."

"That's okay," she'd reply, "I just needed to say it." Then we'd both go back to working on our stories.

As you may have gathered, newsrooms are also not overly serious places, and there is a lot of joking around. I've returned to my computer terminal after forgetting to log off and found that someone had invited the entire station to my house for dinner. Another time I returned to find that my story script had been altered and now included a line about mice smoking marijuana. Unfortunately, I didn't notice this alteration until I was voicing the story live on the air. I didn't voice it out loud, but it was close, and there was a lengthy pause while I tried to figure out why my story had references to doped-up rodents. I delivered the rest of the story in mortal

185

terror, sure that a few other "script improvements" were bound to be in there.

Part of the casual atmosphere is due to the nature of the TV news business, and part due to the type of people that go into it. TV types are generally not straight-laced nine-to-fivers, and almost everyone has a sense of humor. I guess you need it. Otherwise, you might get overly upset by the errors and mistakes you just made in front of thousands of people. Sometimes Mike Cihla, an anchor I worked with who rarely took anything seriously, would return to the newsroom after a blunder-filled broadcast, toss his earpiece on my desk and start quoting lines from *Top Gun*. "I'm turning in my microphone Paul, I've lost the edge. I'm holding on too tight."

"You can't quit Mike," I'd explain. "Who else can we send to *Top News*?"

Another reporter I worked with, Heather Donald, would cackle like a witch and start reciting Glenn Close lines from the film *Fatal Attraction*. "I won't be ignored, Paul," she'd yell from across the newsroom as I tried to focus on my story. Heather was tough to ignore. She was six feet tall and striking and had an outsize personality to match. Heather needed a bit of turmoil to get her out of bed in the morning. But like everyone else, she rarely took anything too seriously.

It is fair to say that in local TV news there are not a lot of people on a mission to save the world. I don't know if that's because it attracts the cynics, or, more likely, because after seeing TV news up close most idealists and crusaders get out of the business. But the end result is that most people don't take anything too seriously and are fun to be around, especially in small markets where everyone is young and in roughly the same boat. In the Wilmington newsroom, most of us were in our early to mid-twenties, making very little money, struggling to learn the business but dreaming of the big time. At 28, I was one of the oldest. Small- and middle-market TV is a young person's game.

Of course, there are a few older authority figures around to keep watch on the youngsters. The assignment editor, for instance, is often older than the rest. Assignment editors (also called assignment managers, or simply "the desk") are in charge of keeping track of everything and everybody in the field, and making sure that all the news worth covering that day gets covered. They have to have a keen sense of what makes a good story and is worth devoting resources to. Assignment editors also have to keep a close ear on the police scanner and react to breaking news by switching news teams from one story to another.

Being an assignment editor is a very difficult job and includes many of the hassles of the TV business without a lot of its rewards. It's also a position that gets very little recognition, even in the business. No one watches a newscast and says, "Man, that assignment editor did a bang-up job today." Even assignment editors can't tell how good a job their counterpart at another station did that day. You would have to know not just what they covered, but what resources they had available. Because it is the assignment editor that often decides what gets covered, who will cover it, and how it will be covered. To be an assignment editor, you have to love directing traffic; moving chess pieces around without getting to see or report the news yourself. I've worked with assignment editors who had never been out in the field but had a great sense for what could or should be covered. I guess it's comparable to being an air-traffic controller, who may not know how to fly the plane but who is the one you want telling the 747 where to land.

An assignment editor position is often a stepping-stone to the position of news director, or sometimes a step down for a former news director who was fired. It was the latter case at WWAY in Wilmington, where our assignment editor, Tom Lamont, had been the news director at the rival station before he lost his job in one of the various management shuffles that occur with amazing regularity. So our news director gave Tom a position as our assignment editor.

Tom did a pretty good job, too, and never seemed bitter about the fact that he had moved from being the number one guy at the number one station to being the number two person at the number two station. Or at least he never expressed resentment publicly. But it wouldn't have surprised me if he truly had taken it all in stride. You can't have a big ego to be an assignment editor, and because it's the kind of job where everyone else gets all the credit.

A good assignment editor is invaluable, though, because TV stations have a very limited number of news crews. In Wilmington, we generally had three reporters during the day, one at night, and one on the weekends. Later, when I was in Knoxville, it was about the same, sometimes fewer. So someone has to decide what stories are worth spending time on. Should you pull Heather off the school uniform story — the one she set up a week ago — to cover the tractor accident? Does Marguerite have time to swing by the university and get a comment about the tuition increase, or will that cut into her story about the police department slush fund? Can you send a crew to a distant county to cover a trailer fire when they might be your only crew that day, leaving you empty-handed should a school bus get into a fender bender nearby?

Most reporters and photographers respect the assignment editor, but at the same time there are lots of conflicts that arise between the desk and field crews simply because the folks ordering you around may not have a ground-level understanding of what's going on.

This happened a lot with one assignment editor I worked with in Knoxville who had a habit of distorting time and facts to suit his purposes. A trip that might, in actuality, take a news crew 45 minutes would somehow get described to you as a quick 20-minute jaunt when he wanted you to go cover something. Yet if he then had to explain to the news director why we hadn't been able to cover something, that same trip might somehow morph into an hour and a half each way.

That assignment editor also had a habit of telling you that he had "set up" an interview when all he had done was leave a message on the person's answering machine. When he was the assignment editor, reporters did a lot of apologizing for arriving late or showing up to interview someone who had no idea they were coming.

Another assignment editor I worked with, Angela Lindenberg, was better about time, but would explain things in ways that were often hard to understand. Her written directions, for instance, practically took a PhD to decipher. I copied one down that reminded me of stream-of-consciousness poetry:

Paul.

Take 33 north. Thru New Tazewell and Tazewell.

6 Lights. The 5th light 25 east straight toward Kentucky. 3 miles construction.

Thru.

Three bait shops. Three lane hill. At the top of hill 3 lanes go to two.

Sign for Oxford Bolton road. Turn and down bank.

Circles up by house. 11:30.

About the only thing missing was, "Darkness. Blood. Mother, put down that axe ...."

On the other hand, Angela had an amazing ability to monitor the police scanner and not overreact. Overreacting is a

189

constant danger for assignment editors, because lots of things sound dramatic and newsworthy over the scanner. One time half the Knoxville newsroom went into a frenzy when someone heard a dispatcher say, "Police officer down." Two or three crews were headed out the door to cover what they thought was a police shooting before someone figured out there was a police officer with the last name Down or Downs and there wasn't anything the matter with him. Or nothing worth reporting about in any case.

It's easy to overreact when something like "Body seen floating in river" comes blaring over the scanner. But you are in trouble if you pull your crew from an important mayoral news conference to cover this apparent murder and it turns out the floater is a wooden log with a baseball cap stuck to a branch. Angela was always cool and collected, and wouldn't send a crew until she confirmed that the floater was a genuine decedent with at least one arrow sticking out the back. I've worked with assignment editors who weren't as circumspect. They would send you to cover every parking lot fender bender that sounded moderately serious over the scanner.

The dilemma for field crews is that no matter how good or bad an assignment editor's judgment, it's the reporter and the photographer that have to deal with the consequences, because in local TV news, you *always* have to come back with a story. If you show up late for an interview and the person you need to talk to has already gone, or didn't know you were coming and doesn't want to talk to you, you can't just call the station and say you don't have anything. Instead, you may have to track the person down or figure out a way to do the story without that interview. In other words, if the floater turns out to be a wooden log and it's too late to return to the mayor's news conference, you may have to make a story out of that log. That's why you end up with stories like "Dangerous

Debris Threatens Boating Safety," or "Rising River Level Imperils Shoreline Development."

This sort of switch happens every day. It's not unusual to get sent on two or three different stories in one day before settling down to the one that actually ends up in the newscast. Sometimes I would spend several hours working on a story, gathering interviews, b-roll and background information, only to have the desk decide at 3:30 that they wanted me to cover something else for the five o'clock show. That's why complaining about the desk is sort of your God-given right as field crew. It's like the infantryman's privilege to gripe about the generals. You are allowed to do it, just not too loudly.

But conflicts between field crews and the assignment desk don't even compare to the tension that exists between reporters and producers. Producers are the ones that take up where the assignment editor left off. They "stack the show," meaning that they determine which stories go where in the broadcast and how much time gets allotted for each piece. Producers also write segues and voice-overs for the anchors and have final script approval over stories written by reporters. Then, during the show, the producer sits in the station control room and monitors everything to make sure it's all going according to plan.

Producers in local TV news are usually young, and, for some reason, generally female. I've worked with 40 or 50 show producers and can count on one hand the number of male ones. I guess male college broadcasting majors don't find it appealing. It's not a glamorous job. But as I've noted, there's an inverse ratio in TV news between recognition and control. Local news producers rarely go out in the field or interview anyone, but they have near absolute control over the overall look of the show. And while local news producers may

191

not write a lot of stories themselves, they control everyone else's.

This is where most of the reporter/producer conflict originates. It can be tough for reporter out in the field to swallow criticism and changes imposed by a producer who has never left her desk. And while assignment editors help field crews by finding stories and setting up interviews, producers rarely assist field crews in any way whatsoever. It's not their job to do so, but the result is a one-way street in which producers demand a lot from reporters but don't give much in return.

Producers may also have different goals than reporters. The field crew wants to do the best story possible. The producer wants to do the best show possible. These goals are not always mutually inclusive. Sometimes they are not even remotely similar. A producer, for instance, might decide that the show needs a live shot or "reporter presence" to spice up the newscast. But getting this reporter presence may require pulling the reporter and photographer off the story they were covering so they can travel to the live-shot location, set up the camera, lights, and live-truck (a van with a big antenna on the top that rises and collapses like a telescope and can transmit video and sound back to the station tower), do the live shot, and then take everything down. This can take a couple of hours. And if the reporter can't go live from a live-truck because of geography, weather, or lack of available live-trucks, the crew may have to return to the station to go "live from the newsroom." The show may look jazzier that way, but it's tough to cover stories from the newsroom.

Take the time I was covering a story about human bones uncovered in the woods near Oak Ridge, Tennessee. When my photographer and I arrived, all we could get was a shot of a couple of police officers standing by the side of the road. The officers refused to let any news crews into the woods, and they wouldn't do interviews or provide any information. They said, however, that forensic experts were expected at 5:00 and might be willing to talk to us and show us the discovery site.

I was the night-shift reporter that day and was principally doing the story for our eleven o'clock newscast, but my photographer and I couldn't wait around until 5:00 because the producer of the five o'clock newscast wanted a live reporter update in her show and we couldn't get a live signal out of Oak Ridge. So at 3:45, the photographer and I had to leave the scene and drive 40 minutes back to the station so I could go live from the newsroom with little video and even less information. Afterward, we drove back out to the scene in Oak Ridge, but by the time we got there the forensic guys had come and gone. So my five o'clock newsroom shot kept me from getting the interviews and video I needed for my eleven o'clock story. I ended up having to track down one of the forensic experts at his home and interviewed him on his front lawn. I was lucky he was willing to do it. If he'd eaten out that night I might have been out of luck.

This sort of thing happens all the time, which is why reporters are invariably complaining about some "stupid" thing the producer wants them to do, while producers are constantly complaining that reporters don't have the overall interests of the station at heart. Both are right. It's a wonderful relationship.

The only thing you can do is try to see it from the other person's point of view. I'd like to say I've always taken this mature approach, but I haven't. I've gotten into some nasty arguments with producers, and I once yelled at a producer so much I made her cry. I felt bad about it so I bought her a bag of gourmet jelly beans afterward to say I was sorry and was promptly ridiculed by other reporters for not standing firm.

Another time I simply refused to do what a producer wanted and got in trouble because of it. I was out by the side of an interstate doing the ritual crowded-highways-before-Thanksgiving story when, about three minutes before I went on, the producer told me they had heard over the scanner that there had been a fatal accident on some road in another county. She wanted me to talk about this in my live shot. I didn't know anything about it, and as I've noted, it's not always a good idea to go live with unverified scanner reports. More to the point, I just didn't know what to say. So I told her I didn't feel comfortable ad-libbing about a fatality. The producer kept insisting, and I kept saying no. Finally, she relented, but said ominously, "This isn't over."

Sure enough, it wasn't. When I returned to the station, I found a note from my news director (a former producer, mind you) stating:

"When a producer tells you what to do, do it. It's absolutely ridiculous that you would question what [she] asked you to do, then refuse. It's unacceptable."

The note ordered me to appear in the news director's office to account for my actions as soon as she returned from her Thanksgiving holiday. Evidently my reprehensible behavior wasn't reprehensible enough to merit delaying her holiday plans. So after an uncomfortable long weekend, I returned expecting to be flogged, suspended, or even terminated. You can lose your job for "insubordination" and this qualified.

I decided, however, that instead of appearing in the news director's office as instructed, I would wait and let her bring up the issue on her own. I was hoping that maybe she had overdosed on tryptophan over Thanksgiving and forgotten the whole thing. Here, I got lucky. On the first day back the news director was too busy to bring it up, and on the second day she was fired in a management shake-up brought on by low ratings. Saved by the bell.

Looking back on it now, I realize I could and should have done what the producer wanted. I could have said in my live report, "We've heard there was a fatal accident on such and such road, we're looking into it and we'll have more information as soon as it's available. Meanwhile here on I-40 …." That would have been enough. You don't have to know every last detail about a topic to talk about it. But back then I was still new at live shots and scared stiff to stray from my prescripted remarks.

I ended up working with that producer for another year or so, and I can't recall getting into any other big arguments with her. And although arguments happen all the time in the newsroom, for the most part, everyone gets along. You spend so much time together that you really have to. This is especially true when it comes to working with photographers. Reporters and photographers spend more time with each other than they do with their spouses.

Chapter 13

Photogs

TV news photographers (or "photogs," as they are often called) are a very strange breed. They seem to see the world a bit differently, perhaps because for so much of the time they are viewing it through a camera lens. Possibly this gives them a unique perspective and colors the way they look at everything else. Or more likely they were just a little bit odd to begin with.

In the inverse hierarchy of TV news, photogs are considered slightly lower down than reporters. They usually get paid less and are accorded less respect by station management, which tends to view them as interchangeable. This view may arise from the fact that it is the reporter's name and face that go on the story, and thus, in theory, ultimately the reporter's responsibility. The reporter is responsible for putting everything together; for finding the facts, getting the necessary interviews and video, writing the script, and figuring out how to manage the time effectively so that all of this gets accomplished by deadline. When push comes to shove, as it sometimes does, the reporter usually gets the final say. Likewise if the story turns out badly — if you get back too late and miss your deadline, or if there's a factual error or you're badly beaten by a competing TV station — it is the reporter who gets called into the news director's office to answer for this, not the photographer. The photographer can always say he or she was just doing what the reporter said to do.

I use the words *in theory* because in local news the photographer is actually more important than the reporter much of the time, and any reporter with half a brain understands this. A photographer usually has much more of an impact on how a story turns out than the reporter does. Good photogs don't just shoot pretty pictures, they think through the story and recognize what the reporter needs. The best I've worked with didn't stand around and wait for me to direct them like I was Francis Ford Coppola, they shot the story without any guidance and then told me how to write my script.

"You can start by talking about the school," Jay Kaley would tell me. "I got a shot of the broken roof, then you can move from that to talking about the upset parents, and we'll go to the sound bite with Papa Joe Schmuckatelli [Jay's catch-all name for all interview subjects] about how upset he is. That's where your stand-up will come in in the empty cafeteria."

"Great." I'd say. "I'll go get lunch. Let me know when you need me."

By comparison, I once worked with a not-so-good photog who shot the prettiest pictures in the world but didn't have the slightest idea how to tell a story. We'd cover a fire department ceremony honoring a life-saving officer, and the photog would come back with 40 minutes of b-roll showing tinkling glasses and glimmering reflections off the silverware, but he'd neglect to get a shot of the firefighter hugging the rescued baby's grateful mother as tears ran down her cheeks. This photog was an *artiste*, and while he probably would have done well shooting music videos, he was frustrating to work with in TV news. He saw the pictures but never the story.

Another photog I worked with once sat there with her camera turned off while a Knoxville sports agent I was about to interview began diagramming the NFL salary structure with a piece of chalk on his office window. You shouldn't have to tell a photog to start shooting video in a situation like this. Because when you speak up, the person doing whatever it is they were doing starts to feels self-conscious and stops doing it, and there goes your b-roll. Some photogs have to be told what to shoot, whereas the best are one step ahead of the reporter all of the time.

That's why I cringe when people refer to TV reporters as *the talent*. Reporters may have one type of talent, but in local TV news it is not the most important one. A station is better served by a talented photographer and a mediocre reporter than the other way around. I can readily concede that some photogs have a much better idea of how to do a story than I do. When I worked with Mike Pelzer, for instance, WWAY's chief photographer, I was just along for the ride. Mike had been at WWAY for several years before I arrived, and while WWAY is a small market, Pelzer was not a "small-market photographer." In fact, Mike had worked at a station in Charlotte but returned to Wilmington to be closer to his family.

Working with Mike was the easiest reporting experience I ever had. First off, because he was an extremely nice guy and very easy to get along with. He had a warm, friendly demeanor and a great sense of humor, even about somewhat touchy issues. I remember when we once did a story about a Coast Guard training exercise where they dropped a mannequin out of a helicopter and into the ocean. It so happened that, for whatever reason, the mannequin was dark skinned. Mike, who's black, saw this and immediately commented, "It's always the black guy that gets thrown out of the chopper. Back of the bus isn't bad enough, we get tossed out the window."

Sometimes Mike would amuse himself by putting himself into a story without telling anyone. One day, I was reviewing some video Mike shot of a rare North Carolina blizzard, and I saw a man bundled up and noticeably shivering as he walked by the camera in the snow. Wait a minute, I thought, that guy looks familiar. Sure enough, it was Mike. He had set the camera on a tripod, snuck down the other side of the street and walked back past it, shivering and letting his teeth chatter loudly as he did so. Mike just grinned when I called him on it.

Mike was also easy to work with because he knew everybody in Wilmington and already knew how to do every kind of story. That's because he'd done them all before, usually multiple times. He would ask me what we were doing that day, and I'd tell him I had come up with this great idea for a story about gun sales to senior citizens scared about crime. Before I could launch into a more intricate explanation, he'd say, "Oh yeah, old people and guns. I did that four years ago. We'll go to the firing range out by the airport, and I know this old lady who has an AK-47 ...." Or I'd tell Mike we were doing a story about the struggles of small businesses, and he'd say, "I know a woman who runs a beauty salon, she's always a good interview. Plus, I can get a little off the top while we're there ...."

Mike never seemed the slightest bit concerned about whether we would be able to get a story finished in time. Whether we were covering a horrific drive-by shooting or doing a feature on jumping-jack competitions, Mike always had the same calm demeanor and would usually decide that there was plenty of time to swing by Hardees for a burger on our way. "Just to tide me over until lunch," he'd explain as we waited in the drive-thru, fire engines screaming by in the background.

Working with Mike also meant making various unscheduled stops at rental properties he owned around Wilmington. Mike owned seven or eight small houses in what could be described as the less fashionable sections of town. He had purchased the houses on credit and then leased them out, which meant he had to stay on top of his rental income so he didn't fall behind on his loans. Sometimes en route to a story he'd take a brief detour so he could check on some electrical problem or make sure an evicted tenant was actually leaving. "Are you sure this is the way to Wrightsville Beach?" I'd ask, confused about our unfamiliar route. "We've just got to swing by a house for a bit. Shouldn't take long. They'll still be there for us out at Wrightsville."

With another photog I might have been concerned, but with Mike I was never worried about finishing my stories. He always knew how to get a story one way or the other. In fact, he was so experienced that he rarely had to exert himself. Doing a story one day about mosquito infestation, Mike refused to get out of the car when an insect control officer took us to a marshy area where the bugs fed and bred with gusto. Mike had been there before, of course, and didn't feel like getting bitten again. I got out with the officer and was engulfed by a swarm while Mike shot the entire story through the windshield. Amazingly enough, his video looked pretty good, although there were a disproportionate number of shots of bugs crawling on a window.

Mike was also the most economical photographer I've ever seen. Most photogs take dozens and dozens of shots and then use only a small percentage in the finished story. Mike would come back with 15 shots and use 14 in the story. He once told me that if I had written one more sentence he'd have run out of video. Of course, Mike had backup systems on hand should this occur. These were his N&E tapes; tapes which, Mike explained, had file video footage that could represent "nothing and everything" at the same time. Need a few shots to cover a story about rising cancer rates? Mike would pull some generic video he had of people in Wilmington walking down the street. "Perfect," he'd say. "Some of these people could get cancer, but we're not saying any of them do." Or, if I needed video for a story about the homeless, Mike would pull some wide, sweeping shots of Wilmington that he had shot a few years before while doing a story atop the city's highest building. At first glance, you wouldn't think this video had much to do with the homeless, but as Mike explained, "Somewhere in this city, there are homeless people. So this shot works." And it did.

The shot could have worked equally well for a story about an increase in crime, or about the annual goose migration through North Carolina. You couldn't do a whole story with N&E shots, of course, but if you needed to cover a few seconds of script they were invaluable.

I don't want to leave the impression that Mike did just enough to get by, because he cared quite a bit about the finished piece. Good photographers always do. There is an enormous amount of pride that goes into shooting and editing a news story, even a story you don't care about, sometimes to the extent that photogs and reporters end up yelling at each other because they disagree over some minor detail. I've gotten into plenty of arguments with photographers, even ones I got along well with, over silly issues like which hand you should use to hold the microphone. The relationship between photog and reporter is similar to what I imagine it's like between patrol car partners, except that in news, neither of you is carrying a loaded weapon. Which is a good thing, because you spend so much time together it's impossible not to get on each other's nerves. You spend hours and hours driving from place to place, working the scene of a story, eating together, editing together, sometimes even sleeping together in the same room or the same bed on a road trip. It is natural to get a bit tired of the other person.

Yet in the end, reporters and photographers know that to succeed they need each other. As a reporter, you need the photog to take good pictures, monitor the sound, edit the story, and act as your eyes and ears when you're off scribbling down notes, writing your script, or using the bathroom. The photog needs the reporter to locate the people to talk to, get the pertinent facts, and write a script that matches the video and makes some semblance of sense.

If all this seems like the basis for a studious team — a partnership based on a shared seriousness of purpose between two dedicated professionals — that might be overstating it a bit. Let's just say it is closer to Seinfeld/Costanza than McNeil/Lehrer. Most of the time field crews spend together they are talking about things that have absolutely nothing to do with the news story of the day. There really isn't a lot you can talk about before you arrive at the scene of a news story. "Okay, when we get there, you get shots of the overturned school bus and I'll try and round up a couple of witnesses and the school's public information officer." That pretty much covers it.

In fact, you really don't need to say that sort of thing, because if photographers and reporters have been in the business for any length of time, they know what their respective roles are. The reporter gets the info and corrals people to interview, while the photog gathers pictures and sound. There's obviously some overlap in that a good photog passes along information he or she picks up to the reporter and a reporter explains to the photog what sort of shots he or she might need. But in general, you both know what you're doing, and you don't spend a lot of time chatting about it beforehand.

So instead, you talk about whatever else is on your mind. Sports, politics, religion, relationships — everything is fair game. Sometimes I would spend half the day with a photog named Jason Hensley joking around in Australian accents as we tried our best to imitate *The Crocodile Hunter*. "Look at the deadly foam on this microphone. One bad sound bite could kill a roomful of scribblers. Crikey!!!" Or we'd trot out lame imitations of Christopher Walken and Jack Nicholson just to pass the time. Sometimes we'd spend so much time fooling around it was hard to switch back and speak normally when we had to do the real interview. I'd have trouble not berating the school board president with "You want the truth? You can't handle the truth!!"

Working with another photographer, Jules Smith, we'd occasionally pass the time playing off lyrics to popular songs from the '70s and '80s. "Jules," I'd say. "You may be a good photographer, but you're as cold as ice. You just seem willing to sacrifice our story."

"Paul," she'd reply, "Someday you'll pay the price. I've seen it before, it happens all the time with reporters. You're losing control, you'll leave the story behind." A photographer well versed in old Foreigner songs can't be overvalued.

It wasn't all lighthearted chatter, of course. Sometimes you'd get into deep philosophical discussions while driving around. Jules and I, for instance, discussed everything from the pop takeover of country music (she was against it) to the validity of same-sex marriages (for it). On the way to a news scene with another photog, Josh Liner, I once got into an involved theological debate about whether Judas went to heaven after he died. This had little to do with the story we were working on, but Josh's father was a minister and it somehow came up. By the time we'd arrived at the scene, we'd settled on the conclusion that Judas was not in heaven since he didn't fully repent and committed suicide. Josh and I then got out of the car looking for people to interview.

If it seems odd that the son of a minister became a TV photog, well, all I can say is that you never can tell what sort of background people had before getting into TV news, and that goes double for photographers. They are the most diverse bunch in the business. Besides a minister's son, I've worked with photogs ranging from a 20-year veteran of the Marine Corps to a die-hard Deadhead to a photog who actually *was* a minister on his time off.

The minister's name was Jason Grant. He was from East Tennessee (the buckle of the Bible Belt) but told me he had not been raised in an especially religious household. He also said that when he was younger he had raised hell like a lot of other teenagers, although I expect it was a relatively mild sort of hell. He told me stories about pranks he and his friends used to pull, such as the time they walked into a hotel kitchen in the nearby resort town of Gatlinburg and started to wash the dishes. After 10 or 15 minutes, Jason and his friends walked out, leaving the staff wondering who they were and what in the world had been going on.

At some point, Jason found faith and became an ordained minister. On his days off from TV news, he delivered sermons and handed out religious literature. Once, when I asked him if he ever read any good books, Jason replied, "Just the Bible. It's the only one I have time for."

TV seemed a peculiar profession for deeply spiritual people such as Jason and another Knoxville photographer I worked with, Brud Gann. I got the sense that they grappled a bit with questions while out covering our sordid stories of sex, lies, and videotape. It must have been hard when we had to cover the murder of a family of Jehovah's witnesses, or report allegations of pedophilia in the church, or even just cover a crime occurring on a religious holiday. I remember once having a lengthy discussion about faith and the meaning of Easter with Brud while on our way to cover a big drug bust.

Journalism can be a cynical and callous profession, and it is impossible not to feel as though you are exploiting people, especially following a tragedy. Yet both Brud and Jason seemed able to incorporate their faith in such a way that it did not hinder their ability to be news photographers. That's not to imply that they were hypocrites, but rather that their spiritual beliefs didn't prevent them from doing a job that, admittedly, is not always about helping people.

Instead, Jason, for one, would use his faith to provide comfort whenever he could. I recall more than once when, after interviewing some family experiencing a tragic loss, Jason would give them a hug and say with utter sincerity, "God Bless You."

Jason was the chief photographer when I was there, and Brud had been the chief before Jason. Both were excellent photographers who cared about their craft. Jason may have been the best news photographer I've ever worked with. He had a tremendous visual sense combined with an intricate understanding of how to tell a story. He was also incredibly inventive and resourceful, particularly at using wireless microphones. While doing a story on the circus, for example, Jason would put a wireless microphone on a six-year-old boy and then take his camera to the other side of the arena, leaving the boy and his family alone until they forgot about the microphone or the camera crew filming them. Then Jason would start shooting and end up with all sorts of wonderful video and sound of the six-year-old laughing at the clowns, begging his parents for Cotton Candy, and being told to shut up and enjoy the show.

Once, while doing a story about a snowstorm in the Smokies, I wanted to do a stand-up that would show how difficult it was to drive in near white-out conditions. So Jason put a wireless microphone on me and stationed me outside of the vehicle behind a road-closure barricade. Then he got into the news car, pointed the camera at me through the windshield and slowly drove forward through the snowfall, steering with one hand and shooting video with the other. In the story, you could hear me speaking but couldn't see me through the snow until the car nearly ran me over. It nicely imparted the message that conditions made it very difficult to drive.

Another time, I was out doing a live shot and our phone communications went down, so I couldn't hear the station (channel 6) in my ear. Jason happened to remember that a TV channel 6 can also be picked up on the radio at 87.7 FM because of frequency proximity (this is true for any analog channel 6 anywhere in the country). So he turned the radio on in our car, put a wireless microphone on a seat nearby, and rigged the wireless receiver into to my earpiece out on the live shot. Everything the anchors said came over the car radio, was picked up by the wireless microphone in the car and transmitted to me out on the live shot. I couldn't hear the producers give me cues, but I could hear everything that went out over the air, and so knew when to talk.

That was very typical of Jason; he was always thinking. Another photographer like that, but a polar opposite in terms of personality, was Jay Kaley, who I've mentioned before. Kaley was about as laid-back cool as you could get; the ultimate hipster with a goatee, a busy cigarette habit, and a way of striding through the newsroom with a rolling lackadaisical gait that made it seem as though he'd stopped by because he felt like it, not because he actually had to work there. Jay would also disappear from the newsroom for long stretches, then stroll in just in time to go cover the story, walk up to my desk, and say, "Giddy'up, Spell-Man. Time to go."

Jay always had an ultracool way of saying something. When I asked him if he'd ever been to England, his response was, "Never been across the pond." Another time, when discussing the various uncertainties surrounding a body found floating in an East Tennessee river, Jay remarked, "That's the wild and wacky thing about dead people. They don't answer questions, leaving you to surmise and speculate." Jack Nicholson couldn't have said it any smoother.

Yet despite this laid-back persona, Jay was one of the sharpest photogs I've ever worked with, and not just about photography. He was a veritable encyclopedia of popular culture, and watching *Jeopardy* or *Who Wants to Be a Millionaire* with Jay was an awe-inspiring experience. I lost more than a few bets to Jay over arcane trivia. In fact, I may still owe him some money.

He also knew how to craft a news story, and would have been a great reporter if he felt like being on camera. He didn't want to, explaining to me once that he didn't want to deal with on-camera stuff and have to worry about his appearance all the time. He was somewhat dismissive about the need for on-air types to be well groomed. If I had the impertinence to ask Jay if he had gotten a particular shot, or remembered to bring a piece of equipment, he would typically respond with, "Don't tell me my bidness, boy. You just stand there and look pretty. Got your pencil?" He was just joking around, but he was such a good photog that really all I had to do was stand there and look pretty. He did all the rest.

As for this sort of joking around, it's pretty standard fare between reporters and photographers. With another photog I worked with, Kevin Umberger, a typical greeting might go something like this:

"Hey Kevin, are you with me today?"

"No, I'm against you. I've never liked you. But I am paired with you today, if that's what you mean."

Or we might have this discussion on the way back from a story:

"Kev, did you get a shot of that girl who started to cry during the memorial service?"

"Oh, did you want me to roll on that? I would have, but my reporter didn't say anything to me about getting quality emotional video. I thought I was just supposed to get some pretty shots of the flowers."

"Well," I'd reply. "I was going to suggest the crying shot, but I know how stressed out you photogs get when you have to use your eyes and ears and shoot pictures at the same time. That whole focusing and pushing the on and off button sure gets tricky. I didn't want to put any added pressure on you."

"Thanks. I appreciate that, especially coming from someone whose primary concern is to make sure his tie is on straight."

"So did it look good?"

"What? Your tie? No, it was slightly askew, as usual."

"The video."

"The video was great, you can see the girl's eyes get all misty as they talk about her teacher. It's pretty powerful. I'd start the story with it."

"Excellent. Burger King for lunch?"

"Taco Bell."

I don't recall that precise conversation taking place, but I wouldn't be surprised if it did. We had dozens of conversations of that character. Of course, a lot of this back-and-forth banter depends on how well you get along with your photographer. I generally got along pretty well with them because I let them do their own thing. As long as they got the job done I was not going to argue with their methods.

With Jay for instance, I knew to give him a long leash and not get worried if he disappeared for a while. I'm still not sure where he went all the time, although he only lived a couple of blocks from the station, so he probably just went home to hang out and play video games or something. It didn't matter because I could always get him on the pager, and Jay was so fast at shooting, editing, and setting up live shots that he could always make up time.

Jay and I once left the station at 5:53 for a 6:05 live shot and made our slot. One hour beforehand is the recommended minimum amount of time to arrive and set up for a live shot, even for one just around the corner, as in that situation. But Jay knew a place where we had a clear line-of-sight shot at our station tower — located on a hillside above the city — and we wouldn't have to raise the mast on our live-truck, which can take an eternity. All he had to do was fire up the truck's generator and point the transmitter at the tower. Jay really saved my butt, because it was my fault we were so late getting out the door.

Despite his photography talent, I never got the impression that TV news was Jay's primary passion. Instead, it seemed like he viewed it as something interesting to do for a while. Jay also loved to play pool and cards and video games, and he was constantly telling me about some complex wager that offered him a chance to win thousands of dollars. Last I heard, Jay had gone out to Vegas to get closer to the action. I heard he played in some poker tournament and outlasted Chris Moneymaker, the former World Series of Poker Champion.

At least Jay's wagering was relatively "legitimate." Another photog I worked with was running a plainly illegitimate scheme to rip off a bookie. That photographer, who I'll refer to as "Alex" for his own protection, had gone to one of those big Division I schools where sports betting among fraternity students is rampant. There was so much betting going on that a college friend of Alex's had gotten a job collecting bets for a bookie in New York. I guess this campus collecting served as an internship of sorts, for after the friend graduated, he moved to New York to work for the bookie full-time.

The bookie used a system in which all bets placed over the phone were tape-recorded, and the bookie would then pay off on those that won. So Alex's friend came up with a scheme whereby his college buds would phone in bets for both sides of a big game, and afterward, the "inside man" would erase the tape recordings of the losing bets. They could only do this when there was a lot of betting going on and the bookie wasn't going to notice a few lost wagers. When this situation arose, the friend would page Alex, telling him how much to bet and on which game.

I didn't know this, of course, when I first started working with Alex. We were on our way to cover some breaking news when Alex got a page and suddenly pulled out a personal cell phone, punched in a number, and started speaking in a strange accent. You can imagine my confusion when I heard this clean-cut all-American type put on a thick Middle Eastern accent and say, "Yes. Dis is Dakota. I want to put 15-hundred American dollar on LSU please in game with Tulane." Then, a minute later, Alex dialed in again and, in an exaggerated hillbilly drawl, declared, "This is Rampage. Gimme Tulane to win. 15-hundred smackers!"

I thought he was crazy. I still think that, even after he explained what he was doing. I mean, bookies are often *connected*, if you know what I mean, and it occurred to me that Tony Soprano might try to break Alex's legs, or worse, if they found out. This concerned me, if for no other reason than that I might have to go back to one-man banding if the station unexpectedly went short a photographer. Alex insisted that the bookie wasn't connected to the Mafia and claimed the bookie made so much money he wouldn't care much even if he found out. I didn't buy this (everybody minds being ripped off), but I wasn't going to rat him out to the mob. And maybe Alex was right. I can't speak for his friend in New York, but I know

Alex is still alive and well, although I don't believe he deals with bookies much anymore.

Whether I was with Alex or Jay or Jules or someone else, one nice thing about being a reporter was that I got to pair up with a different photog every day. Some stations keep photogs and reporters in permanent pairings, much like police partners, but at most places, you swap around. This has its good and bad sides. The good is that you get variety and don't get on each other's nerves quite as much. The bad is that some pairings don't work as well as others.

It's the same for any team; there are just some people you work well with and some you don't. Sometimes another reporter I worked with, Wanda Williams, would actually barter with me and trade me her photographer if she was stuck with someone she didn't work well with. "I'll trade you Angela for Jules," she'd say, to which I'd respond, "Throw in a photog-to-be-named-later and it's a deal."

Every reporter had his or her own favorite photog, sometimes for peculiar reasons. One of my all time favorites was a guy named Mark Brown, who was really just subbing as a photographer while he applied to law school. Mark had been a sports anchor at a very small-market station in West Virginia before deciding to give up TV and pursue a legal career. He needed something to do while he went through the law school application process and took a job as a photographer because he knew how to shoot, having been a one-man band at the West Virginia station.

Mark would be the first to admit that he wasn't the most artistic photog in the world, but for me he was just my lucky photographer. Every time I worked with him things turned out well. I still recall a story we did about a flu epidemic in a rural county. The county had shut down its entire school system because so many kids had the flu. So naturally, I had to go

211

there and find someone with the flu. Normally to do this, you go to a doctor's office to find some infected people, but I was working the night shift and couldn't make it into the field until after 7:00 p.m. All the doctor's offices were shuttered, and due to the distance and my deadline, I had less than two hours to track down enough child flu sufferers to make a good TV story.

Just as Mark Brown and I arrived in the county, we spotted a local pharmacy and I yelled, "Stop. Pull in here." I had this notion that someone might have gone there to get medicine for a sick kid. We pulled in and spotted a minivan parked outside with a woman getting in with a small bag of supplies. I approached and explained that, no I wasn't about to carjack her, but was instead a TV reporter looking for someone with the flu, preferably someone of school age. She pointed over her shoulder and said, "I've got five kids in back and all of them have the flu." I've never been so happy to meet such sick people.

Mark and I then followed her to her house and got all sorts of great video of her spoon-feeding the kids cough syrup and treating their sniffles and runny noses. It was perfect. Then we quickly swung by a county school board meeting and got a sound bite from the school superintendent. I did a stand-up showing the shuttered classrooms and empty school hallways (which would have been empty anyway, of course, since this was well after school hours), and we high-tailed it back to the station. Not counting drive time, the entire story took an hour and fifteen minutes to come together. I know this sounds silly, but I firmly believe that if I had been with another photog, the minivan driver would have been alone and buying toothpaste and the school superintendent would have refused to talk to me. Mark was just my lucky photographer.

Another time working with Mark, I was doing a holiday-away-from-home story about college students unable to return to their parents for Thanksgiving. Mark and I only had an hour to find someone, and the university public information office was shut down for the break. So we went over to campus and spotted a pizza deliverer on her way to a student's room. We followed her and got some great shots of a lonely student eating a holiday meal of pizza and wings in front of a dormitory TV set. I started my script with the line, "For this college student, Thanksgiving dinner this year came with sausage and extra cheese ...." Had I been with another photog, I might still be out throwing pebbles against dorm windows trying to find someone to talk to.

Of course, I didn't always get to work with Mark, and working with different people, I had to learn to get along with different personalities. The Foreigner-friendly photog, Jules Smith, for instance, was a good photographer and a really fun person to hang out with, but she could also be a bit intense. Jules was a die-hard UT football fan, and every Monday morning during football season she would arrive at the station without a voice, having screamed herself hoarse cheering on her Volunteers over the weekend. And that was after games in which UT won by 30 points. When UT lost, you were better off not even trying to talk with her.

Jules was also a bit high strung on the highways. On our way to a story, Jules would be flying down the interstate cursing every car in front, beside, or behind us, even if it was a van full of nuns. Jules would yell at the slowpokes and resort to maneuvers that left me grasping for the safety straps.

In general, it is the photog who does the driving and is responsible for the news car. Which also means that photogs control the car stereo, so, as a reporter, you have to get used to some diverse musical tastes. When working with Kevin

Umberger, for instance, it helped if you shared his affinity for *The Grateful Dead*, *Phish*, and *The Allman Brothers*. Kevin followed those bands with something bordering on obsession, and literally followed them from city to city on his vacation time, which he made sure to coordinate with the bands' touring dates. Kevin was a "taper," in band lingo, and had something close to 4,000 live shows on tape. The most expensive piece of furniture in Kevin's apartment was a custom-built dresser filled with nothing but audiotapes of live concerts. A lot of those Kevin had taped himself.

I once asked Kevin if he ever got bummed out thinking about the death of Jerry Garcia, and he replied, "Every day. Every damned day." When I left Knoxville, Kevin gave me 10 live shows on tape as going-away-gift. I still play them sometimes.

By contrast, photog Dave Wignall worshipped the Spice Girls with a sustained reverence that seemed remarkable for anyone over the age of 13. Dave had seen *The Spice Movie* five or six times, and could describe pretty much every last detail of the Girls' personal and professional lives. Meanwhile, another photog I worked with, Randy Stephens, was a bluegrass picker who spent his weekends playing music around a campfire. Working with Kevin, Dave, and Randy, you really covered the musical spectrum.

I was pretty flexible in my choice of music and got along with almost all the photogs, but even the mildest personalities start to rub you the wrong way when you're in such close proximity for an extended period of time. I'm sure they tired of me as well. I often heard them complain about other reporters and have no reason to believe they spared me the same treatment when I wasn't around.

For the most part, though, disagreements between reporters and photographers are based on small matters that really aren't important. I've probably worked with 40 or 50 different photographers, and only really had trouble working with one. I won't name him, because it's not really fair to slam someone who doesn't have a chance to respond. Plus, he would probably try to hunt me down.

This photog could hold a grudge like no one I've ever met, and he took offense at nearly everything I said. If I offered a suggestion about what to shoot, he accused me of ordering him around. If I didn't say anything, he complained I wasn't treating him as an equal partner. If I tried to help carry his gear, he thought I was hurrying him along. If I didn't offer to carry anything, he'd accuse me of treating him like a pack mule. He once told me never to speak to him again, and then a few weeks later berated me for ignoring him.

I later found out that he acted this way toward almost every reporter he worked with, but at the time I didn't know this and he made my life miserable. I didn't feel I could approach station management over a petty personal conflict with a photog. News directors and general managers don't like to be bothered by these sorts of things. Besides, they figure that you are working with a different photographer every day and can stand a rough pairing every now and then. The problem in this case was that I was working the nights-and-weekends shift, and he was the only photographer on that shift, which meant I was stuck with him nearly all the time. It was a very unpleasant experience.

We'd get into fierce arguments, and sometimes I literally dreaded going to work, knowing I'd have to work with him. He once called me the worst reporter he'd ever worked with. Later on, when he was feeling more charitable, he amended that and said I was the *second* worst reporter he'd worked with, the first being a reporter named Jim Acosta. Since Acosta is now a national correspondent for CNN, this may tell you something about this photog's news judgment. Perhaps if I'd only been a little bit worse, I might have gone farther in the business.

Chapter 14

All in the Family

"I have never slept with a photographer," says the female anchor, looking at me with a grin. Well, hey, that's no secret. Everybody here knows I dated a photog for a year, so I take a sip from my beer. But surprisingly, a few other people drink up too.

"You slept with a photog? Tell us. Who was it?" everyone demands of the other drinkers. "Female or male?"

It's a Saturday night in Wilmington and we're playing "I never," a silly drinking game in which one person states something that they've never done, and everyone who can't truthfully make the same claim takes a drink. There are about 10 of us playing; a few reporters and photogs, the station sports anchor, a couple of producers, and one or two people who don't work in TV. They are the odd ones out. Everyone else here works at WWAY. We've gathered to celebrate the anchor's new apartment, and after a few drinks the party has degenerated.

"I've never had sex with more than one person at a time," declares one of the producers.

For good or bad, I'm not drinking for that one, but one of the other reporters is taking a big gulp. Really?

"That's not news. I told you all about that," he says, in response to all the curious glances.

"That's true, he tells everyone he can," comments one of the photogs. "I've heard the story three or four times."

"This is boring," chimes in someone else. "Let's play 'Truth or Dare.'"

"Why don't we just skip all this and go straight to the group sex?" says the anchor. She's joking, but don't think it hasn't crossed anyone's mind.

You would think that with the amount of time reporters, photogs and others in the newsroom spend together, you would not want to hang out with each other when you're not on the job. The opposite is actually the case, especially in small markets where most staffers are young and dislocated. This was certainly true for me in Wilmington, where pretty much my entire social life revolved around the people I worked with.

On Friday nights, a group of us would gather at my apartment for Margueritas and Martinis before strolling over to the nearby bars and nightclubs. On weekends (after covering my festivals), I'd watch football games with photogs. I went to movies with producers and minor league baseball games with the sports anchors. I even celebrated a few holiday dinners with co-workers. There's nothing like spending Thanksgiving dinner with a bunch of TV news orphans to give you a strange sense of family, but a family it was in many ways since we were all displaced news junkies with nowhere else to go.

Besides the fact that you often don't know anyone else in the community when you work for a local TV station, when you're new to the business, TV news is all you want to talk about, so you gravitate toward people who can relate. Non-TV types just don't grasp the significance when you brag about how your live package was better than the other station's newsroom VOSOT, or truly appreciate how much of an accomplishment it was to get the truck driver to do an interview as he was being strapped onto the stretcher.

That may be one reason why so many people in TV end up dating and even marrying someone else in the business. Apart from the entertainment field (and admittedly, some view it as the same business) TV news is about the most incestuous industry you can find. In almost every TV market, reporters are dating producers, photographers are fooling around with assignment editors, the anchor might be married to the news director, or perhaps the graphics editor is sleeping with the whole promotions department. This is particularly true for small markets. As a friend once put it, small-market TV people tend to be young and attractive and attracted to each other. Intra-office romance is rampant and routine, even for co-workers who aren't playing "Truth or Dare" and "I Never."

A number of these romances result in nuptials. At one of the other stations in Wilmington, for instance, one of the sports anchors was married to the meteorologist. Their marriage endured a couple of station moves until the meteorologist had an affair with a studio camera operator and things fell apart. Which must have led to an awkward scene in the studio as the now-divorced sportscaster and meteorologist sat beside each other at the news desk while their home-wrecker stood behind the camera.

At the station I worked for in Knoxville, two of our reporters were dating station producers, our assignment editor ended up marrying a photographer, our main female anchor was married to a freelance cameraman, and our main male anchor was married to a former radio reporter. Another Knoxville station had just five on-air people and four of them were dating each other. The married sportscaster was shacking up with a reporter and ended up divorcing his wife to marry her, while one of the anchors abandoned her fiancé for the weatherman, whom she ultimately married. The male anchor was the only one not involved with someone else at the station, at least that I know of. He must have felt like the odd man out, and I imagine his wife was a bit anxious.

219

I didn't marry into the media, but as I mentioned, I did date a photog for a while. Her name was Beth and she worked at a competing station in Wilmington, WECT. We hit it off while covering a drug bust. They can be terribly romantic, you know. For two hours Beth and I were stuck at the scene waiting around for the police to finish searching a house and arrest someone. We just sat and talked and talked. A couple of crime stories later we were an item.

This was a bit complicated in that, technically, we were competitors. My news director, who was aware of the relationship (everyone was aware of the relationship), always made a point of declaring, "What I'm telling you is not for the other station. Paul, keep it to yourself." Working at different stations led to situations in which one of us would be called out to a breaking story while we were together, and we couldn't tell the other why we were leaving or where we were going.

One time I ran into Beth in the field when she was on her way to cover a big story about a fatal accident at a manufacturing plant. I was on my way to cover another fish festival. Did Beth tip off her main man about this big news story? Nope. I found out about it watching her station's evening news, just like everyone else. Did she apologize for keeping me in the dark? Nope, she lorded it over me for days.

On the whole, though, there weren't many conflicts for Beth and me since neither of us was fiercely competitive. That's in stark contrast to a couple who worked in Wilmington before I got there. I never met them, but their rivalry was legendary. They were at competing stations and were so fiercely competitive that supposedly when one got paged in the middle of the night and used a notepad to write something down, the other would wait until the spouse had gone and then scratch the pad with a pencil in order to trace out the imprint of what had been written down on the torn-off page. I'm told that marriage didn't last.

My relationship with Beth didn't last either. There were a variety of reasons for that, but hanging over us the whole time was the realization that at some point one or both of us would have to leave Wilmington if we wanted to stay in TV. It is very difficult to stay in TV news in a small market because of the low pay and lack of career-advancement opportunities. To move ahead, financially and otherwise, you have to move up to a bigger city and a bigger TV market. As a result, if Beth and I were to stay together, we'd both have to find new jobs in the same place. There aren't a lot of openings in TV news, so the chance of finding two jobs in the same market at the same time are slim. It happens, but it's hard.

This probably isn't the main reason Beth and I didn't stay together, but it may have been a factor. I know I thought about it a lot. It makes it very tough to commit, emotionally or otherwise, when you know you may ultimately have to choose between your relationship and your career. I once had another girlfriend tell me she withdrew emotionally in part because she knew I would ultimately leave for another job in another place. A preemptive strike I suppose, or else just a creative excuse on her part. It's not you, it's your job. Whether that line was true or not, it is definitely true that maintaining a relationship, and figuring out where things are going, is tough enough without the specter of a job-related departure every two or three years.

It might be different, of course, if TV news people earned enough money that one spouse didn't have to work. For reporters that really isn't possible until you reach the top 30 markets. For TV photogs it may never be possible.

The best way to stay in a relationship may be to date someone with a job outside of TV that is easily transferable. Teachers and nurses are ideal, as are lottery winners and other independently wealthy individuals. The problem with finding these individuals is that when you're in TV news it is hard to meet people outside of the business. You're working odd-hour shifts and moving from city to city and rarely get a lot of time to put down roots or get to know people in the community.

When you work nights and weekends, as I did for a while in both Wilmington and Knoxville, you are working during precisely the hours that most people socialize. When I dated Beth, she was on a different shift than I was, so for the first six months we didn't have a single whole day together. Every day at least one of us had to go to work. The only full day we got to spend together was when we both called in sick and snuck out to the beach.

Beth at least got her weekends off, whereas I had off Mondays and Tuesdays. Having weekdays off is great for taking care of errands and visiting the dentist, but it kills your social life. Sunday night was my Friday night, and it is tough to find people eager to hit the town on Sunday nights. Even if you can, there's not a lot going on.

My big end-of-the-workweek celebration was to go out to a Darryl's ribs restaurant, sit at the bar, and watch sports by myself. It became my Sunday night ritual, to the point that the bartenders knew what brand of beer I preferred and would start pouring one as I pulled up a stool. I felt a bit like Norm on *Cheers*.

After you've been at a station for a year or two, you generally move off of nights and weekends and to a better shift with more regular hours. But just when you are settling into the new schedule and making a few friends, it is probably time, career-wise, to move to a bigger market. In 10 years, I moved five times, and switched shifts eight times. At one point, after working nightside[*] for over a year, my station

---

[*]The "nightside" shift generally works from 2:30-11:30 p.m.

hired a new reporter and promoted me to dayside,[*] to my great joy. Two or three months later, the new reporter was fired and I was sent back to the nightside, where I remained for another six months. I have never forgiven that reporter for losing her job.

The result of all this is that, as a TV reporter, you have limited opportunities even for a social life that doesn't involve other people in TV. So even if you don't want to date others in the business, you probably still end up relying on colleagues to fix you up. TV fix-ups are dangerous, if for no other reason than that people in TV are amazing gossips. It's the nature of being a reporter, I guess; you just love to pass along juicy stuff.

I was on the receiving end of this one time when a sheriff's department public information officer (a former TV reporter himself) encouraged me to ask out a woman he knew. She was a fitness instructor for the local YMCA, and I was not opposed to the idea. But as soon as I asked her on a date, the PIO proceeded to announce this development to all of my co-workers, competitors, and everyone I knew at the sheriff's department.

During the daily morning meeting at my station, instead of discussing the news of the day, everyone instead deliberated on where I should take the fitness instructor, what I should wear, and whether I should attempt a kiss on the first date. It was also suggested, only half jokingly, that I do a live report for the eleven o'clock show to update everyone on my progress. I can see it now: "We're at the scene of Paul's latest rejection, let's go live for the latest ...."

---

[*] The "dayside" shift generally works from 9:30 to 6:30, although I usually started an hour earlier to do my courthouse rounds, which I discuss in Chapter 22.

Later that same day, I attended a sheriff's department press conference and had to endure 20 minutes of the sheriff's secretary, the chief deputy, and six local reporters and photographers sitting around evaluating my prospects. When the sheriff came out, he looked at me, smiled, and nodded knowingly.

After that, I swore that not only wouldn't I date anyone in the news business, I wouldn't date anyone who knew anyone in the business. As you can imagine, this starts to limit your opportunities. Before you know it, you are into your thirties and spending a lot of time by yourself.

In Knoxville, my closest companion for much of my stay was a stray cat who started showing up at my apartment. I gave him some food one day and, from then on, he'd be waiting in the parking lot whenever I arrived home. I named him Lenny, and he would come inside and hang out for a few hours, then he'd go and stand by the door until I got the message and let him out. In some ways I guess it was the perfect noncommittal relationship for a nomadic TV reporter.

Not to belittle that man-feline bond, but sometimes I felt that working in TV news kept me in a state of arrested development compared to friends who took stable jobs and stayed in the same location for a while. This hit me when I visited a former college roommate around the time of my 30th birthday. Here I was, driving a beat-up old pickup truck, renting a small apartment with just two or three pieces of furniture, and I hadn't been on a date in months.

My former roommate, by comparison, was living in his second house (having already moved up from the starter home), with a swimming pool, a nice car, and a beautiful wife, seven months pregnant. They're telling me about the baby on the way and I'm thinking, "Well, I just got cable ...."

By that point, I had been to the weddings of at least 10

college buddies and had begun to notice that the so-called singles tables got smaller and smaller and farther from the head table each year. It was almost as if the hosts were getting embarrassed of us. There weren't many singles left, anyway. At one friend's nuptials, I counted 20 women my age, with 17 of them wearing diamond rings. Of the other three, I later found out that two were gay. Unfortunately, I only learned this pertinent fact after I'd spent an hour or so getting drinks for one of them. To borrow a line from TV critic Tom Shales, I was barking up the wrong she.

By that point, I had gone to so many weddings unaccompanied that my friends were starting to get suspicious about *my* preferences. "Is there something you want to tell us, Paul? We're very open minded." Good for you. I'm not gay, I'm just in TV.

But every time you move in TV, you start over from scratch, and contrary to what you might expect, it gets harder each time to make new friends and join a new community. After a few moves, I found myself less eager to make the effort, having been through the whole gain and loss process a few times before. It's hard to commit to anything when you know that eventually you'll be faced with the choice of sacrificing your dream. So instead, you tend to view things as a short-timer, and think, what's the use?

Should I join that swing-dance group I read about? Should I join a book club or get involved with a local volleyball team? Should I introduce myself to that comely neighbor? Nah, I'm probably going to move in a few months anyway, why bother? Before you know it, you're a hermit, and your neighbor thinks you're a jerk.

This isn't inevitable, of course, but you have to make a concerted effort to avoid it if you move around a lot in TV news. Because in stark contrast to the so-called glamour of being on TV, the life of a roving reporter can get pretty solitary, even when you have friends at the station.

Sometimes in Knoxville, returning to Lenny the cat and my otherwise empty apartment with a six-pack and some take-out Chinese food, I couldn't help wondering why I was enduring this. One night I opened up a fortune cookie and read, "There is a true and sincere friendship between you both," only to look over at Lenny and wonder, "Is this really worth it?"

Just to provide some brief psychological comfort, I had what I called my "fall-back dream girl." No, it wasn't a blow-up doll, just the memory of a girl I dated for a short period of time when I was 14 or 15. I hadn't seen her in over a decade and had no idea what she was up to. Perhaps 300 pounds. Or her seventh kid. It didn't much matter, because I wasn't going to actually look her up. The idea was to have someone to daydream about when I was feeling lonely. I would imagine running into her. She'd have seen me on TV, we'd rekindle that lost flame, marry, have kids, etc. She would also have inherited a lot of money.

At a particularly low moment, I made a brief stab at locating her via her college alumni office, but wisely aborted the effort before I learned anything. Because if I did find her, and she turned out to be married, or now calling herself Steve, or worst of all, didn't remember me, then what dream would I have left to fall back on? If a dream is sustaining you, you don't want it crushed by reality.

The fact is, it is very unusual to make it to the big time in TV without changing cities, stations, and jobs at least three or four times and changing schedules two or three times at each station. You have to get used to spending a lot of time alone, even if you are fortunate enough not to get exiled to a remote outpost like Whiteville for a while.

Sometimes I think that those who achieve the greatest success in TV news are those able to withstand solitude and instability the longest; those able to put off the yearning for family and friends and financial stability. Either that, or those who have a spouse who doesn't mind living on food stamps and relocating every two or three years. I know an enormous number of TV reporters who gave up their dreams of the big time because they or their spouse simply got tired of moving around, tired of living at age 35 as though you were still 24.

A few years back, I spoke to an ambitious young reporter, probably not more than 24, who firmly declared that she intended to make it all the way to the networks. I didn't try to dissuade her, but privately I thought, "Give it a few more years, a few more moves, and see if you still feel the same way." You have to be willing to make a lot of sacrifices to make it to the top. Makes me wonder sometimes about the people who make it.

Chapter 15

Life as a Quasi-Celebrity

Despite the solitude, there are some unusual benefits from working in TV; mainly that there is a quasi-celebrity aspect to the job. I didn't go into TV with that in mind, but I have to admit that, in the beginning, it did seem like a bonus. Be on TV, impress your friends, attract beautiful women! I guess I thought hordes of scantily clad females would be calling me up at the station after seeing me on TV. It didn't happen. I am still awaiting the arrival of the Paul Spelman Fan Club.

Any fame and glory I experienced as a local TV reporter was nothing to write home about. To this day, if someone asked me what my greatest claim to fame is, I'd probably say it was getting tossed into a glass table by Barney Miller's son when I was seven. *Barney Miller*, in case you aren't aware, was a popular TV sitcom in the 1970s starring Hal Linden as Barney, a police captain for a bunch of oddball detectives. Hal's son Ian was an elementary school friend, and we were watching karate on TV one day when we decided to act out a few moves. Ian proved a faster learner than me, and my forehead went into a glass coffee table. Hal took me to the hospital to get stitches. Sometimes I wonder if it's too late to sue. I haven't seen Hal or his son since I was 10, but the very faint scar I have on my forehead still tops all the fame and celebrity I achieved as a reporter in TV news.

It is true that telling people you are a TV reporter sounds impressive. Whenever I would state my occupation, the usual response was, "Really? You're actually on camera? Wow!" It is the kind of job that makes for impressive cocktail party conversation. I've been at parties where the conversation

228

would suddenly shift to a lively discussion of TV news as soon as anyone learned I was a reporter. Not that I volunteered this information, but it often seemed to come up. Friends were often to blame. They had an unfortunate habit of making sure other people knew what I did for a living. "Have you met Paul? He's on TV," was a common introduction. People seemed to think I wanted to be introduced like this. Once, I recall, I was introduced to an attractive young woman with, "Do you know Paul? He's on TV. You may not recognize him, though, because he looks different. You know, my wife asked me just the other day, 'How old is Paul? He must wear a lot of makeup because he seems younger on the news.'" The really ironic thing was that the guy thought he was talking me up.

His comment about looking different in person was not unusual. People always say you look different in person than on TV. I was never sure if this meant that I looked better or looked worse, or which one I would prefer. It seemed like a choice between being unattractive in real life or looking bad at my job. In either case, the recognition I got as a TV reporter had less of a star-struck celebrity aspect to it than a "Don't I know you?" quality. Most people didn't think I was a big star, they just thought I looked familiar. "Gimme a second, I'll get it, you work at Ken's Auto, right?"

Or if they did know who I was, they seemed to think that I knew them too. It was a peculiar phenomenon to have people I'd never met before say, "Hey Paul, what's going on?" and expect me treat them as lifelong chums. Yet if I failed to act as though I recognized and remembered them, they thought I was giving them the cold shoulder. It didn't help that I tended to get recognized at inconvenient moments, such as when I was at the drugstore buying condoms, or a tube of Preparation H. "Aren't you on the news?" they'd ask, glancing at my checkout items. "Looks like a fun night for Mr. TV Man ...."

This must happen to genuine celebrities all the time. Not the Preparation H part, just the one-sided familiarity. I recall when I lived in Telluride, a place frequented by honest-to-goodness movie stars, a ski area lift operator once told me that Sylvester Stallone had ridden his chairlift and was arrogant and conceited.

"Why do you say that?" I asked.

"He didn't say anything to me. Acted like he was too good or something. Next time, I won't be cleaning the snow off his chair."

At the time, I thought, "What a jerk. It'll serve Rambo right to get a cold butt next time." But working in TV made me realize how ridiculous this is. I mean, how often do you engage in chatty conversations with people you've never met before? How often does anybody? When you do address strangers as if they are your lifelong friends, that's when they think you're odd and start edging away from you. But when people see you on TV, or in the movies, they think they know you and that you must know them back. It's such a common phenomenon that even people in the TV business forget that they really don't know the on-air folks from competing stations. Whenever you run into another TV reporter in the field, you tend to call them by name and ask how they're doing, even if you've never met them before.

As for those hordes of scantily clad females, I found that being a minor celebrity really wasn't helpful. Few women were truly impressed, and those that were were not women I generally wanted to go out with. This may sound like the Groucho Marx line about not wanting to join any club that would have him as a member, but it was more that the type of woman who was impressed by the fact that I was on TV turned out to be significantly less impressed when she realized how little I earned, how much I had to work, and how little influence I had with the restaurant maitre'd'.

Apart from women in the news business themselves, most of the women I dated had no idea I was on TV before I told them. When they did spot me on screen, they usually laughed. I guess it's because they weren't accustomed to seeing me in my "Paul Spelman, TV Guy" persona. In general, I much preferred that they didn't view me as a TV celebrity, although I have to admit I was a bit taken aback when a woman told me, "I saw your little story. It was cute." I'm not sure if she used the word "little" because the story was unimportant or because I looked diminutive on her screen, but either way, it wasn't the adulation I'd been hoping for.

Perhaps that should have been my cue right then and there that we weren't right for each other. The mismatch must have been obvious to others, because when we went out for our date another guy actually came up and asked for her number while I was sitting there. I guess he wasn't awestruck by my stardom either. She had the courtesy not to give him her number, at least in my presence, but when we said goodnight, she gave me a brief hug and said, "Thanks for playing." I felt like a game show contestant taking home a year's supply of Turtle Wax as consolation for coming in second.

The only real time that being on TV made me feel like a celebrity was when I played for the Knoxville station's basketball team, the 6-Shooters. Our station meteorologist, Matt Hinkin, organized the team in order to raise money for local charities and garner publicity for the station. Schools and church groups would challenge the 6-Shooters and get to keep the proceeds from concessions and ticket sales. WATE used it as a promotional tool, and the players used it to get some exercise.

231

Since our basketball skills were marginal at best, I guess the appeal for spectators was getting to see TV "celebrities." If that was the case, they were undoubtedly disappointed. Besides our weatherman, I was usually the only on-air person who played. About half of the team, including all of our best players, didn't work at the station. Which made for some amusing introductions before the game. "Number 4 is Paul Spelman, a Channel 6 reporter. Number 3 is Matt Hinkin, Channel 6 meteorologist. Number 7 is Doug Blair, a ... really nice guy who works down the street from the station."

I always wondered how the fans felt when they turned out expecting to see our main anchors and got me and the promotions editor instead. I can't imagine paying to see TV people play basketball anyway. I mean, why would you pay to see a bunch of mediocre athletes play basketball. You can see that at the YMCA any time you want. Half the people in the stands were better players.

An astounding number of people did pay to see us, though. The 6-Shooters were extremely popular, especially in small towns. Each year, the team played about 40 games, raising close to $25,000 in the process. We actually had a waiting list of groups that wanted to play us.

Sometimes the crowds were pretty thin, but in other places they would pack the gym with a thousand people or more. This was especially true for the more remote locales. The general rule was that the farther we'd go, the bigger the crowd would be. A game in Knoxville might draw three or four people (and they were usually related to one of the players), but if we played in a small town an hour and a half away, we'd arrive to find a packed gym with screaming crowds. It was surreal.

As for the games themselves, they could be fierce, despite our lack of athleticism. I guess the players didn't want to lose to these TV big shots. The player guarding you might be the local dentist or church pastor, but he competed as if you had just insulted the town womenfolk. I was pushed, elbowed, shoved, and even had my finger broken during a game. At times you had to remind your opponents that, uh, Mr. Minister, this game is for charity, right? This, after you'd been struck in the face for the fourth or fifth time as you went up for a layup. In all fairness, I have to admit I got a bit overheated by the competition too. I knocked over a few elementary school principals here and there.

Win or lose, the games were certainly gratifying to our egos. I was always amazed that all of these people had come out to see us. Kids would line up for our autographs, and somewhere in the hills of East Tennessee, dozens of youngsters have my signature on crumpled paper napkins. The really funny thing is that when they asked for your autograph, most of the time they had no idea who you were.

Thinking that you are "somebody" but not knowing who you are is quite common since, as I mentioned, even when people recognize you they are not always sure why. Sometimes people would know that I was on TV but thought I was the sports guy or the meteorologist. I'd have to explain that I had no idea who won at Darlington, or what the forecast was for this weekend.

Another time, I actually heard two guys arguing over whether I was on TV. "No. I'm telling you, he's on TV. I'll bet you 10 bucks," said one.

"You're on," said the other, and they turned to me and asked if I was on TV.

"Yes I am," I said, "You owe him 10 bucks."

"We'll who are you?" he demanded.

"I'm Paul Spelman," I replied.

"Who the hell is Paul Spelman?" remarked the loser of the bet.

"He's on TV, he does news," said his friend.

"Yeah, well I wouldn't know him from Adam. You can forget your 10 bucks."

Makes a fellow proud to be such a luminary.

To be frank, I don't always recognize celebrities either, even ones I should know because of my job. One time, I didn't recognize the governor of Tennessee, even after working as a reporter in his state for over a year. I'd been sent to the Knoxville airport to cover the return of the University of Tennessee football team after a big bowl game, and was told to look for Governor Don Sundquist. I had no idea what he looked like, and the airport was filled with lots of important-looking people, any one of whom looked as though he could be the governor. Fortunately for me, I had interviewed the governor's wife a few months before at a charity event, so when I spotted a familiar-looking woman standing next to a state trooper, I figured this had to be she. So I sidled over and said, "Excuse me, but aren't you Mrs. Sunkist?"

Just as the state trooper started to push me away, I said, "I'm a reporter. I was hoping to talk to your husband."

"Oh, he's getting our luggage," she replied.

This didn't help, because if he returned with a group of people, I still wouldn't know which one to address. I had visions of interviewing the governor's personal secretary and putting him on the air as "Tennessee Governor Don Sundquist."

So I casually remarked, "You know, I think I just saw the governor go by. Is he wearing a bright orange blazer?"

"No. No. He's in the blue sweater. Over there."

She pointed about 10 feet away.

"Oh yes, I must have gotten confused. You know, everybody looks the same from the back ...."

She nodded and smiled, but I doubt she was fooled. Still, at least I didn't put the governor's cousin on the air.

When you are a TV reporter, encounters with genuine celebrities always remind you of how insignificant your local TV stardom really is. It is impossible to feel full of yourself when some media flack makes you wait 90 minutes to do a four-minute interview with teen actor Jonathan Taylor Thomas from *Home Improvement*, in town to promote some straight-to-video release. Another time I got to interview Dolly Parton and ended up so nervous I had to physically hold down my leg to keep it from shaking. Admittedly, it wasn't just Dolly that had me nervous, but the fact that I had to interview her on stage in front of hundreds of people.

That happened when Dolly stopped by Dollywood at the same time she was promoting an educational program that provided books to area kids. It was a genuinely worthy program and almost made up for the fact that Dollywood is a tacky amusement park with boring rides and more fried food than all the festivals I went to in North Carolina put together. You can feel your arteries clogging up just walking in the gates. Dolly didn't start the park, and probably had little to do with its menu, but she's from that area and gave it her name. She isn't there all that often, but every now and then she comes through and gives an impromptu performance at one of the park's musical venues.

In this case, my station sent me to talk to her about the book program. I thought it would be just a brief interview in an office somewhere, or perhaps in front of the park entrance. But when I arrived, her media handlers informed me that we would do the interview on stage right after Dolly's performance. Nobody had mentioned anything about doing the interview in front of a live audience. But I couldn't argue about it because I wasn't going to get to talk to her any other way. So I watched Dolly sing and dance for a bit, and then listened in horror as an announcer came over the loudspeaker and informed the cheering crowd that Dolly was about to be interviewed by a "local TV celebrity" and everyone was welcome to stick around and watch. They put Dolly, me, and my photographer up on stage in front of three or four hundred people and wired us through the sound system so my voice could be heard throughout the theater. My interview essentially became a continuation of Dolly's live performance.

It is fair to say that I was unaccustomed to performing in front of large crowds. As a TV reporter, it didn't faze me that tens of thousands of people might be watching me on TV so long as I couldn't see them. But with hundreds of people watching me in person, I felt more self-conscious than I ever have in my life. One of my legs was shaking so hard I thought I might pull a muscle.

Fortunately for me, Dolly's a professional and accomplished interviewee, and all I had to do was mumble a question or two about why books are good and she ran with it. In no time at all, she was prattling away about her Tennessee upbringing and what it was like to be raised in a poor family of fourteen with little reading material (or indoor plumbing, for that matter). I'm told Dolly is at her best in front of large crowds and I believe it. I imagine it also helps keep her interviewers in line. When you are on stage in front of Dolly's faithful, you are less likely to hit her with tactless questions about how much she earns off the fried onions, or the details of her cosmetic surgery. I hadn't planned on asking those questions anyway, but I wasn't going to improvise with hundreds of her fans sitting in the audience a few feet away.

The only celebrity encounter I had that was even more humbling for me was when I got to meet the future leader of the free world himself, George W. Bush. That happened before he was president, when Bush was campaigning in Tennessee. At the time, I was my station's "political reporter" (among other things), and so it was presumed that I would get to interview the candidate when he came through Knoxville. I was very excited when my assignment manager told me I would get to do this, and started thinking about all the tough, hard-news questions I could ask. Unfortunately for me, at the last minute my news director decided that our main anchor, Clay Thomas, should do the interview instead. The news director kindly explained that it was not that he didn't think I could handle the job, but that getting to interview Bush would bolster our main anchor's standing and credibility with the public.

Clay is an excellent journalist and didn't need any bolstering, in my opinion, so it is quite possible the news director was just trying to be kind, but I can also understand why a station might want its main anchor to interview the man who might be president. Stations invest a lot in their anchors, both in terms of pay and promotion, and it helps to have the public see these folks actually doing something important every now and then. Besides, Clay was from Texas, and this would give him an excuse to wear his cowboy boots.

Even though I understood, I was quite disappointed and a bit hurt that I had been yanked off a big story. So as consolation, I was allowed to tag along and watch Clay do the interview. As they set up the camera and lights, the photog asked me to help get a white balance, so I stepped forward with a piece of paper and held it out in front of George W.

"Who's this?" asked Bush, looking up at me. "An intern?"

My humiliation was complete. Afterward, when I'd had time to reflect and come up with a response, I realized I should have said, "No, I'm a Gore supporter," or something pithy like that, but at the time I was struck dumb. I couldn't open my mouth to say a word and just stood silently with a pained expression on my face. Clay tried to save face for me by jumping in with, "No, Paul's not an intern, he's one of our senior reporters," which only prompted Bush to ask, "Well then, why isn't *he* doing the interview?" Which made me think that Bush may be smarter than he looks.

I did get a memento from the experience, as Clay insisted that I get my photo taken with the future president. I would have been too meek to ask. In the photo, we are standing next to each other and grinning into the camera. The man soon to be the most powerful person in the world, and a 32-year-old news intern. I still have the photo, but Bush looks so stiff and wooden in the shot that no one believes it is really him. They always think I'm standing next to one of those cardboard cutouts that tourists pose next to one block from the White House. I guess I might as well have been.

Chapter 16

Pay, Perks, and Parking Tickets

I don't think it ever really occurred to me how hard it would be to make a living as a TV reporter. I mean, you always hear that journalists aren't well paid, and I didn't go into it for the money, but there is a difference between knowing something and *knowing* something. Money, or lack thereof, makes it very difficult to remain as a TV reporter, especially in small markets. It is the biggest reason so many people get out of the business.

Local TV stations are just plain funny about money. At WWAY in Wilmington, my station tried to save money in all sorts of ways. WWAY would spend hundreds of dollars to outfit all of the microphones with colorful station logos, known as mike flags, but wouldn't spend a dime for quality windscreens to protect the microphones. So you'd end up with microphones that *looked* great but sounded terrible. The station also tried to save money by not buying individual business cards. Instead, station employees got generic cards and you'd have to scribble your name on one whenever you gave it to someone. "Just start working there?" was a common question. "Just two years ago," was a common response.

But by far the biggest way WWAY and other local stations try to save money is via low salaries for the news staff. I can't think of another profession where there is a greater disparity between what people get paid and what the public *thinks* people get paid. I recall when I was in Whiteville, a local businessman once tried to get me to invest in a real estate venture he was lining up. "You can make some good money with your disposable income," he said as he launched into his sales pitch. "What do earn in a year now?" When I said $17,000, he got a stunned look on his face and said, "Ah, never mind. Maybe some other time."

I had inadvertently stumbled on a foolproof way to discourage people from hitting me up for money – tell the truth about my income. The difference between perception and reality regarding TV salaries is so profound that even many in the TV business have a poor grasp of how little you earn on the lower rungs.

You often hear about the multi-million-dollar salaries commanded by news stars like Brian Williams and Diane Sawyer. Katie Couric, at last report, earned around $13 million a year. Yet you rarely hear about small-market reporters and photographers surviving on government assistance. According to a survey by the Collegiate Employment Research Institute, journalists have the second lowest starting salary of any college-educated profession, and TV journalists earn less than their print colleagues. TV reporters, even in the 21st century, usually start out at under $20,000, and the salary doesn't get much better until you make it to a top 25 market, meaning a city the size of Minneapolis, Cleveland, or Atlanta.

At WWAY, considered an entry-level station, I earned $17,500 in 1997, and that was pretty good for a small market. In fact, this made me one of the highest paid reporters at WWAY. Most of the other reporters earned $14,500. I was awarded $3000 more because whereas the other reporters worked with photographers, I was often a one-man band, acting as both reporter and photographer. So in essence, my pay was for the work of two people.

Some small-market reporters earn less than $14,000. I know a reporter who was told, while interviewing for a job in Montana, that her TV salary would make her eligible for food stamps. This was explained to her as if it was a station-offered job benefit, part of her overall employment package. "We have a 401(k) plan, and along with our station's health and disability insurance, you'll qualify for welfare ...." And this wasn't a case of "yes, but back then you could buy a steak for a nickel." It wasn't that long ago, and $14,000, or my salary of $17,500, was as low as it sounds. In 1997, the average full-time male worker in the United States made $46,120. Averaging isn't the best way to look at salaries, since there is always some billionaire or pro athlete around to skew the scale. But the median, or midpoint, salary for full-time male workers was still $35,248. To compare TV reporting to another low-income profession, teachers in 1997 earned, on average, $38,436, according to the American Federation of Teachers. Beginning teachers *started out* at $25,012.

Even America's *per capita* income in 1997 was higher than my $17,500. Per capita income includes every man, woman, child, retired grandparent, prison inmate, and hobo riding the rails. Including all of those, the per capita income in the United States in 1997 was $19,241. So I was working 50–60 hours a week as a TV reporter and I was still dragging down the national average.

The really funny thing is that I actually made more at WWAY than I had as a newspaper and radio reporter in Colorado. That's because in Colorado, my jobs were both considered part-time, which really means you're only paid part of the time. At the newspaper, I got paid by the inch. It was undoubtedly the only time I have ever had anything in common with adult film stars, although my rate did not measure up.

Every column inch I wrote, I received $1.50. The day the newspaper came out, all of the reporters would get out our rulers and measure what we'd written in order to submit our weekly invoices. This pay model did not encourage brevity in storytelling. I wrote as long-windedly as possible and included every trivial bit of information I could dig up. The town planner's middle name was Alphonse? Throw it in, it's worth a nickel and the public has a right to know.

I once even charged for writing a correction to my own mistake in an earlier story. I had incorrectly described the mayor of a nearby town as a "former mayor." She was upset about my decision to evict her from office and asked the paper to issue a correction. I had to write it, so I charged for it. I earned about $2 for it. Not much, but it raised the interesting notion of improving my finances by making more mistakes. I never tried this, though, because I had a feeling any financial improvement would be short-lived.

I did, however, get into arguments with copyeditors intent on cutting my stories. I'd explain that while I agreed my story could use some trimming, my rent was coming due and I couldn't afford to let them exercise their editorial prerogative. A typical story ran 12–15 inches, and writing five or six articles for each issue, I earned a little over a hundred dollars a week. Combined with my radio work, for which I got paid about $15 dollars a story, my annual income in Telluride was generally between $7,000 and $8,000. With no benefits.

Even so, at that point I was still in the "college mode," sharing a shack with two or three other people and eating peanut-butter sandwiches for dinner every other night. I had few real wants or expenses. So long as I had my ski pass and enough money to get a beer every now and then, I was okay with it. The issue of being a starving journalist didn't come up that often.

Naturally, I assumed the money situation would improve dramatically in the glamorous world of TV. I'd heard the stories about Tom Brokaw and his $7 million-dollar salary and was therefore quite surprised to learn that local TV pay at lower levels isn't much different from newspaper and radio reporting and in some instances is worse. This is another area where TV is a lot like pro baseball; unless you make it to the major leagues you don't make major league money.

When I left Wilmington for a better job in Knoxville in 1997, moving up some 90 markets in the process but remaining firmly in TV's minor leagues, my salary jumped from $17,500 to $26,000. I rejoiced at this figure, though, because it meant that eight years after graduating from Colgate, my income had finally surpassed what I earned as a bartender's assistant during my college summer vacations. It also finally exceeded the *starting* salary for a teacher. Although when you took into account the fact that by this point I had signed with a TV news agent and had to give him eight percent of my salary, I still took home less than starting teachers. And a lot less than teachers with six years of experience, as I had in news by that point.

There are a couple of reasons why I sometimes compare reporters' salaries to that of teachers. The first is simply that teaching is not known for its generous compensation. But another reason is that, as a news reporter, I'd end up having to do at least one story a year about the despicably low wages paid to those who educate America's children. Don't get me wrong, I believe educators deserve more and am sympathetic to their plight. But it was grating to have to do stories decrying low salaries for people who earned significantly more than I did. I mean, compared to me, teachers seemed to have high pay and benefits, not to mention their summers off. Whereas not only did I not get summers off, but my first year in Knoxville I had to work on Thanksgiving, Christmas, and New Year's Day, and didn't get a single day of vacation because I had started at WATE on January 15th and the station had a policy that you had to be employed as of January 1st in order to qualify for that year's vacation time. WATE's management graciously let me "borrow" a week of vacation from the following year, which meant that I only got one week off the next year.

I probably shouldn't complain too loudly about reporters' incomes, however, because reporters are not the lowest paid in local TV news. That dubious distinction belongs to photographers. At WWAY, photographers were paid $12,000–$14,000 a year, and due to a pernicious work rule, they had to cover the cost of all equipment they damaged or lost. This meant that if they misplaced a camera battery, or accidentally broke a microphone part, they had to pay for a new one.

This rule hit me as well since, as a one-man band, I also used and abused the equipment. One day in Whiteville, I was in a hurry to get back to my bureau and accidentally left a portable police scanner on top of the car when I drove off. It cost me $80. A few months later, I tripped over a loose cable and damaged a TV monitor. Another $100. It would have cost even more had I told the station about it and paid for a new one. Instead, I bought a used TV at a local pawnshop and substituted it before the station found out.

This station reimbursement policy also applied to vehicular damage. Which is why, when I got into a car accident one day coming back from a story, I was required to reimburse the station for the $500 insurance deductible. This was a bitter pill to swallow, even though the accident was, admittedly, my fault. I rolled through a stop sign and was T-boned by another driver. I was lucky my car got hit on the passenger side or I probably wouldn't be here. As it was, the WWAY station vehicle, a clunky old Lincoln Town Car nicknamed "The Battleship," was totaled. Everyone in the newsroom thanked me for getting rid of it, but I wasn't feeling all that super afterward. My head had gone into the steering wheel, and I had a number of other cuts and bruises. Still, I wrote up my story for the day before heading to the hospital to get checked out. It turned out I was fine, at least until my station hit me with the insurance bill.

I had to pay this $500 deductible at a time when my entire take-home pay — after deductions for taxes, social security and health insurance — totaled $250 a week. It took me two and a half months to pay it off, paying in $100 installments every biweekly paycheck. I still have hard feelings towards the WWAY general manager for that. She had the idea that if workers had to pay for damaged equipment, they would take better care of it. Which is undoubtedly correct. You treat the equipment much more gingerly when you realize you'll eat Ramen noodles for a month if you drop a microphone.

But equipment tends to get broken whether you are careful or not, and accidents happen. During my two and a half years at WWAY, nearly every photographer on staff had to shell out for something, and I know of at least two, in addition to myself, that had to cover the $500 auto deductible after fender benders. Between the insurance deductible, the scanner, and the TV monitor, my job at WWAY cost me $680. If I'd worked there a little longer I might have had to take out a loan just to keep paying the station.

I tried calling up the North Carolina Department of Labor to see if I was legally obligated to pay these bills, and they explained that by law, the station couldn't force me to cover the cost of equipment damaged on the job. Unfortunately, they also said that by law, there was nothing to stop the station from firing me if I didn't cough up the money. So I could either pay and keep my job, or leave and try starting over at another station. That wasn't much of an option. It had taken me months and thousand dollars to find an on-air job in the first place, and it wasn't going to help this time around that I'd have to explain that I lost my job because I wrecked the station's car.

In small- and mid-market TV news you are in a bind. As a reporter, you need a place where you can hone your skills, get on-air experience, and put together a resume reel. There are a limited number of places to do this. There are only about 200 TV markets in the U.S. and not a lot of on-air jobs. In Wilmington, there were nine or ten on-air reporting positions for an area with more than a 100,000 people. If I wanted to keep pursuing my dream of making it in TV news, I had to bite the bullet and pay up. So I did.

I guess it was the prudent thing to do because if I hadn't, I probably wouldn't have landed a job later at WATE in Knoxville, where the station did not make employees pay for damaged equipment. That wasn't as much of a concern for me by then, anyway, since I didn't handle the equipment in Knoxville very often. But I did drive station vehicles every now and then, and WATE did make employees pay their own tickets, which are hard to avoid when racing out to cover breaking news all the time.

Parking tickets, in particular, are almost inevitable. Telling the news director you couldn't cover the big warehouse fire because there weren't any parking spaces is not considered an acceptable excuse. Yet when I presented my news director with a ticket one day, I was told, "It's company policy that employees pay their own tickets." The first time this happened I even got hit with an additional late fee because the news director held onto the ticket for a few weeks "to look into it" before letting me know that I had to pay it myself. After that, I did what most of the other employees did when they got a ticket in a news car — I ripped it up and threw it away.

As for speeding tickets, you couldn't rip those up because they had your name on them, and that's what snared Josh

Liner, a young WATE photographer. One day he was returning late from a long-haul story in Kentucky, more than an hour north of Knoxville, and was going around a hundred (he claims he was going downhill) when he got pulled over. That will cost you.

Liner was a relatively new photographer and probably making in the low twenties, if that, and so a speeding ticket was quite a blow, especially at that speed. So the next day everyone in the newsroom received a creative plea from Liner and his reporter, Kimberly O'Neal:

We all know the pressures and adversity that we, as newsies, put up with every day in this business. Many days, it seems like these same pressures are insurmountable. However, isn't it great to know that through it all we have each other. It is out of this love for you guys that I ask you to read the following poem written by our dear sister Kimberly O'Neal:

The Ballad of Young Liner
There is a young lad that most know as Liner,
As a Channel 6 photog, there are few that are finer.
He was sent on a story, far out of state,
The drive back was long, and he couldn't be late.

Young Liner drove swiftly, because of the need,
But he wasn't aware how that Escort could speed.
He was almost home, and the trip had been super,
When Young Liner looked up, and saw the state trooper.

247

The trooper said, "Son, it's just luck you're
alive,"
Then wrote out a ticket for one-twenty-five.
Young Liner's a photog, as we mentioned before,
With his cameraman's salary, he's really quite
poor.

The ticket's substantial, please understand,
So we're asking his newsies to give him a hand.
A five-dollar bill would lessen the strain,
It would help pay the ticket and ease Liner's
pain.

He's learned a good lesson, that's really on par,
Don't drive like Jeff Gordon when in a news car.

After wiping the tears from your eyes, I hope that you will consider what Kimberly O'Neal has so beautifully put into words. All we need is 18 people to look deep into their hearts and see how much they truly care for this station. Sure, there are some who might see this as begging. They might say, "Do the crime, pay the fine!" However, I think such a coming together will bring us closer as a WATE family. Not only bring us together but propel us over the hump to where we can finally reign supreme over those dogs down the street!! Thanks for your support!!
— Josh "Lead Foot" Liner

I was so impressed with their literary talents (although a bit perplexed as to how eighteen times five equals $125), I contributed five dollars. Unfortunately for Young Liner, his plea was not well received by others in the newsroom, in particular, by other photographers, many of whom had had to pay their own fines. It provoked a response in kind from fellow photographer Jay Kaley, who followed with a note to the newsroom stating:

Fellow compassionate photogs –

I love all of you, I love this station. I am proud to be a part of this big, happy, mushy, lovey-dovey tribe of wonderful picture takers. To be able to do this beautiful job with you wonderful people, I had to find somewhere to live. Now this guy wants money every month for me to live there. He calls it rent or something. It's $400 bucks. But if we all get together we can take care of this and I won't have to pay it. You could all give me $20 bucks or whatever you want to do. If I have any extra, I'll buy clothes or something. Let's pitch in and get me rent free. Josh Liner will be collecting the cash for me. Thanks for your support. – Jay "You gotta be kiddin' me" Kaley

Whether it was Jay's response, or simply self-dignity, Liner was shamed into returning money to everyone who had donated (it was pretty much just me and a few anchors) and ended up paying the ticket out of his own pocket. Kimberly felt bad and chipped in half. Liner told me he worked a second job as a freelance photographer for a day to get money to pay it off.

Taking second jobs and freelance work isn't uncommon in small and medium TV markets, especially for photographers. They often shoot weddings and bar mitzvahs on the side in order to make ends meet. I never felt I could manage a second job, but I knew other reporters and anchors who did. In Knoxville, one of our reporters worked weekends at a department-store cosmetics counter. In Wilmington, the main female anchor sometimes worked as a clerk at a clothing store. It must have been strange for viewers to walk in and see their local anchor behind the counter. "We have some breaking news for you, your credit card has been rejected ...." But with the salaries they offer in small and medium markets, this shouldn't surprise anyone.

The reason the pay is so low is simply that stations know that if you want to be in TV news, you have to get on-air experience and you don't have a lot of options. Some stations feel they're actually helping you out by letting you work there, since they figure you're going to leave in a year or two anyway. And sometimes they *are* doing you a favor. WWAY did me a real favor in taking a chance on me in 1994, because I didn't have any TV experience whatsoever. I didn't even have an internship or communications degree under my belt, and for the first few months at the Whiteville bureau I wasn't able to contribute a whole lot to the station.

I think a lot of station managers and news directors have also been in local TV news for so long that they actually start to believe that the pay scale is appropriate. They get kind of beaten down themselves. I recall a news director at WATE, Brian Trauring, whom I respected immensely for the most part, but who seemed to honestly believe he was being quite generous when he offered to raise my salary from $28,000 to $29,000. This for a 32-year-old reporter with eight years of experience. Brian proudly proclaimed that this increase surpassed the present rate of inflation. He neglected to mention that the inflation rate the previous year had been the lowest rate in 33 years. Brian also made this generous offer at the same time he was continually posting company memos from our owners, Young Broadcasting, trumpeting large corporate profits and detailing Young's latest $100-million-dollar station acquisition.

While the Internet and changes in the economy are now starting to cut into profits, most local TV news operations make a lot of money. In fact, according to most business analysts, the operating profit at a typical local TV station has traditionally been between 40 and 50 percent, higher than most industries not associated with illegal activities. I couldn't help looking at these station memos and thinking, "Someone's making a lot of money here but it sure isn't me."[*]

If you really want to make money on-air in TV news, you have to move up to a big market. In fact, a lot of small- and medium-market stations are genuinely surprised if reporters or anchors want to stay and use higher salaries in bigger markets as a way of getting rid of the competition. In Knoxville, for instance, my station would put popular anchors at competing stations up for sale. When a competing station's anchor grew popular with the public, my station would tape the anchor on the air and send the tape to big market stations, hoping the big-market stations would offer the Knoxville anchor a job. It was simply understood that the anchor would be offered more money by the big-market station and the Knoxville station would never match it.

Other Knoxville stations did the same thing. One of our more popular morning anchors told me he got a phone call one day from a big-market station telling him they liked his tape and wanted him to come interview for a job. "How did you get my tape?" he asked, to which they replied, "We got it in the mail. You didn't send it?" Unfortunately, he was under a contract at the time and couldn't go anywhere.

Contracts in TV news are an insidious form of indentured servitude; they bind you to a station for a set period of time, usually two or three years. In actuality, they bind you for a little bit longer, since it usually takes several months to find a job after your contract runs out, and if you can't find a job

---

[*] However, a few years later Young Broadcasting ended up filing for bankruptcy, so perhaps their projections were a bit too rosy.

quickly enough, you may have to sign another contract. Some contracts even prohibit you from *looking* for another job until the current contract expires. Contracts also usually have no-compete clauses, which prohibit employees from switching to another station in the same city for six months to a year or more. So if a competitor in the same market sees your work and wants to hire you, you not only have to wait until your contract expires, you then have to work as a fry cook or something until your no-compete clause runs out.

I know of one small-market station that even required its reporters to sign no-compete clauses for markets located two hours away. This was to keep big-market news directors from poaching the small-market station's reporters if they happened to be any good. So if a reporter making $15,000 at the small-market station got offered $60,000 by the bigger market, he or she would have to say no. It's sort of like telling an actor at the Pasadena Community Theater that if Steven Spielberg discovers him and wants him for a new movie, he has to turn it down.

I didn't have a contract in Wilmington, but I did have one in Knoxville. This meant that I could get a job offer from the head of ABC News himself and I'd have to turn it down and stay on local news in Tennessee. Not only couldn't I leave for another station, I couldn't even leave to go into the mortgage business or something until the contract ran out. Otherwise I would owe the station liquidated damages. My contract had a complex clause creating a formula that made it costly for me to cut and run. If I left early, I'd have to pay the station $3,500 times the number of months left on my contract divided by the total months of the agreement, plus moving expense reimbursal. In other words, if I had 12 months to go on a 24-month contract, I'd owe them $1,750 in damages, and would also have to give back the $750 I received in moving expenses — money, of course, that I'd spent moving to Knoxville.

My anchor friend Mike Cihla used to keep a running countdown of how much he'd owe if he suddenly bolted. "Down to $2,000," he would announce, "just a little bit less, and I can afford it." Another WATE anchor ended up paying $3,000 to get out of his contract early. The station had demanded $22,000, the full amount left in his salary for the remainder of the year, but after extensive haggling, they settled on $3,000. They reached this agreement late one night when he didn't have his checkbook with him, so he called someone and had it brought to him before management changed its mind.

Unlike modern contracts for pro athletes, local news contracts are almost always for the benefit of the employer, not the employee. For reporters, there are very few benefits to signing a contract. Supposedly, it protects you from getting fired arbitrarily, but in actuality, you can still get fired so long as you give the station "cause." Cause can be anything from tardiness or insubordination to failing to "conduct yourself with due regard to social conventions and public morals and decency," according to the terms of my WATE contract. Other things that could get you fired were drugs, alcohol, uttering an on-air obscenity, and "dishonesty and deceit." One reporter at WATE was fired after she was arrested for driving under the influence on her night off. Her case was later dismissed in court, but she never got her job back.

Some of these clauses make sense, of course, since you don't want your local TV station represented by a bunch of moral degenerates. But because the contract also allows stations to fire reporters for "failure to perform" (and who knows what that means), management has quite a bit of wiggle room to send you packing. I know several reporters and anchors who were "strongly encouraged" to look for a job elsewhere despite the fact that their contracts weren't up and they hadn't robbed any banks or done anything else especially heinous (at least that I knew of).

On the flip side of this, I know a few reporters and anchors who broke their contracts and jumped to a bigger market when they shouldn't have. I also know a reporter who was able to leave before her contract expired because her station forgot to make her sign it. She had to endure a lengthy lecture about ethics and fair play, but legally, there wasn't anything the station could do to stop her.

From a legal standpoint, it's questionable how much a contract really prevents you from leaving anyway. Some employment attorneys have told me that most no-compete clauses, especially in small markets, aren't worth the paper they are printed on and basically amount to scare tactics. Even if a contract is legally enforceable, few small-market stations would want to spend the money to litigate it. Unfortunately, neither do the big-market stations doing the hiring, so sometimes a station offering a job will back down if your current employer calls and threatens a lawsuit. Which happens.

When a contract runs out, you can try to avoid signing a new one, but stations tend to play hardball. One station in Knoxville would post the reporter's job (essentially putting up a help-wanted ad for the position) whenever someone evinced a reticence to sign a new contract. My station did this with our weekend meteorologist after he commented one day that he would rather work weekdays. He thought he was negotiating, and they effectively countered.

Another reporter was told that if he didn't sign a new contract by the day his expired, he'd be fired. So he went all out to find another job and found one. By that time, management had changed its mind (or more likely just couldn't find anyone good to take his place) and asked if he could kindly stick around for a few more weeks so that the station would be fully staffed during ratings. He told them, "See you later."

Despite this kind of heavy-handedness, I have to say that the stations I worked at were relatively fair to me with regard to contracts. WWAY in Wilmington didn't require one when I was there, and WATE in Knoxville allowed me to stay on for a year after my contract expired even though I wouldn't sign a new one. I was grateful to WATE for this, but it was not without advantages for them. The news director explained that if I wasn't going to sign a new contract, he couldn't give me a raise, even one less than that woeful rate of inflation. I was just thankful they didn't force me to leave. I could live without a raise, but I couldn't live without a job.

And despite the low pay, there are a few job perks that go along with being in TV. For instance, some anchors, and even a few reporters, get a clothing allowance that helps them stay well suited. I never got one of these, which was why I had to resort to buying suits from thrift stores and then paying a tailor for alterations. The jacket I wore on TV more than any other cost me all of $27. It was $7 at Wilmington's Salvation Army and then another $20 to have it altered to fit.

The few new suits I splurged on were usually cotton poplin, since they cost about half of what wool suits cost but you can't tell the difference on camera. And since shoes are rarely seen on TV, I bought a used $12 pair from a Wilmington Army-Navy store. They were plain black and had a bulbous round front that gave my feet a vaguely clownish look, but they were nearly indestructible.

While I didn't receive clothing perks, I did get various food freebies that reporters tend to get while out covering stories. These are quite common. In Whiteville, nearly every time I did a farming story I'd return with a free tray of fruit or vegetables courtesy of a local farmer. When a TV crew does a story involving a pizza parlor, they invariably walk away with a free pie. Technically, all of this qualifies as payola, and ethically, journalists are not supposed to accept it. But when you are doing a good-time-was-had-by-all story about the strawberry festival and some farmer offers you a free quart of fresh strawberries, you don't usually feel morally conflicted.

Most people offer these gifts out of simple generosity. Farmers I've met are generally good-natured and proud of what they produce. But a few people, I'm sure, do give gifts hoping the media will present them in a more favorable light. And I may have, although most of the time I wasn't out there looking to do an expose on the strawberry festival in the first place.

Payola can be a genuine problem if it is large enough to truly influence a serious story, and there is one gift I should have turned down. That happened early on when I was a radio and newspaper reporter in Telluride, and the local ski company decided to give free season passes to members of the local media as a "goodwill gesture." These passes were worth about $800, a fairly substantial amount even when you're not earning just $7,000 a year, as I was. Even at the time, I recall thinking that it seemed suspiciously generous on the part of the ski area, but my bosses didn't have a problem with it. In fact, they took the free passes as well. After covering a few news stories involving the ski area, however, I realized that it was nearly impossible to remain as objective about a company that had just provided me with an $800 Christmas present. I'm sure I wasn't the only one. Coverage of the ski area seemed to get more favorable for a while.

The only person this gratuity seemed to have little effect on was my radio news director Jon Kovash. He took the free season pass yet remained virulently critical of the ski company and its operating practices. I would listen with amazement as he would air story after story slamming the ski company for its expansion plans and high ticket prices (which, of course, he was no longer paying), and then go use his pass for a day of fun and sun on the mountain. It seemed the ultimate in either journalistic hypocrisy or integrity. I could never decide which. I'm sure the ski company was perplexed as well.

But after seeing how those passes affected most of us in the media, myself included, I become more circumspect about what I accepted from anyone. Admittedly, though, when you are scraping by on a journalist's income, it's hard to turn down free food. Reporters rarely pass up a free meal, and the quickest way to a reporter's good side is undoubtedly through his stomach. In Telluride, I once even wrote a newspaper article about which governmental meetings provided the best meals.

I called it "The Hungry Reporter's Guide to Good Meeting Eating" and handed out ratings from zero to five stars. The Chamber of Commerce won "the coveted *Edible Gavel* award," since most of its meetings were held at local restaurants and provided relatively high-quality food. The town school board, on the other hand, was panned because its meetings were devoid of food and entertainment and spectators were forced to sit in uncomfortably small kindergarten chairs. My "guide" was meant as a joke (although I charged the paper for the inches), but afterward some meeting organizers actually improved their food offerings in an attempt to move up in the rankings; an effort I did nothing to discourage.

Perhaps TV station owners realize that reporters are easily swayed by food, because they tend to give out food gift certificates in lieu of Christmas bonuses. In both Knoxville and Wilmington, my entire Christmas bonus amounted to a $25 certificate for Honey Baked Hams. Strangely enough, the cheapest ham was priced at $35, which was a dilemma until photog Kevin Umberger discovered that he could use his certificate on a $1 cookie and get $24 in change. That beat eating spiral-sliced ham for a month, but it certainly didn't make up for the lack of real money in local TV news.

Chapter 17

Hurricanes and Heading for Higher Ground

My time in Wilmington was one of the happiest periods for me as a TV reporter. I was able to work with some great people and became much more comfortable on the job. But after about two and a half years at WWAY, it was time for me to go. I'd done pretty much every kind of story you could do in Wilmington, and although I loved the coastal North Carolina area, I found myself increasingly frustrated with the limitations of working in a very small market. The equipment was always breaking, the staff was always changing, and I was always out of money. I also still had my dream of making it to the big time; to a top 25 market, or even to CNN or a network. I would run into network reporters in the field every now and then and think, "Someday, maybe, I'll be on that side of the fence."

What gave me the final push to get out of Wilmington was the arrival of Bertha and Fran. Not twin babies or a juicy love triangle, but two hurricanes that came along in the summer of 1996. Both were originally headed elsewhere, but chose at the last minute to veer off course and slam into the North Carolina coast.

Bertha came first at the beginning of July. It was mostly a Category 1 storm, meaning winds from 74–93 miles an hour, although a small part of the storm reached Category 2 with winds up to 110. This sounds serious, and did cause about $250 million dollars worth of damage, but Category 1 is the lowest level of hurricane, and Bertha really wasn't all that bad. In a lot of ways, it was fun and exciting, being my first hurricane and all.

259

Everyone at the station thought it was going to miss us. We had had plenty of hurricane scares before and had already done to death all the hurricane-prep stories about residents stocking up on plywood and battening down the hatches. I did so many stories from the Wilmington Lowe's, I probably knew the store better than the employees. Certainly the portable generator and masking tape aisles. But in the end, the storms would always miss us or peter out.

For Bertha, the weather service was predicting that it would go south and strike Myrtle Beach or Charleston. Instead, it took a last minute swerve north and plowed right into Wilmington. The authorities evacuated the beach towns and the whole city shut down. Except for us TV folks. We were in the thick of it.

I spent Hurricane Bertha on Carolina Beach, an island community 20 minutes south of Wilmington and separated from the mainland by the Intracoastal Waterway. The town had been evacuated, but along with a photographer, Chad, and a courageous intern named Eric, I hunkered down in the city hall with a few police officers and the town mayor. Every now and then when we got our courage up, we would venture outside to get video, driving around through deserted streets and the flooded harbor area. We could barely see where we were going, and whenever it got really hairy — in other words when a 40-foot-high Wendy's sign came crashing down and just missed us, or when the floodwaters started to seep in through the car doors — we would scurry back into the safety of the shelter.

All in all, it was pretty exciting, and since a Category 1 is the weakest kind of hurricane, we weren't dealing with much genuine death and devastation. Category 1 is mostly a lot of torn shutters and broken windows and a few blown-off roofs.

The hurricane didn't even last that long; just a few hours. Which was long enough to make for good TV.

Hurricanes are practically made for TV, which is one reason they get so much coverage. What could be better than a natural disaster with tremendous visuals and just enough advance warning to get your crews into place? The irony, of course, is that if you are a local reporter, most of your viewers lose their power and can't see your splendid reportage. Still, you get as much footage as you can, figuring you'll have plenty of opportunities to show it again afterward.

And you do. Too many opportunities, actually. The big-time network reporters go cover a hurricane and then leave town afterward, on to the next story. But when you work as a local TV reporter in the community that gets clobbered, your station runs nothing but hurricane stories for the next month. I did follow-up story after follow-up story, all related in some way to Hurricane Bertha. I started with the damage — first to homes; then to businesses; then to the beach, the crops, and the golf courses. Then I moved on to the clean-up — talking about the downed trees, flood debris piling up along the roadside and clogging the gutters, contaminated water supply, etc. Then I moved on to long-range impacts, on tourism, the environment, and shoreline development. Then I did stories about how this compared to previous hurricanes and the likelihood we'd get hit again. This went on for weeks.

If there was a story with the slightest tangential connection to Hurricane Bertha, I did it. It was more than three weeks after Bertha before I did a single story that wasn't storm related, and probably six weeks before hurricane stories didn't make up the majority of our newscast. The United States could have changed its name to South Canada and invaded Mexico and we would have reported it sixth in our newscast behind five stories about storm cleanup.

Despite the repetition, it was a good experience. I got to see what a hurricane was like, and learned a lot about how to cover one. What was not such a wonderful experience was getting hit by another storm just two months later. And a far more severe hurricane at that.

Hurricane Fran was again supposed to hit farther south, and again, it veered north at the last minute and stormed up the Cape Fear River. Many homes and communities were still cleaning up from Bertha when Fran came along and blew everything away.

Fran was a Category 3, meaning wind speeds of 111–130 miles an hour and a storm surge of 6–8 feet, far too serious to spend hanging around in a beach town at sea level. In fact, the storm came up so quickly that I nearly didn't make it back to the station. A photographer and I had gone down to the coastal community of Southport, right where the Cape Fear River opens into the ocean, to get video of residents evacuating. We got footage of the deserted areas, visited a Red Cross shelter, and headed back toward the station. But we stayed too long, and by the time we were halfway back, the wind and rain were so severe we couldn't see anything. We were on a narrow two-lane road and it was a race back to the station against the storm, which was following us right up the Cape Fear River.

It was one of the scariest car rides I've ever had. It was sort of like driving through a washing machine on full agitation cycle. We drove about 15 miles an hour most of the way, and every now and then a big gust of wind would push the car onto the side of the road.

We finally made it back, and I wrote up our story for the newscast and then bedded down with everyone else at the station, which had an emergency generator. For the rest of the night, it was too severe to go out, so we mostly just sat around eating peanut-butter crackers and taking calls from people phoning in to report what was going on in their neighborhoods. "So you're saying it's windy where you are? Any roofs blown off? Great, stay on the line, we're going to put you on the air."

Occasionally, I'd venture out to do live shots from the station parking lot. Even sheltered by the station building, I could barely stand upright. And nobody could hear a word I was saying. Which didn't matter a whole lot, since nobody could watch our news anyway, what with the power out from Charleston to Winston-Salem.

The only time I left the safety of the station was when the hurricane's eye arrived. A photog and I took a chance and drove around, shooting video of the damage in the dark. It is very odd when you are in the eye of a hurricane because it is remarkably calm. All the winds died down, and we could see the moon and stars up above. But the eye of a storm is very dangerous because it only lasts for a short period of time, and then you get hit by the back side of the hurricane, which is almost as fierce as the front. So you have to make sure you don't get lulled into thinking that it's okay to stray far from safety.

I got about two hours of sleep that night and awoke to a completely different city. The often overused cliché "looks like a war zone" really applied; there was debris everywhere. Some houses near the shore had been swept away or torn to shreds, with some areas suffering 90 percent damage. A number of large boats were overturned, and there was a pretty big sailboat sitting in a grass field several hundred yards inland. My apartment was fine, but a historic church steeple just four blocks away was lying in rubble in the street.

The damage was so bad that we couldn't get a lot of video of it on the first day because so many of the roadways were blocked or flooded. My photographer and I nearly got marooned when we went out to shoot storm damage and floodwaters rose before we could get back.

When we finally made it out to the coastal community of Topsail Beach two days after the storm, we had to sneak in to get footage, because the damage was so bad that the National Guard had set up a roadblock and wasn't letting people past for fear of looting. My photog Chad and I left our car by the side of the road and snuck in via the beach, lugging all our equipment more than a mile on foot through the sand so we could get video. Apparently the Guard felt that looters weren't either that smart or energetic.

The difference between a Category 1 and a Category 3 is incredible, because at Category 3 you have surpassed the threshold where many buildings can sustain that kind of wind strength. So instead of a Cat 3 being three times as bad as a Cat 1, it is 20 times as bad. The damage from Fran was over $5 billion in North Carolina, and 27 people died.

Looking around at the destruction from Fran made me feel humble and insignificant. In my story the day after, at one point I simply shut up and didn't say a word for several seconds, just letting the camera sweep across the devastated coastline. The video alone had a far greater impact than anything I could say.

Whereas Bertha had been exciting, Fran was kind of scary, and afterward, a huge hassle. Besides all the usual follow-up stories, the same ones I had just finished for Bertha, I didn't have power in my apartment for eight days. I had to take cold showers in the dark and dine on crackers and potato chips. When my power returned, it came on unevenly and blew most of the light bulbs, as well as the circuits in my TV, VCR, and phone answering machine. It wasn't long before I was experiencing a little tropical depression of my own.

I decided that Hurricane Fran was a signal for me to move. I had learned a lot at WWAY and really liked the eastern North Carolina area once I made it from Whiteville to Wilmington. But it was time to head for higher ground, professionally, monetarily, and geographically. In Wilmington TV news, I had become a moderately big fish in a small pond, but I was bumping into the pond's limits. It was time to test my skills at a higher level. So, armed with a new and vastly improved resume tape filled to the brim with my hurricane coverage, I started sending my reel to bigger-market stations. But even after all of my experience from Telluride, Whiteville, and now Wilmington, moving up in TV news would be no easy task.

Chapter 18

Moving Up and the Name Game

"The TV business is uglier than most things. It is normally perceived as some kind of a cruel and shallow money trench through the heart of the journalism industry, a long plastic hallway where thieves and pimps run free, and good men die like dogs for no good reason." –Hunter S. Thompson.[*]

I've seen this quote posted in numerous newsrooms around the country. Sometimes the posting includes the punch line, "There's also a negative side," which is a good line, although Thompson didn't write that part. But even without the added line, there's definitely some truth to the comment, especially when it comes to moving up as a reporter. TV news is a harsh, often unfair business, and good doesn't always triumph.

Even armed with my best hurricane stories and several years of reporting experience, moving to a bigger market from Wilmington would be difficult. That's because stations tend to hire and fire reporters for innumerable reasons, many of them inexplicable or nonsensical, and TV news is one of those peculiar professions where the cream does not necessarily rise to the top. That's not to say that most reporters at the networks and in top local markets are not smart and talented journalists. But many equally talented reporters never make it there, and there are also a few top TV folks for whom you can't help but wonder, what did they do to land that job? Getting ahead in TV requires more than just talent; it requires a combination of

---

[*] Reprinted with permission of Simon & Schuster, Inc. from "GENERATION OF SWINE: Tales of Shame and Degradation in the '80s" by Hunter S. Thompson. Copyright © 1988 Hunter S. Thompson. All rights reserved.

skill, stamina, luck, and looks, not necessarily in that order. It also helps to have a sugar daddy around to support you in the early stages and a family member working at or owning the network.

The reason that making it in TV news is so challenging (apart from the obvious fact that there are few jobs and many applicants) probably lies in the fact that judging the quality of a TV reporter is entirely subjective. Unlike, say, pro baseball, there are no statistics a reporter can provide to show that he is doing a swell job. You can't point to your batting average or home run total, or show all the widgets you've sold or the legal cases you've won. Even if a station improves in the ratings after you start working there, it likely has very little to do with anything you did as a reporter. Or if it does, the connection is so tenuous that it would come across as an enormous stretch to try and persuade a big-market news director that you were responsible.

Oh, there are plenty of awards you can win to demonstrate how talented you are. In all likelihood, the journalism industry hands out more self-congratulatory honors than any other profession on the planet. If a station is aggressive about entering its staff in these contests, which require entry fees, it is almost difficult not to win an award every now and then. The stations that win the most awards are invariably the ones that enter the most contests, which may explain why it is usually the lower-ranked stations in a market that win a majority of the awards, because the top-ranked stations don't feel this need for constant validation.

News contest judging is also highly dependent on subject matter. If I sent in a story about a very interesting event, I might win an award even if I did a terrible job covering that event. I won or shared four or five awards from organizations such as the Associated Press, the Radio & Television News

267

Directors Association, and the Society of Professional Journalists, and while I am moderately proud of these honors, I'm not always proud of the stories that won them. Don't get me wrong, it's better to win awards than not to, but you have to recognize that winning doesn't always have a lot to do with the job you did.

Perhaps that dynamic is emblematic of the TV news industry as a whole, because advancing as a reporter in TV seems to have about the same level of arbitrariness to it. It is highly dependent on snap decisions made by a news director or executive producer who reviews a tiny fraction of your work. That's the way you apply for reporting jobs in TV; you send out tapes or DVDs with four or five stories on them and hope to catch a news director's eye. Each tape takes several hours to put together, costs several dollars each, and almost never gets returned.

It is an arduous and expensive process, and the 10-minute tapes may not be a very accurate reflection of your overall skill as a reporter. If you do between 250 and 300 news "packages" a year, as I did in Wilmington (I did even more later on in Knoxville), and write two or three times that number of stories in total, your four-story resume reel is hardly representative of the job you're doing.

Even if the tape does showcase some genuine high points, most news directors won't watch the whole 10 minutes. They'll watch 10 to 20 seconds of it. That's right, 10 to 20 seconds. If they like what they see, they'll watch a little bit more. If they actually make it to the end of the tape, start making moving plans because you're probably going to get an offer.

I received an instructive lesson on how arbitrary this process can be when I applied for a job at WAGA-TV, a Fox affiliate in Atlanta. At the time, I had a TV news agent to whom I handed over eight percent of my $26,000 salary. This agent was supposed to scour the country for openings and find me a better job. He had heard that there was a reporter opening at WAGA and sent in my tape. It just so happened that I had a friend at WAGA, a producer by the name of Amy, with whom I had worked earlier. So I sent her an email asking if she knew anything about this job opening. She didn't know much, but suggested I send a tape to her boss, the executive producer. My agent had already sent him a tape, but I figured it couldn't hurt to send another one, so I fired one off, this time mentioning Amy's name in my cover letter.

About two days later I got a call from the executive producer telling me he loved my tape and wanted me to come interview as soon as possible. WAGA flew me to Atlanta the next week, and I endured a marathon round of one-on-one interviews. They called the process "running their gauntlet," and it involved meeting with about 10 different station managers and producers, one after the other, for about 20 minutes apiece. It was exhausting, but also encouraging, as several praised my "strong tape" and told me how impressed they were with my demonstrated writing ability and on-camera presence. I was really excited. Atlanta is big time. I would have been in the major leagues.

After my final interview, I ended up back in the executive producer's office. Sitting there while he dealt with some paperwork, I noticed a huge stack of resume tapes, probably 60 or more, piled up on the floor beside his desk.

"Are those my competitors for the position?" I asked, trying to sound casual about it.

"No, those are all the bad tapes," he replied dismissively.

I laughed heartily, and tried to look confident without appearing overly smug. But as I glanced over at the stack of tapes, I saw that right in the middle, with very large black labeling on its side, was a tape with my name on it. It was the resume tape submitted by my New York agent. It wasn't 100% identical to the tape I had sent, but it was pretty close; maybe one story on it was different. The real difference between me being a good reporter and a bad reporter had been the mention of Amy's name.

It was then and there that I decided to get rid of my agent, a decision reinforced by the fact that I could see that my tape wasn't even the only tape from that agent in the "bad tape" pile. There were tapes for several other of his clients, all consigned to WAGA's dustbin.

I had signed with this agent out of desperation and naiveté. I had been in Wilmington sending out my hurricane-filled resume tapes for several months without any luck when a friend of the family suggested I send one to an agency he knew in New York. When the agency agreed to represent me, I was thrilled. A "talent agent," wow, that's something movie stars and pro athletes have. I must be really good. Why else would a New York agent want to represent me unless he thought I was going places? I must be the next Matt Lauer.

Unfortunately, I later learned that agents in the TV news business operate very differently than agents in pro sports or Hollywood. Instead of focusing on a few select clients who make loads of money, TV agents tend to take on a large stable of reporters and anchors, send out mass mailings of tapes, and hope that a fair number pay off. TV news agents generally get between 5 and 10 percent of a reporter's salary, which is a lot of money for the reporter but not a lot for the agent. If I landed a reporting job in a top 25 market making $60,000 a year, the agent wasn't going to get rich from my $6,000 annual contribution. Which means TV agents have to have a lot of clients and can't spend an inordinate amount of time or effort on any one of them. Some agents put multiple reporters on the same tape sent for the same job opening. Take your pick, the agent is saying, they're all the same to me.

My agent didn't do that, as far as I know, but in the three years I was with him he never got me a job. (No, I didn't get the job in Atlanta. I had one lackluster interview near the end of the gauntlet when I was running out of steam, and, unfortunately, it was with the person that really counted, the news director.) In fact, if you exclude job interviews I got through my own devices, my agent only secured me one interview during the entire three years. For this, I gave him eight percent of my earnings. What did I get out of the arrangement? One time I was in New York visiting my family and he took me to lunch. In some ways, it was the most expensive lunch I've ever had. Over the course of three years that lunch cost me $7,219.97. Obviously, I should have ordered the steak.

My experience with the TV agent is not uncommon. I'm sure some agents do a good job for their clients, and they do come in handy when you have to negotiate terms with a big market. They can provide very useful advice about contract language *once you've been offered a job*. But as far as finding you that big-time position, they generally don't do a whole lot, from what I've seen, heard, and experienced. Every now and then I'll talk to someone who thinks a TV agent is great and helped land him or her a big job, but I've heard many, many more negative stories than positive ones. But in TV, you become so desperate to move up that you'll try almost anything, even if you've heard all the stories beforehand.

To make the moving-up process even more frustrating, it is very rare to get any sort of response from a station or news director to whom you have sent a tape. You could have been their second choice out of the 150 or so who applied, but you might never know how close you came if their first choice

271

takes the job (which their first choice usually does, since he or she is as desperate as you are to get out of market 147). Most of the time, your tape gets a brief review and ends up in the newsroom recycle bin for employees to take home and use to record their favorite TV shows. I know this because that's what happened to discarded resume tapes at my station in Knoxville, and because out of the 200 or so resume tapes I sent over the years, I only got four or five back.

You could be a 20-year veteran of the news business, and if nothing in the first 10 or 20 seconds of your tape catches the news director's eye — if he or she doesn't like your hair, disfavors reporters with glasses, or is looking for a different gender or ethnicity — your background, skill and experience will mean nothing and your tape goes into the discard pile. I firmly believe that if Tom Brokaw or Diane Sawyer sent a tape to 10 local TV news directors who somehow didn't know who they were, neither one might get an offer. "Nah, this guy's got some sort of speech impediment, keeps slurring his "l"s. And she's okay, but we already have seven blondes on our newscast. Who's next?"

If you think I'm exaggerating about the arbitrary nature of TV hiring and firing, consider the number of reporters and anchors who "fail up," as it's sometimes called. Failing up refers to getting fired by one station only to land a better job in a bigger market. It happens all the time. When I was in Knoxville, my station decided not to renew a weekend weather anchor's contract, much to her dismay. She was then immediately hired in Indianapolis, market 26, nearly 40 markets ahead. I know a reporter let go by a station in Miami who was then hired by the Fox News Network. The most famous case is probably Matt Lauer. Lauer was fired five times in five years, was unemployed for 15 months, and had actually applied for a job as a tree trimmer when he got hired to anchor a weekend morning show for WNBC in New York. That job led to *The Today Show*.

It is the nature of the TV news business to have one person think you're great and another person think you're rubbish. A network reporter once told me that she cautioned aspiring TV reporters, "How would you like to go into a field where a hundred people will tell you you're not good enough? That's what it's like working in TV." A hundred is a low estimate. Of course, most of the time they don't bother to tell you.

When I first decided to get into TV news, my friend Jon Dienst told me I would have to apply to 50 stations before I got a job. I don't know where he got this number, but it actually made me feel better about the process because even when I got turned down, I viewed it as one rejection on my way to 50. I even applied to a few stations where I really didn't want to work just so I could get a few more rejections.

I borrowed this get-your-rejections-in approach from a cousin of mine who claimed he used it when he was feeling forlorn about a particular love interest. He would go to a bar or party and deliberately try to get turned down by 20 women, on the premise that after 20, what was one more? Even though the original rejection was the one he initially cared about, that rejection became just one out of two dozen or so. You're going to dump me? Get in line. It sounds absurd, but it can be a peculiarly effective way to minimize the importance of one particular setback. Besides, my cousin told me he never made it past nine before a girl said yes.

To get my first TV job took me 53 rejections, and despite my experience covering hogs and hurricanes and festivals, getting out of Wilmington for my second TV job took me about the same number. If I hadn't approached it with this get-your-rejections-in method, I don't think I could've stomached it. I never knew if I was getting turned down because my writing was poor, my delivery wasn't right, or because they already had three white male Colgate grads with brown hair and suits from the Salvation Army.

I also usually had no idea what a station was looking for when they posted an opening. News directors will tell you that they just want talented journalists, but that's not the whole story. They are seeking talented journalists all right, but talented journalists who fit whatever preconceived images the news director or station manager has for the on-air team. Usually that image involves a certain combination of looks, genders, and ethnicities. It's often like filling a slot, the *Mod Squad* approach to TV news — you have to have the blond woman, the white guy, and the minority. If you are a white guy and the station is looking for the blond woman or the minority, well, you're out of luck.

Sometimes they'll even tell you this. One time, interviewing for a job in Greenville, North Carolina, during my Great Job Tour, I interviewed with a news director for 45 minutes and everything seemed to be going well. Then he lowered his voice and told me that he really wasn't supposed to be talking to me until I had been selected by his human resources department as part of an "ethnically diverse pool" of job applicants. "If anybody asks," he said, taking a sidelong glance down the hallway, "we've never met." He encouraged me to reapply to the station's human resources department, and said if I made it through their vetting, I had a good shot. I guess I didn't make it through because I never heard from that station again.

This color-by-numbers approach can be exasperating, especially if you are a white male. There are already an awful lot of white male reporters on TV, so most stations aren't looking to add more. When a job opens up, they would usually prefer to fill it with a minority in order to increase newsroom diversity. I had news directors tell me flat out that if I were Latino or Asian or African-American they would hire me. This prompted friends to suggest I change my name to Pablo Spelmanez, but with blue eyes, fair skin and a poor understanding of Spanish, I don't think I could have pulled it off. Maybe I should have tried Running Bear Spelman. That at least would have gotten past the language dilemma, since most news directors don't speak Navajo or Chippewa any better than I do.

As a white male, it was hard not to feel a bit resentful about the fact that it was so much harder for me to find an on-air job than it would have been had I been a minority, but this is just a part of the TV business, and there are some justifiable reasons for it. Besides the fact that there is a long history of job discrimination against anyone who *isn't* a white male, there can be a genuine value in newsroom diversity if journalists from different backgrounds provide different perspectives. A Latino reporter, for instance, may know more about what's going on in Miami's Latino community than an Irish Jew from New York. Furthermore, most viewers instinctively identify with people who look like themselves, so if your news team resembles the populace, it is more likely the populace will identify with them. So for a news director, it's not always a question of getting the best on-air people; it may be a question of getting on-air people that viewers want to watch.

Does that mean that reporters hired because of their ethnicity are not as talented as non-minorities? Not usually, but it means that they get a chance a lot faster than non-minority reporters, and tend to move up much faster than non-minorities, spending far less time in the news minors, especially the middle markets. It is not uncommon for a minority reporter to jump from market 130 to market 20 in one leap. It's quite rare among white males. But once a reporter makes it to market 20, he or she still has to do a good job to stay there. To use a baseball analogy, left-handed pitchers are in demand in the majors, so they may spend less time in the minors. But if your left-handed pitcher keeps getting shellacked, it doesn't matter which arm he throws with, he's not going to stick around very long.

The *Mod Squad* approach also creates a real dilemma for everyone in TV in that you can become pigeonholed to your "ethnic slot." If a station already has its female minority anchor, it may not want another one, even if an applicant is fantastically qualified. The same attribute that helped accelerate a person's progress can end up as a hindrance when station management views its staff in terms of ethnicity and gender.

For example, I know of a station that had a very charismatic and successful black male sports anchor. Unfortunately for him, the station went out and hired an even more popular black male main anchor. Station management then decided it needed a white male to round out its look, so the black sports anchor had to go. The station managers are never going to publicly admit that's why they made the change, but everyone who works there knows that that's what happened.

When it really comes down to it, newscast diversity is extremely superficial. The focus is on the appearance of diversity, and diversity as an image, rather than on diversity of thought, background, or experience. If a TV station appears diverse on-air, many feel the problem of minority representation is solved. That's why stations tend to have far greater on-camera diversity than they do behind the scenes. The minorities fill the reporter and anchor slots, not the producer, assignment editor, or news director positions, where they can't be seen on-air. There might be three minorities sitting at the anchor desk, but off camera, the crew is mostly white.

In Wilmington, we had nine anchors and reporters and two of those were minorities, 22 percent. Meanwhile, of the 30 or 40 people who worked at the station off air, just two were minorities. So was the station to blame for not hiring more minorities off-camera or for focusing on its on-camera team in terms of racial and ethnic slotting? Slotting is so accepted that some media watchdogs count the number of minorities on TV and issue critiques when the percentage isn't high enough. They're not looking at whether the news *coverage* is diverse, just the color of the team covering it. That sort of assessment has more to do with ethnic appearance and identification than with genuine diversity. But that's the way a lot of people look at it, viewers included. And if I were a station owner, I'm not sure I would want to argue that while my news team was mostly white, it included some really diverse thinkers. Still, as a college-educated Northerner working in the South, I often felt I had much more in common with the minorities I worked with in the newsroom than I did with the rural white Southerners I encountered in the field. But that's not how a lot of people saw it, including a lot of those Southerners.

And admittedly, I've never been a member of a racial minority, so I don't know what it's like to stand in those shoes. I've never had someone look at me differently because of my ethnicity, been stopped by a police officer because I fit a racial profile, or had someone cross the street when they saw me. I've never felt uncomfortable because of my skin color. Perhaps if I had, I would see more value in diversity by pure numbers.

On the other hand, I do know firsthand the frustration of applying for a TV news job when another applicant is from a preferred group. I can't deny it, as a white male applying for a reporter position your heart just sinks when you hear that another candidate has this innate "diversity advantage." I am sure it is how minorities felt just a few years ago applying for jobs in TV; trying to gain acceptance in a system that was essentially closed to them. The deck is stacked against you, and you know you are going to lose most of the time.

That is probably why some reporters change their names or appearance to make themselves appear more "ethnic." It is ironic, really, because in the past, American immigrants would change their names to appear less ethnically identifiable. That's how Joan Molinsky became Joan Rivers and Frederick Austerlitz became Fred Astaire. My grandfather, Henry Spiegelman, changed his name to Spelman in order to appear less patently Jewish.

In TV news these days, you find the opposite, as reporters and anchors try to appear as ethnic as possible. You may have heard the story of Jerry Rivers changing his name to Geraldo Rivera. This is legendary, although not entirely accurate. Rivera is the son of a Jewish mother and Puerto Rican father, and his father's last name was, indeed, Rivera. So if he ever went by the name Rivers (and he denies it), he simply went back to Rivera. But others openly admit adopting ethnic names or changing their names to appear more so.

Adele Arakawa, for instance, an extremely popular anchor in Denver (she also once worked in Knoxville), is of Asian ancestry, but was born Adele Hausser. When an interviewer asked about her change of surname, Adele explained that she was proud of her Asian heritage. I have no doubt this is true, and her last name has nothing to do with her anchoring skills. But I do wonder if she would have kept Hausser were it as advantageous in her profession.

I've even heard of Irish-American reporters putting an extra O' in front of their name, and Jews switching from Green back to Greenberg to make sure their Semitic side is recognized. That may seem odd, but in a multi-ethnic city where a TV station wants to appeal to every demographic, it helps to ensure sure that every demographic knows it's been covered. I might actually have been better off if my family had kept Spiegelman. But probably only in Miami and New York.

Sometimes it's the anchors and reporters themselves who decide to alter their names; other times it's the station that makes the suggestion. No one has ever seriously suggested that I go by anything but Spelman, but an anchor I knew with the last name of Trentham told me she was asked, when at a station with a large Latino viewership, if she would change her last name to Vega or Fuentes. It is hard to believe that the station management thought a pale blonde from Kentucky might be mistaken for a Latina, but in any event, she declined.

It is easy to decry this sort of thing as false and shallow, but it should be noted that there is a long history of people changing their names, even for non-ethnic reasons. In Wilmington, for instance, three of the four main anchors didn't go by their given first names and it had nothing to do with ethnicity. The female anchor Margaret Callaham went by her middle name Jill; the sports anchor Columbus Motley went by Gene (I might too, in that circumstance); and the main male anchor altered his on-air name from John Evans to *Jon* Evans. He told me he did it to make it more memorable, and the funny thing is he was absolutely right. Jon Evans *is* more memorable than John Evans.

The Wilmington station also persuaded our weekend sports anchor, Steve McGehee, to shorten his name to McGee so it would be easier for viewers to remember. Steve did but hated it, and changed back to McGehee when he switched stations a few years later.

Sometimes on-air people change their names because of other anchors or reporters at the same station. Knoxville anchor Clay Thomas was originally Clay Loney but changed his name so it would have a more alliterative ring when paired with his co-anchor, Lori Tucker. In Wilmington, a male reporter with the last name Barker changed it to Bauer because a female reporter at his station already had the surname Barker when he arrived. I don't know if the station didn't want viewers confused, or the female reporter didn't want people to think they were married or related, but from what I understand, he was not given a choice. So he went by Bauer for a few years until he left the Wilmington market.

All of this focus on names and image in TV news seems kind of ridiculous, but there's no getting away from the fact that in TV, a reporter's image and appearance matters. You could do the best story in the world, and yet if your name is odd, or your appearance peculiar, that's probably what viewers will notice and remember. In addition to gender and ethnicity, this also applies to things like how you speak, dress, and comb your hair. A sports reporter I worked with once told me that if he had to choose between getting a late game score or spending time primping in the dressing room, he would make sure he got the score. At the time, I thought this was the admirable decision. Now I know better. He should have combed his hair and put on makeup. Because the audience isn't going to pay attention to his scores if it thinks the sports guy looks unshaven and wonders why his hair is sticking up in back. There is a lot of truth to a *Peanuts* cartoon I once saw in which Charlie Brown encountered his sister Sally watching TV news.

"Well! I'm glad to see you're watching the news … What's going on in the world?" he asks.

"The anchor person looked better when she had long hair," is her reply.

How many of us watch a news station because we truly admire the anchor's journalistic skills and credentials? Very few. You watch because the anchors seem trustworthy, attractive, or just make you feel comfortable. Working in TV, you have to get used to the fact that news directors and the public are less interested in the work you do than in how you come across.

I was both helped and hurt by this. Helped in that, while I'm no George Clooney, I don't resemble Quasimodo either. On the other hand, I'm a relatively generic looking white male who resembles the majority of other white males on TV. This point was driven home to me one day when I did a story about a new facial-recognition technology designed to match up criminals on a computer database. They used this kind of technology at the Super Bowl to alert them to possible terrorists in the crowd. When we entered my face into the computer and searched for a match, up popped the likeness of another white male TV reporter who had done the same story a couple of days earlier. I would not have picked him as my twin, but the computer did, and probably so would thousands of TV viewers.

I am also aware that something about my appearance makes me come across as overly serious. I might be reporting a story about watermelons, yet one look at me and the viewer immediately suspects that something must be wrong with the fruit; that I am about to warn them of a cancer-causing fertilizer or watermelon seed toxin. Why else would I look so grave? Oh, I would put on a big smile and try to look as friendly as possible, but it didn't help much. Then I just looked like I was trying a put a good face on this cancer-causing fertilizer. It's just the way I come across on TV.

And had I remained in TV, I would have had to accept that fact, and the fact that my gender, ethnicity, and general appearance would always play a part in how I would be judged. It is the way of the world in TV news, and it is likely to stay that way, at least until people as a whole stop judging others by their looks or identifying with people who look like themselves. Let me know when that happens.

Chapter 19

Knoxville and the Nightside

I'd been sending out hurricane-filled resume tapes from Wilmington for a number of months before I got any sort of response. That response came from a news director at WATE, the ABC affiliate in Knoxville, Tennessee. I didn't know much about Knoxville, but had heard it was a pretty good local TV news market. It was a medium-sized market, about the TV news equivalent of a double-A minor league baseball team. In fact, Knoxville had a double-A minor league baseball team, the Knoxville Smokies.

I had sent WATE my tape shortly after Hurricane Fran, and then, quite honestly, had forgotten about it. In the meantime, I had sent out another 25 or so tapes, all to no avail. As I mentioned earlier, I had also signed with a New York agent. This was a mistake, but I didn't know it at the time.

Just a few weeks after signing with the agent, I was sitting at my desk at WWAY, mulling over the fact that for the first time in months, I had failed to turn a package that day. Every piece I'd worked on had fallen through, and for some reason the station had a lot of stories that day and let me get away with not doing one. Not turning in a package was very very unusual, and very frustrating for me by then. Unlike my early days in Whiteville, I had reached a level where I felt a bit worthless if I didn't do at least a package or two a day. So I was sitting there in a bit of a funk when my phone rang.

"Is this Paul Spelman?" asked a pleasant sounding voice, which seemed more and more pleasant when the news director said she wanted to fly me to Knoxville as soon as possible to talk about a reporting position. Fly me to Knoxville? Here I was at a station where I had to pay for my own business cards, and these folks were ready to shell out $600 for airfare just to meet me.

I went out the next week, and everyone at WATE seemed very friendly and welcoming. They treated me to a nice lunch at one of the better restaurants in town, showed me around the station, and boosted my ego by telling me how impressed they were with my resume tape. Then they offered me a job, at $26,000 a year. That was a full $8,500 more than what I earned in Wilmington. After months of not getting a single return phone call from news directors, here I was getting an offer to jump 90 markets and increase my salary by 50 percent.

It took a great deal of restraint on my part, but I told them I needed time to think about it. I didn't really. I was so desperate to move up I probably would have taken a job for the same salary I received in Wilmington. WATE also had a fairly good reputation in local news, so it looked like a promising career move. The station was number two in the Knoxville TV market, a market reputed to be slightly better than its mid-market number would indicate. Better in terms of the quality of its reporting, its photography, and its aggressive use of live shots.

I waited a couple of days to savor the moment and show Knoxville I wasn't overeager, and then said yes. My Wilmington station made no attempt to change my mind or offer me more money to stay. I knew they wouldn't. But they were nice about it, and actually took time during a newscast to announce that I was leaving and wished me well. The news director even wrote a kind note stating I had been one of the best reporters he'd had come through Wilmington. I found this unlikely, but it was nice to hear nonetheless, and almost made up for that car insurance deductible thing. Almost.

A few weeks later, I packed up my things and drove 10 hours over the Appalachian Mountains to Knoxville. Unlike when I had left Colorado, this time I couldn't fit all of my belongings into the bed of my pickup truck. But it wasn't like I had to a rent a big moving truck, either. At 29 years of age, my worldly possessions consisted of one twin-size mattress, a writing desk of the type you'd find in a sixth-grade classroom, one small chair, and a 19-inch TV set with a wavy line through the screen courtesy of Hurricane Fran. My life sure had been prosperous so far.

I rented a small trailer from U-Haul (mostly for the mattress) and threw everything into the back. Proud Mary pulled it over the mountains and through a snowstorm without complaint, but when I arrived, I found the truck's rusty rear bumper had split in two from the strain. Another 10 miles and I would have been driving down the highway without any belongings whatsoever. I ended up having to pay the U-Haul folks an extra fee to come pick up their trailer. But I had made it to the next level in TV news. I was moving up. I was now in double A and felt I was on my way.

As for the area, I didn't know much about East Tennessee, but figured it couldn't be worse than Whiteville. While Knoxville is an urban metropolis, East Tennessee, as the area is known (never "eastern"; for some reason referring to it as eastern Tennessee is a grave faux pas), is quite rural once you get 10 or 20 minutes outside of Knoxville. It is a beautiful part of America, filled with gently rolling hills and lush green valleys, winding rivers, and deep blue lakes. The Great Smoky Mountains National Park is just 40 minutes southeast of Knoxville (less as the crow flies), and if you're at any elevation in the city, you can see the Smokies off in the distance. Thirty minutes to the north of Knoxville is the historic Norris Dam.

To me, the area conjured up images of the old rural South, as depicted in the film *O Brother, Where Art Thou,* or its inspiration, *Sullivan's Travels*. Driving along two-lane country roads across railroad trestles and through the hills and hollers was like stepping back in time. Everywhere I went, I saw dilapidated old barns and ancient tractors, and there are places not far from Knoxville where you can still leave money behind a tree and return later to pick up a jug of moonshine. Or as the East Tennessee anthem "Rocky Top" puts it, "get your corn from a jar."

The residents in the areas outside of Knoxville often wore farm overalls and chewed tobacco as they drove around in old pickup trucks with gun racks mounted in the back. They also spoke with what, to my ears, was a barely comprehensible dialect. Even after nearly three years in North Carolina, I had enormous trouble comprehending what Tennesseans were saying. Asking for help, as I had become so accustomed to in North Carolina, was much less effective here, because I often couldn't understand the reply. One resident, for instance, directed me to "Jes' go down side of there road there past my aint's house, cain't miss it." Getting information I could comprehend was at times akin to pulling teeth, although that's not the best analogy in this area, since, as a colleague of mine (who grew up in East Tennessee) once put it, "In some parts around here, having teeth means you're middle class."

Quite simply, some residents would say things to me that left me baffled as to how to respond. Once, while doing a story about a county that had taken the step of jailing parents for their children's truancy, an upset father complained to me, "You get thrown in jail either way. If they don't go to school, they jail me. If I get 'em up and beat 'em, they jail me. You can't win for losing." All I could do was nod my head and agree it was a tough situation.

Nearer in to Knoxville, residents were not country bumpkins. The folks in and around the city were often very well educated, and East Tennessee has a fair share of PhDs, since the University of Tennessee is based in Knoxville and Oak Ridge National Laboratories, home of nuclear arms research and development, is just 25 minutes up the road. But you really didn't have to go far from Knoxville to find true hillbillies. Let's just say I was not surprised a few years later to spot an article in the *Weekly World News*, that pantheon of groundbreaking journalism, stating that Tennessee had declared a three-month long "Bigfoot Hunting Season" after several "7-foot-plus man-beasts" were spotted near Knoxville. The article quoted a "Knoxville hunter" stating, "A Bigfoot head mounted over our fireplace and a Bigfoot rug on the floor of our den would be something our whole family could take pride in."

I never spotted any such man-beasts while I was in Knoxville, but the fact that the *Weekly World News* selected East Tennessee as the site for its creative fabrication surely says something about the area.

Despite this, I came to love the Tennessee countryside, and really enjoyed talking to people once I was able to figure out what they were saying. I actually preferred doing stories in the really remote areas. Much the way I had been so impressed by the Whiteville farmers, here I was fascinated to see something so removed from my upbringing. And the scenery was plain gorgeous.

The city of Knoxville itself was not. In fact, some might say quite the opposite. It is an old industrial city, filled with train yards, decrepit warehouses, and a small, sparsely populated downtown with shuttered department stores and dilapidated office buildings. Knoxville might well be called the "Milwaukee of the South," a comparison that would likely offend residents of both cities. In truth, it is actually nowhere near as big as Milwaukee; it's more on the order of Harrisburg, Pennsylvania.

Knoxville does have a few things to be quite proud of; in particular, the University of Tennessee is based in Knoxville. UT-K, or UT, as it's invariably called everywhere but Texas, takes up a large part of a neighborhood overlooking the Tennessee River just across a hill from downtown. Renowned author James Agee grew up in the neighborhood and the area is reportedly the setting for his classic *A Death in the Family*.

Knoxville also has the headquarters for the Tennessee Valley Authority, a depression-era bureaucracy that now has hundreds of employees in two downtown buildings referred to as the TVA towers. Calling them "towers" provides some indication of Knoxville's overall stature and skyline, since neither building is more than twelve stories tall.

The city also houses the new Women's Basketball Hall of Fame and the remnants of the not-so-new 1982 World's Fair, Knoxville's last glorious moment in the sun (if you don't count gridiron heroics as great city moments). By most accounts, the '82 Fair was a big success, but by the time I arrived, the only remaining attractions were a large, rarely used park and wading pool, a run-down convention center, and an odd golden mirrored-glass globe called the Sun Sphere sitting atop a five-story pedestal. It looks like one of those disco balls from the 1970s plopped down on a giant Pez dispenser.

The Sun Sphere is Knoxville's version of the Seattle Space Needle; it defines the city skyline, and from a distance it appears moderately attractive. On closer inspection, I found it was virtually abandoned, with a dirty old elevator that creaked up to a cramped and barren observation area. The view from up there was impressive, but everything else about the place was not. At least during my time in Knoxville. They closed the Sun Sphere for renovations shortly after I arrived, and it hadn't reopened by the time I left three and a half years later. Last I heard, they were having a problem with birds using the Sphere as a guano dumping ground.

Knoxville also has a small historic section called the Old City, with a wonderful old tavern that dates back to the days when, in a strange Telluride tie-in, Butch Cassidy's gang member Elzy Lay used to be a frequent customer. Lay was captured by the authorities in Knoxville but somehow managed to escape from jail. Legend has it he was last seen heading across the Tennessee River on the Knox County sheriff's stolen horse. Unfortunately, besides the tavern, there's not much of that historic character left in Knoxville, and while one area may be called the Old *City*, it's only two blocks long and is largely underutilized.

Underutilization seemed to be a trait all too common to many of the more interesting parts of Knoxville. The city has several nice parks and bike paths, as well as a scenic river walk just a few hundred feet from downtown. Yet you could go there on a sunny Saturday afternoon in May and find the place virtually empty. The parks and pathways always had that desolate midwinter feel, even in mid-July. I got the impression that Knoxvillians weren't big on frequenting public spaces, apart from their football stadium.

There wasn't much to do in private spaces, either, since Knoxville has relatively few museums, theaters, nightclubs, or other cultural attractions. Far fewer than existed in Wilmington, a city about a third of Knoxville's size. I guess I should have suspected this dearth of entertainment when, during my job interview at WATE, an executive producer kept telling me how much I was going to enjoy the local mall. About the most enlightening cultural event I experienced in three years in Tennessee was the Great Smoky Mountain Rib Fest, where the featured entertainment was the '70s Southern rock band Molly Hatchet. They came on stage and yelled out, "Hello Rib Fest!!! How are the ribs?"

"Come back tomorrow," urged one of the festival vendors as we were leaving, "Eddie Money's playing!"

That memorable moment wasn't even in Knoxville; it was in Pigeon Forge, a remarkably tacky tourist town near the entrance to the Great Smoky Mountains National Park. Pigeon Forge is the Myrtle Beach of the Mountains, with innumerable putt-putt courses, bungee jump rides, go-cart races, and outlet malls. Pigeon Forge was often bustling with activity, whereas Knoxville had the feeling of a city that lost its mojo somewhere along the way.

What happened to Knoxville, of course, is the same thing that has happened to a lot of American cities. The middle class left Knoxville's city core and moved out to new residential developments closer to the malls, shopping strips, and golf courses. You could say the residents moved to the suburbs, except that in this case, the suburbs were still within Knoxville's urban city limits, north and west of the city center along the two major interstates that intersect in Knoxville, I-75 and I-40.

Those interstates are among the busiest in America. While few people I've met have actually spent time in Knoxville, it seems nearly everyone has driven through it at one point or another. It is quite centrally located. From Knoxville, it's a three-hour drive south to Atlanta, four hours north to Cincinnati, two hours east to Asheville, three hours to Charlotte, two and a half to Nashville, two to Chattanooga, six to Memphis, and so on. For that reason, Knoxville is a huge trucking juncture. Twenty-four hours a day, seven days a week, trucks rumble down Knoxville's interstates, and the

Department of Transportation once told me that during non–rush hour periods, as much as 25 percent of the traffic consists of tractor-trailers.

Despite its less attractive qualities, Knoxville did have some genuinely good things going for it in my book. It was very inexpensive, the climate was moderate, and it was a very genuine town in many ways, inhabited by down-to-earth people with old-fashioned jobs and old-fashioned families. There aren't a lot of celebrity publicists, hedge fund titans, and people who wear black for breakfast. In fact, most people wear orange. That's because the area is inundated with all things Vol.

"Vols" is the nickname for the Volunteers, the name for UT athletic teams, and in particular, UT football. People in East Tennessee are simply nuts about college football. It doesn't matter whether you went to UT or have never set foot on the campus, if you live in East Tennessee you are a rabid Vols fan, and this infuses itself into everything. To cite just a few examples, when Knoxville added another area code, the public phone company chose 865, or V-O-L, as the prefix. When the local CBS station decided to change its call letters, it chose *WVLT* and started calling itself *Volunteer TV*. And the local daily newspaper, *The Knoxville News-Sentinel*, begins running Vol football stories in June, two months before the season starts, and then literally runs at least one Vol story every single day right through January. There must be a quota, because the paper never skips a day.

Anything to do with the Vols is big news in Knoxville. One of the biggest stories I ever covered concerned the theft of the Vol mascot costume, a big dogsuit, which was stolen from a student's apartment after a game. (In another example of how seriously UT took its team, the student who wore the suit was on an athletic-related scholarship, as were many of the cheerleaders).

Once a Vol, always a Vol, and always identified as such in the local media. You could become Surgeon General and you'd be referred to on Knoxville TV as "former Vol, and now Surgeon General, Frank Smith ...." A mild fender bender might make front-page news if either car was driven by a Vol or former Vol.

Apart from the Vols, the only other truly unique feature to the city was its religious enthusiasm. Knoxville was a very Christian town. It is sometimes referred to as the buckle of the Bible belt. It seemed like very few cars didn't have a fish emblem or two, and as I drove down the Interstate I often passed billboards proclaiming, "Don't make me come down there – God," and "When I said, 'Love Thy Neighbor,' I meant that!" A few Knoxville supermarkets even sold "Holy Cross Soda," complete with the words "Jesus Saves" and "John 3:16" on the sides of the cans.

Knoxville may not have had as many churches per person as Whiteville, but the ones it had were often enormous. A few were so big they were dubbed "Super Churches." One had three thousand seats, three racquetball courts, an exercise and weight room, and a full-length basketball court that doubled as a roller-skating rink on Friday nights. When I interviewed the pastor about his remarkable facility, he told me that when he walked in for the first time, "It just felt like home."

"It's a little bigger than my home," I replied. He laughed, but you had to be very careful making those kind of wisecracks in Knoxville. Not long after I arrived, I made the mistake of flippantly remarking to a woman reading the Bible, "Good book. I can tell you how it ends." She didn't crack a smile, and responded with utter seriousness, "I already know how it ends, and believe me, the end is near." That ended my attempt at small talk.

Faith was a big part of the Knoxville culture, and even the Knoxville news anchors would mention it every now and then on the air. I recall one time when one of the anchors declared, during a story about the death penalty, "This is a difficult question for everyone. I mean, how can we, as Christians, decide what's right?" It occurred to me at that time that not everyone watching or working alongside that anchor was necessarily a Christian, but from a ratings standpoint, I guess that demographic wasn't large enough to worry about. The majority of people in East Tennessee support God, guns, and UT football, just not necessarily in that order.

As far as the TV news in Knoxville, I quickly recognized that the overall quality of reporting was far more advanced than what I had been doing in Wilmington. The Knoxville stories had impressive photography, with fast editing and lots of natural sound. The reporters wrote creative pieces interspersed with quick sound bites and great matching words to the visuals. They also did many more stories in far less time that I was accustomed to. It took me a while to adjust, and it was trial by fire.

It is another of the ironies of local TV news that the reporter with the least experience invariably gets the most difficult shift; the night shift. Working the night shift (or "nightside") in Knoxville meant that I came in at 2:30 p.m. and usually did reports for the five, five-thirty, six, and eleven o'clock newscasts. Sometimes I did different versions of the same story for each newscast, sometimes I'd do one story for five, a different topic for six, and a completely unrelated story for eleven. The nightside reporter does more stories and has less time to do them than dayside reporters. I was also the only reporter on duty after 6:30, which meant I always had the main story for eleven, and thus it was even more vital that I not fail.

Even after my training in North Carolina, I found this to be a strain. I wasn't used to turning stories that fast, and I had some rough moments. At one point early on, I almost had a nervous breakdown. I was covering the bust of a methamphetamine lab in a rural county about an hour from Knoxville, and by the time my photographer and I made it out to the scene, there wasn't anything to shoot or anyone to talk to. We drove to the police station, but the chief investigator was off trying to get a search warrant, and none of the other officers were allowed talk on camera. They wouldn't even provide me with background information, saying they had to wait for the chief to come back before releasing any details. So I waited. And waited. And watched the clock move closer and closer to my deadline.

I called my station and told them I couldn't get anything, and the producer replied, "You have to get it. It's too late to send you anywhere else."

"But there's nothing here and nobody will talk to me."

"Paul, I can't do the story for you," she replied. "But you're all we have tonight and you have to come back with something."

I started getting very agitated. I went in and begged the officers to talk to me. "Please," I pleaded, "I won't make you look bad. I promise. Just say you made an arrest and you're happy about it. Say whatever you want. Talk about the weather. I don't care. I just can't go back without anything."

They refused, and out of frustration and stress, I finally threw up my hands, slid down the wall, and just sat there on the floor. I wasn't crying, but I sure felt like it. The strain of having to come back with a story and not having the time or the know-how to pull it off was bearing down on me.

One of the officers finally took pity on me and promised that if I could stick around a bit longer, they might have something good. I knew I had to leave for Knoxville by nine p.m. in order to get back in time, but as 9:00 rolled by, I still didn't have anything. No video, no sound bites, not even any information. I sat in the car and watched the clock. Every time it ticked off another minute felt like a blow. Finally, at 9:14, the chief arrived and agreed to talk on camera. Even better, he said we could ride along while he and his officers raided a storage facility rented by the alleged meth lab owner. That's what the search warrant was for.

So with cameras rolling, the officers broke open the storage unit and discovered all sorts of bottles and tanks and chemicals, most likely for making drugs. It was a nice bust, and made for great TV. Now all I had to do was get it back in time. My photographer drove like a madman and I wrote the script on the ride back. We got back with about 25 minutes to go until air, and my cameraman quickly threw together some video from the storage-unit raid along with a sound bite from the chief. I don't know how he got it all together that fast, but he saved me. At 11:00, I went live from the newsroom with the story.

It turned out to be a pretty good story, and a bit of a scoop because none of the other stations had it. They either hadn't bothered sending anyone to follow up after the initial bust, or had wisely given up long before 9:00. But I'm still not sure it was worth it in terms of my mental state. I was a wreck. And ashamed of my conduct at the police station.

Even after my years in Telluride, Whiteville, and Wilmington, I just wasn't used to having that little time to do a story, having to change gears that rapidly, and having to always come back with something. The last item is really the true test of a local TV news reporter; it's not how good a job you do on a big story, it's how dependable you are in terms of bringing something back day in and day out. In local TV news, there's a constant struggle between quantity and quality, and quantity usually wins out. So as a reporter, you have to be able to figure out ways to do a story with very little time. In Knoxville, it was months before I got accustomed to this, and even longer before I got accustomed to going live.

Chapter 20

When Bad Live Shots Happen to Good People

"I'm not a reporter, but I play one on TV" – common joke among TV reporters

Live shots can be painful experiences. That, of course, is because they're live, so when something goes wrong there isn't much you can do about it. And no matter who caused the problem, the reporter is the one that ends up looking foolish.

I'd done the occasional live shot in Wilmington and Whiteville, but they were nothing compared to Knoxville. In Knoxville, reporters went live almost every day, often several times a day. This was one of the hardest things for me to get used to. I might only have to be live for fifteen seconds, but the simple knowledge that I was live without a net was hard to get out of my mind. The same two or three sentences that I could repeat ad infinitum when rehearsing off camera became a tortured tongue twister requiring near photographic recall when I heard the anchor say, "Let's go live to Paul Spelman ...."

To make matters worse, when you're on camera you are the only thing in the picture, and so everything you do is magnified. The slightest stutter, twitch, or movement becomes extremely noticeable. For instance, I tended to gesture with my left arm during my live shots. In everyday conversation, few would have noticed, but on TV, it looked like I was directing planes at the airport. I also tended to lean slightly to my left side. Again, hardly noticeable if I'm sitting there in person. It wasn't like I was falling off a stool. But when your face takes up half the screen and you tilt a few inches, everyone notices.

They start to wonder if you've been drinking, or are braving gale-force winds even when you're inside. When I tried to counter my natural lean by remaining rigid, I looked it, and it looked as though I'd been impaled on something. It is a difficult balancing act; standing completely still yet looking completely relaxed. I never got it completely right.

Despite this, most TV live shots aren't really that difficult and usually go according to plan. That's because 90 percent of local news live shots aren't all they are hyped up to be. By that I don't mean that they're not live, I mean that the actual live part is all of 15 seconds, and everything the reporter says in that 15 seconds is scripted and rehearsed. There's also usually little reason for being live in the first place.

The idea behind a live shot is that when there is breaking news, viewers want the most up-to-date video and information possible. When there is something going on right at that instant, such as a celebrity murder suspect fleeing in a white Bronco, live coverage is incomparable. Using remote live-trucks and helicopters, TV news can provide instant updates on fires, accidents, courtroom verdict etc. Live TV can air important news conferences and events as they unfold. There is nothing wrong with the basic concept of going live.

The reality, however, is that in local TV news, the vast majority of live shots don't need to be live. Reporters go live even when a story is as far from breaking news as you can get. You do live shots when the story is about ancient Indian basket weaving. "Let's go live to Paul Spelman to talk about how strong those threads were …."

You also go live to talk about things that happened hours and even days earlier. A lot of times I would go live to talk about things that hadn't happened yet, and wouldn't for some time. I once went live from an empty baseball stadium to talk about a big Powerball lottery for which the winning ticket wouldn't be drawn for another two days. The reason for me being in the stadium was so that I could say how much money you could leave in every single seat if you won the jackpot. The reason for me being live was to be live.

Most live shots are what are known as "live wraps," meaning the reporter does a brief live intro, usually about 10 or 15 seconds, then "tosses" to a pretaped story that the reporter has already voiced and edited. This taped story, or package, which may have been done hours or even days earlier, lasts a minute-fifteen to a minute-thirty or so, and then the reporter comes back out live for another 10 or 15 seconds for the "outro" to wrap it all up and toss back to the station with a "live from the stadium, I'm Paul Spelman." Of the roughly two-minute length of the whole story, less than a third of that is actually live, and that third is prewritten, memorized, and rehearsed. Most live shots have less spontaneity than a telephone answering machine.

Still, you do them all the time. In some markets, nearly every single story is introduced live, and stations will go live 20 times a day, if not more. I personally have done more than 20 live shots in a single day, providing updates every few minutes.

This preponderance of live shots came about in local news because at some point media consultants and news directors figured out that because viewers associate live shots with important events, whatever news you're covering will be deemed important if you do live shots for it. Even the most routine school board meeting will appear more urgent and relevant if the reporter is live. That's why station producers schedule in live shots before they even know what stories their reporters will do that day. In Knoxville, I would arrive at 2:30 to be told I was going live for the five, five-thirty, and six o'clock shows, and when I asked what story I was doing, the producer would say, "We haven't figured that out yet. Any ideas?" That's also why I once went live from the Knox County courthouse at 6:00 p.m. for a jury verdict that had come down seven hours earlier. Everyone at the courthouse had gone home by the time I went live, and I had to ask the custodial crew not to run their vacuum cleaner during my shot.

I've also gone live from the scene of a truck accident that took place two days earlier. My story was what's called a "sidebar," meaning it wasn't about the details of the collision — the "nuts and bolts" in news parlance — but rather about a related issue, in this case the difficulty big rigs have in coming to a full stop. This is a legitimate news story; it takes a lot longer for these trucks to stop than most people realize. So I persuaded a truck-driving school to put on a demonstration in which they slammed on the brakes and skidded to a stop. It made for great video.

They did this, however, on a road near the truck-driving school, which was nowhere near the scene of the accident. The station producers wanted a live shot from the accident site, so after getting all my interviews and video at the driving school and writing and editing my story at the station, my photographer and I drove 45 minutes out to the crash site so I could go live from the side of the highway. This, for my 15-second live intro and outro. My photographer and I hadn't been in the same county as the live-shot location until we went live, but I dutifully stood there so the anchors could say, "Let's go live to Paul Spelman at the scene of Tuesday's horrific accident ...."

I mention this simply as one example, but it's not a rare occurrence. This sort of thing happens every day. It's why so many reporters go live from the side of the road. It's all for those few words at the bottom of the screen that say, "Live from ...." Sometimes reporters will literally drive across a county line and immediately pull over to the side of the road to go live, just so the station can say it is "live in such and such county" where a news event occurred.

One time I did a story about farming conditions (either too wet or too dry, I can't remember which) in a remote county that was too far away for a live shot. So after returning to the station and writing and editing the story, my photographer and I got into a live-truck and drove around looking for a nice farm I could stand in front of. We finally found a picturesque grain silo about 15 minutes from the station. It was no longer operational, since the farm had shut down a few years earlier. But that didn't matter; I never referred to the silo or said anything about that particular farm, but the silo looked great behind me as I talked about all the area farms suffering from the worst drought/rainy season to hit the area in weeks. The shot looked so good that when we got back to the station we told all the other photographers where it was located so they could use it whenever they needed a live backdrop for a farming story. That silo probably still shows up every now and then, unless it's been torn down by now to make way for a housing development.

As I mentioned earlier, one irony of going live is that it often means you have to leave the scene of the story you're covering. That's because you usually can't simultaneously go live while watching something. As a TV reporter, you often go live about some news event you can't see because you are off going live. The worst instance of this happening to me was when I was covering a tragic murder case in a distant county surrounded by tall hills. The hills blocked our live-truck's signal, so the only way we could do a live shot was to drive 20 minutes up a winding country road to the top of the highest hill in the area. So just minutes before the judge's sentence came down, my photographer and I had to leave the courthouse so we could head to the live-shot location, and I went live without knowing what had happened.

Despite these issues, I do understand why stations want so many live shots, because the word "live" still does command attention from viewers. Even from me, who ought to know better. When I'm watching TV and something comes on advertised as "live," I still sit up and take notice. That's because I hear the word "live" and wonder if, by some remote possibility, it really does have to do with something important. It's also because there is always the chance something unexpected could happen. It's live, maybe something will go wrong. I've had nearly everything go wrong for me.

I had anchors call me by the wrong name; I called anchors by the wrong name. I mixed up the station call letters, "going back" to channels that did not exist. I had my lights go off in the middle of a live shot, and had my microphone stop working. I also forgot to put on my microphone one time and had to try to find it during the middle of my shot. I also had cars drive through the middle of my shot, and had people heckle me and talk loudly while I was on the air. I hemmed and hawed and stumbled my way through live shots where I was ill prepared, or when a person I was supposed to interview didn't show up, leaving me to fill the time by myself.

I'll never forget the first time that occurred, when a person I was scheduled to interview got stuck in traffic. My station decided to go live to me anyway. "But there's no one here, and I don't have anything to say," I protested to my photographer. "Then it's going to be a long two minutes," he replied unsympathetically. "Here we go, 3, 2, 1...." It was long, and brutal.

I've also completely spaced out once or twice as my mind went blank after too many live shots and too little sleep. One time I stood there for about 20 seconds of pure silence. The photographer was frantically waving at me to start talking, the producer was yelling in my ear, and the anchor was repeating, "Paul, Paul, can you hear us?" Oh, I heard them, I just couldn't think of anything to say. My mind had gone blank. After about five or ten seconds, I figured the best thing to do was to pretend that my earpiece wasn't working. I put my finger in my ear, a tortured expression on my face, and pretended as though I was bravely trying to decipher their words through radio static. Eventually they cut away to another story. Afterward, the cameraman came running over trying to figure out what the problem was with the equipment. I waved him off. "Everything is working fine." At least with the equipment.

I should probably feel guilty about leaving the anchors and producers hanging in a situation like that, but stations have done similar things to me plenty of times. That happens when you finish your live intro and toss to your pretaped segment, only to have the tape jam, or the station control-room director push the wrong button, or the tape operator put in the wrong tape. You're left standing there waiting for your story to start and all you hear is silence. You might even being scratching your nose (or worse), thinking that the taped part is rolling and you are no longer on camera. And then it slowly dawns on you that the on-air broadcast you are hearing through your earpiece is identical to the street noise going on behind you. That the bird you can hear in your earpiece is the same one you can see in the nearby tree. That the car you hear is the one that just drove by.

Your stomach sinks, knowing you are still on the air, standing there looking like an idiot. It is a remarkable feeling, really, because time and motion suddenly slow to an absolute crawl. Every second feels like an hour, and every sense becomes heightened. I recall hearing the wind whistling

303

through trees in the background, the sound of a person laughing far off in the distance. If your senses were this keen all the time, life would seem completely different.

What breaks this dreamy reverie is the panicky voice of your producer yelling, "Talk!! Talk!! The tape jammed!!! Say something!!" So you try to ad-lib the entire story, fumbling at your notes and trying to paraphrase sound bites. "And then his neighbor Mr. Johnson said that he was shocked by the crime ...." It's the kind of experience that makes you consider getting out of the business.

Probably because of these constant opportunities for screwups, and also because live shots aren't always possible due to geographic and logistical limitations, a lot of stations do "look-lives," or "as-lives," instead of actual live shots. These are taped shots, in which the reporter stands there as if he's live, and acts as if he's live, but the whole thing is prerecorded. As a reporter doing a look-live, you may be told beforehand who the anchor will be, so you start by saying the anchor's name. "Randy, the latest here at city hall is ...." Then you record the outro side of the wrap, ending with, "Back to you, Randy." The station getting the look-live pastes the two ends onto the pretaped part of the story and has the anchor act as if he was just talking to you. "Thanks, Paul. Looks might windy out there. In other news ...."

This is considered ethically okay as long as neither the station nor the reporter ever actually uses the word "live." Everything is kosher so long as they just say, "Let's go to Paul in the field," or, as New York's NY1 station used to do, "Let's go to Frank *on scene*." Failure to use the word "live" is often a dead giveaway that a story isn't live, because if a station can use the word "live," they are generally going to do so. Another giveaway is if the newscast doesn't show both reporter and anchor on screen at the same time. Having both up at the same time is called being in "dual-boxes," but the difficulty with dual-boxes for a look-live is that since the reporter part is pretaped, the reporter won't wait for the anchor to stop talking before launching into his intro. So for look-lives, most stations simply show the anchor on screen by him- or herself until he or she finishes introducing the reporter, and then the station cuts to a shot of the reporter "on scene." In local TV news, if they don't do dual-boxes, it's probably not live.

Another live technique is what's called a "generic" live shot. A generic live shot is genuinely live, but it's not done solely for one specific station. Instead, it's done for several stations at the same time. In a generic, the reporter doesn't report for that one station you're watching, but rather is going live for 20, 50, sometimes 100 stations, all at the same time. The reporter in the field doesn't hear the individual station anchors and producers, he just hears a single producer counting down in his ear. "Three, two, one ...." When the count reaches zero, the reporter starts talking. The reporter also makes sure never to mention specific station call letters or an anchor's name, and simply ends with, "Now back to you at the station."

At which point, the local anchor says, "Thanks, Paul. Looks mighty windy out there. In other news ..."

With a generic, every station can look as though it has its own reporter going live in Nome, Alaska, or some other far-flung location, even though, in reality, there was only one reporter doing the same thing for dozens of stations. Sometimes you'll even see the same reporter doing a generic live shot and appearing on competing channels in the same city at the same time. Since only people who work in TV news watch more than one channel at the same time, most viewers are none the wiser.

The difficulty with generic live shots is the timing. If the local station's central clock isn't synchronized with that of the producer running the shot, or if the local anchor doesn't stop speaking on cue, the "toss" from anchor to reporter won't match up smoothly and they end up either stepping on each other or leaving dead air in between the time the anchor stops talking and the reporter starts.

Anchors also can't ask questions and "interact" with the reporter in generic live shots. In terms of providing information, that doesn't matter a whole lot, since most live questions are scripted. By that, I mean that 80–90 percent of the time in local news, the reporter told the anchor what to ask, which is why the reporter happens to know the answer. On occasion, I would get questions I didn't know were coming, but most of the time I'd write my own questions for the anchors to ask me and for me to answer. Prewriting the question is done partly because anchors may not know enough about a story to come up with a good question, and partly so the anchors don't look bad by not knowing what to ask and the reporters don't look bad by not knowing the answer.

At WATE in Knoxville, the station even had a rule that anchors weren't supposed to ask questions, they were supposed to make "declaratory statements," to which the reporter would respond. The idea being that we didn't want the anchor appearing so uninformed that he or she had to rely on someone else for information. So instead of having the anchor say, "Paul, is the fire under control yet?" I was supposed to write a statement for the anchor such as, "Paul, I understand the fire still isn't under control ...." or "Paul, they've been working on that fire for 6 hours and 43 minutes now ...."

"They sure have, Mark, and it's really taken a toll on these firefighters ...."

Making the anchors appear omniscient always kind of annoyed me, so occasionally I would write inaccurate declaratory statements for the anchors that I could then correct. "Paul, I understand the fire still isn't under control …."

"I don't know where you heard that, Jane, it's been under control since Tuesday. What the fire department is doing now is searching for signs of emollients …." Naturally, the anchors didn't think much of this, and they sometimes responded by ignoring my prescripted questions and introductions.

You have to be careful messing with an anchor, because if an anchor wants to get back at a field reporter, all he or she has to do is ask about something that he or she knows for certain you won't know. "Paul, we all learned in grade school that paper burns at 451 degrees Fahrenheit. But why don't you remind the viewers about the melting point for a steel/carbon/fiberglass composite, as is so often used in these late model neo-Gothic structures?"

One WATE anchor, Lori Tucker, would often disregard my prescripted question and ask me something I couldn't answer. Most of her questions were good ones, questions I should have asked myself before I went on the air. The problem was that I hadn't. Which is why, for instance, I was a bit flummoxed the time Lori asked me during a live shot about an apartment fire, "Paul, we know there were two families living there and they managed to get out safely. But where will they spend the night?" Very good question. Unfortunately, I hadn't thought of it beforehand. "Um, your guess is as good as mine, Lori. With relatives?"

Doing shots with Lori, I had to be on my toes. I got adept at speaking without saying anything, or switching the subject to something I did know a little about. "That's a very good question, Lori, one that, as you know, will have to be resolved

307

before the night is through. Because looking at this apartment building, it's obvious they won't be staying here anytime soon. This building has been burning for four hours straight, and all that's left is rubble and ash. Firefighters have been combing through the wreckage looking for signs of emollients ...." Perhaps I learned something from that public relations manual after all — listen, answer, bridge.

Some anchors also like to throw out a final declaratory statement at the end of every live shot, something like, "And we're all praying for their recovery," or "It really shows you the importance of checking the batteries in a smoke detector." I'm not sure if they do this to demonstrate their concern, to bring closure to the piece, or simply to show that they get the last word. As a reporter, all you can do is say something to the effect of, "That's right."

At WATE, every reporter on staff had his or her own pet way of responding to one anchor who *always* made these kinds of statements. One reporter always used, "You bet," while another said "Certainly" or "That's for sure." I always wanted to reply, "If you say so," but I never had the nerve. Conclusory comments became such an expected part of live shots with that anchor that one day a field reporter, Mike Cihla, responded even though his earpiece wasn't working and he couldn't hear the anchor on the other end. But Mike *knew* the anchor would make one of these comments, so after finishing his report, Mike waited a few seconds and then pursed his lips and nodded in agreement as if the anchor had just said something truly profound. It worked perfectly.

Another anchor I worked with used to steal reporters' lines. I'd write an introduction for him, and he would read his intro and then continue on and read all of my lines, leaving me to say something like, "Well, as you said ..." or "And that bears repeating, ..." After a while I started writing a fake intro for myself in the script for him to steal and secretly writing another one, a real one, that I could say after he had taken my lines.

While I may gripe a bit about anchors ad-libbing or stealing lines, I actually think that most of the time unscripted questions and comments are fair game. My feeling is that as a reporter, if I really know the story as well as I should, I should be able to answer or comment about whatever I'm asked. And if I know the subject well and still can't answer, it's probably something I shouldn't be embarrassed not to know. The melting point for steel/carbon/fiberglass composites, for instance. It's kind of like when I was a fledgling bartender in college and didn't know how to make a lot of drinks. My first few weeks, I was terrified someone would ask for something I didn't know, so I kept a bartender's guide in my pocket and would kneel down behind the bar to peek at recipes. But after a while, I'd memorized enough cocktails that if someone asked for something I didn't know, I would just admit it. "A Grumpy Muppet? Never heard of it. What's in it?"

When you're just starting out in TV and doing live shots for the first time, you tend to think you have to know everything, and think you look terrible if they ask you something you can't answer. It's only when you get more confident and comfortable that you realize it's okay to admit ignorance every now and then. When I finally became able to do that, I knew I was getting better. In some ways, the live test for TV news people isn't how perfectly they recite their lines, it's how calmly they react when something goes wrong, as it inevitably will.

The best reaction I ever saw was from Roger Grimsby, the legendary Eyewitness News anchor for WABC in New York. Roger introduced a story one day and went to a sound bite, only to have the audio malfunction, leaving viewers with video of people talking but without any sound of their voices. After a few seconds of this, the camera cut back to Grimsby, who simply remarked, "Apparently they whispered," and moved on to the next story.

Chapter 21

Death, Dogs, and Racking Up the Points

"With violent crime rates up over the past several years, reporters must be both emotionally and psychologically stable, so they can report from gruesome crime scenes." – The Princeton Review Guide to Your Career[*]

I'm riding around Knoxville with photographer Jay Kaley. He's driving, and I'm poring through newspaper apartment listings. We're on our way to cover some uninteresting story, but what I'm really focused on is finding a new place to live. My apartment lease is up, and Jay's been in Knoxville a lot longer than I have, so I'm getting his take on various neighborhoods and locations as I spot listings in the newspaper.

"What about Woodbine, you ever been to Woodbine?"

"Yeah, did a story there when some woman got her throat slit around Woodbine. Nearly beheaded, yet somehow survived. By her boyfriend, no less, who doubled as her crack dealer. Poor choice of companionship on her part. On the other hand, living there you wouldn't have far to go for a little pick me up."

Woodbine is out.

"How about Chilhowie Hills? There's a listing here for a one-bedroom. Ever done anything over there?"

"Some parts are really nice, but you'll recall that's where the Zoo Man took his hookers and strangled them in the woods. Of course, he's in jail, so that not's a concern."

"What about Third Creek? That seems nice."

"Well, remember those rapes we covered on the Third Creek trail? That goes right through that neighborhood. And, of course, Christa Pike killed that girl near Third Creek, although that was over on the UT campus part."

Okay, forget Third Creek. "What about Mechanicsville? There's an apartment listing here in Mechanicsville."

Jay turns and glances over at me. "You don't want to be there, Spell-Man," he says with some gravity. "That's near College Homes. We cover stuff there *all* the time."

Perhaps only for folks working in law enforcement or TV news does nearly every neighborhood bring to mind some calamity. I can't tell you how many times someone told me where they lived, and my first reaction was, "Oh yeah, I know that area, I covered a murder over there," or "Oh, you must live right behind that house where the gas heater blew up." If I have never been to your neighborhood, that's a good sign.

The reason, of course, is that TV news focuses so intensely on these kinds of events. I keenly recall the first time I had to cover something truly horrific. It was when I was working in Whiteville. Two men had been working on what they thought was an empty gasoline storage tank. A spark ignited some leftover fumes and the tank exploded. One man was killed instantly; the other suffered massive burns and died a short time later. When I arrived there was still blood all over the grass where they had been standing. I was walking around trying to get a good shot of the gas tank when a police officer said to me, "You might want to move, you're standing in someone's gray matter." I was horrified, both by the accident and by the casualness of his remark. To think that two men

312

had been working away one second, and then were blown to pieces the next was really disturbing to me. What is in some ways more disturbing, however, is the fact that after a bit more time in local TV news, I pretty much got used to this sort of thing.

*   *   *

"We got the bubble-headed bleach blonde who comes on at five, she can tell you 'bout the plane crash with a gleam in her eye, it's interesting when people die ....." — from the song "Dirty Laundry" by Don Henley and Danny Kortchmar[*]

It is a disconcerting fact that nearly every line in "Dirty Laundry," Don Henley's diatribe about the media, rings true. People do find it interesting when people die. Not just the bubble-headed bleach blondes, of course, but everyone else in TV news and the public as well. As a local reporter, my job was to feed that appetite. To some extent, I knew this going in, and actually looked forward to covering gritty stories about life-changing events. But I never imagined I'd cover violence and death to the point where I couldn't even begin to guess how many victims I've written about. The other day a friend (who's not in the business) mentioned a story I had once told him involving a woman who killed her neighbor over some borrowed silverware. I couldn't remember any of the details. I vaguely recalled spending a few hours interviewing neighbors in some trailer park near the Tennessee–Kentucky state line, but that's about it. Everything else about that murder blurred in my mind with dozens of similarly graphic and gruesome cases I had covered. Only the details were different.

Was it Suttles who stabbed his ex-girlfriend to death in the Wendy's parking lot while her children were inside staring out the window, or was Suttles the one who killed his wife and put a rose on her body? Was it the Cone service station story where the assailants shot someone for a dollar and his wristwatch, or was Cone the case involving the murdered store clerk, where the killer lived 50 yards away and had strolled home afterward with the robbery proceeds? Or what about that guy who buried his ex-wives in the backyard and constructed a cement porch over them? He wasn't the same one who dumped his girlfriend down a well, was he?

All of these events took place in and around Knoxville in the three years that I was there. I'd covered the occasional homicide or fatal accident at WWAY in Wilmington, but these sorts of events weren't a common enough occurrence there to cover on a regular basis. In Knoxville, covering death and destruction was so common that more than once I ran into family members of crime victims and couldn't recall which story I'd interviewed them for.

"Who was that?" I'd whisper to my photog after encountering a familiar-looking woman in the county courthouse.

"Jeanne something or other. She's the daughter of the Dotts, killed out in Farragut by the Gagne gang."

"Oh, that happened before I got here," I'd respond, relieved, thinking I couldn't be blamed for not remembering her name.

"Yes, but you interviewed her last month about victims' rights. I was with you."

Damn.

The amount of violence I covered was especially remarkable considering that Knoxville was not exactly the murder capital of America. It wasn't even close. When I was there in 2000, Knoxville ranked 53rd in the United States, with 12.7 homicides per 100,000 people. That was more violent than Houston and Charlotte but well behind the killing streets of Milwaukee (20.9 per 100,000), Birmingham (31.1) and Gary, Indiana (59.4).

Even so, I covered enough tragedy and sorrow that at one point I calculated that roughly 60 percent of my stories were somehow related to someone dying. Whether it was a murder, the trial of an accused killer, a funeral of a crime victim, a fatal fire, a hiker mauled by a bear, a wrongful death lawsuit, a baby left in a dumpster, a deadly school bus crash, a drowning … it went on and on and on. It seemed I was always interviewing someone in mourning. To quote "Dirty Laundry" again, "Get the widow on the set …."

Covering death and misfortune all the time forced a real transformation on my part. I had to get used to tragedy and get accustomed to approaching victims' family members to see if they would talk on camera. Sometimes I felt like an ambulance-chasing attorney or funeral home salesman, except that what I was selling was public exposure. These kinds of sales calls can be unpleasant experiences, to put it mildly.

The hardest thing I ever had to do was call up the families of four people killed in a fireworks factory explosion in LaFollette, Tennessee, and ask if they would do an interview with me and, more importantly, provide me with pictures of their loved ones that I could put on TV. I had to make these calls just 45 minutes after the families had been formally notified by the coroner that their husbands or wives or children weren't coming home. All I had were the names of the victims, so I borrowed a local phone book and called everyone in LaFollette with the victims' last names, asking if they were related. At one point, I got one of the victim's cousins, who provided me with the number for the victim's parents. When I called them, they hung up on me before I could even explain why I was calling. All they heard was "from Channel 6 News" and there was a click on the other end. I can't say I really blame them.

But I had to ask. Viewers want to see what victims look like and I needed photos to show them. Eventually, I was able to obtain pictures of three of the four people killed in the explosion and got an on-camera interview with a grieving family member. My station was the only local channel to get that much on the first night, and I was hailed as a hero by the newsroom. But I felt ashamed.

What helped me eventually get used to this sort of thing was a nice juicy rationalization about the job. I came to view my role as that of someone performing an unpleasant but necessary chore. It was the embalmer's job to prepare the body. It was the priest's job to preside over memorial services. It was my job to tell the victim's story. Like most good rationalizations, there is some truth to it.

The idea behind telling the story of the victim is to let viewers know that it was a genuine person who died, and not just a name or character like those on some TV show. Covering one of my first homicides back when I was in Wilmington, I overheard a more seasoned reporter tell the mother of a teenage boy who had been killed that she should do an interview because he "didn't want her son to be just another statistic, a faceless victim like so many others killed every year." At the time, I thought his comment was self-serving and revolting, but there is some truth to it. I guess the only really disingenuous thing about the reporter's remark was that he claimed *he* didn't want her son to be another statistic. I think he just wanted to get the story.

Still, the truth is that a crime or accident has greater relevance if you can tell viewers about the people affected. If you report that "one person died in a fire," it doesn't have the same impact as if you say, "12-year old Jamie Stevens was killed," and show a picture of a sweet young girl with a gap-toothed smile. That's why you need the photo. But whenever you see a victim's photo on TV or in the newspaper, remember that most of the time, the reporter had to get that picture by asking for it from the person's family. To tell the victim's story, you also need their friends and family to talk, because unless the victim was a celebrity, you probably don't know anything about them. You need someone who does. It may come across as rude and insensitive to approach grieving family members, but if they won't talk about the person and describe what they were like and how much they'll be missed, no one else can.

And quite frankly, family members were not always unhappy to talk to me. When I first had to approach victims' family members, I assumed that they would view me as an unwanted invader of their privacy. Sometimes I wouldn't even attempt to contact a victim's relatives and felt I was doing them a favor. The funny thing is that I was wrong, because while some people don't want to talk, a surprising number of people do. A remarkable number of people welcomed me with utmost sincerity, and thanked me afterward for listening and showing an interest in the loss of their loved ones. Some even called me before I contacted them. Perhaps they found it cathartic or therapeutic. Usually, I didn't have to ask more than one or two questions before all their emotions and grief poured out, and they would end up talking for 40 minutes.

Of course, some reporters get good at pushing emotional buttons and deliberately getting people to cry. I can't say I've never done it, but I usually don't have the stomach for it. Once, I recall, a photographer jokingly chastised me for changing the subject when I could have pushed a grieving family member over the edge and prompted a few tears. "You had it but you pulled away," he said. "One more second, we would have needed a towel."

"I know," I replied, sheepishly. "I couldn't do it. I'm weak."

Often I think the news story is better without the tears anyway. The Barbara Walters School of Journalism seems to teach that tears make good TV, but I think they also make viewers uncomfortable and can distract from what a person is saying. More likely they just make *me* uncomfortable. But there's no question that hearing from someone close to the victim can be powerful and moving. It is here that local TV news is really quite different from fictional movies and TV shows. In most movie and TV shows, the impact of violence is minimized. Someone gets shot and killed, and you never see them again. Or if you see them again, it's in an autopsy lab being clinically dissected. Viewers don't see much about the victim's pain or the grief that the person's family experiences. They're former cast members whose demise has little impact other than as plot development. In local TV news, on the other hand, reporters go out of their way to show every last consequence of a crime; from the children left without a mother to the husband left without a wife to the 17-year-old gang member who will waste the next 70 years in a six-by-10-foot prison cell.

TV news can also be of genuine assistance if the family or the police need assistance. If, for instance, the police need help finding the killer, or the family needs money for funeral expenses or for paying their rent. This is one of those areas where TV news can perform a truly valuable service. It is amazing how the public responds to a plea for help broadcast over the airwaves. Every year, it seemed, I did a story about some family that had its Christmas presents stolen, and every year those kids ended up getting more donated gifts from viewers than they ever would have received from their parents in the first place. If you're a bit low on Christmas gifts one year, arrange to have them stolen and then call your local station. You'll make out like a bandit. (Which is what you are if you do this, of course.)

That kind of impact always makes you feel good about your job as a TV reporter, but I was well aware that I was not doing these stories out of the kindness of my heart. Most people in TV recognize that helping victims is also helping themselves. There is simply no escaping the fact that TV reporters benefit from other people's misery. The more damage, the bigger the story. I once heard an anchor joke to a reporter just back from covering a possible tornado, "Heather, I understand the damage was even worse than we had hoped." I can't think of one line that more succinctly sums up local TV and its approach to covering the news.

I'm not saying this is necessarily a bad thing or a good thing, just that that's the way it is. The line, "If it bleeds, it leads" is such a cliché that no one in TV news ever says this anymore (if anyone ever really did). But most people in local news will admit that the line is fairly accurate. A study a few years back by the Rocky Mountain Media Watch found that 30 percent of local TV news stories dealt with crime and violence. It feels even higher when you're the one covering it.

I think there are two main reasons why death and destruction make up such a large part of local TV news. Part of it is human nature: people have a morbid curiosity about other people's misfortunes. At least one study found that in terms of viewer interest, crime outranks sports, government, and religion. Maybe deep down, seeing someone else's demise makes us feel more alive. I am not a psychologist, but there must be some reason that crowds gather for public executions and that the hot ticket in Rome was to see Christians eaten by lions. Literary classics like *The Odyssey* and *King Arthur* involve a tremendous amount of bloodletting, and eye-gouging seems to be something of a recurring theme in Shakespeare's fine family entertainment.

People have been reporting on murder and mayhem ever since the top story involved a violent family quarrel between two brothers named Cain and Abel. Even in modern society, which some like to think of as more "civilized" than in the past, when someone dies, especially if it occurs in a lurid or unusual manner, people talk about it.

That's a big reason it gets reported on the news. The "talk test" is often how you decide whether to cover something in TV news. "What are people talking about today?" my Knoxville news director Brian Trauring would ask at our morning story meeting, and invariably the answer involved some calamity. That or a good sex scandal, followed closely behind by the weather. Put all three together and you've got a top-rated newscast. The ultimate TV news promo would simply be: "Death. Sex. And the 5-day forecast. Your news is next."

But from a local TV news perspective, just as important is the fact that crime and disasters are easy and inexpensive to cover. Unlike investigative stories and enterprise reporting, which take time and resources, covering tragedy is journalistic fast food. It fills up your newscast and it's quick and cheap. I could run out to a murder scene, interview a shocked neighbor and a not-so-shocked police detective, and get a few shots of a flashing patrol car, and I'm ready to go live for the five, six, and eleven o'clock newscasts. It's perfect for a local TV station with two or three reporters working that day. Which, in many markets, is every day.

With so few reporters, you are simply not allowed to come back empty-handed. I had to complete at least one story, often three or four, every day without fail. So when it came to the choice between having me attempt a complex investigative piece that might fall through or sending me to the latest gang shoot-out, it was a fairly easy decision. And these days, with most local stations cutting back on personnel while simultaneously increasing their number of news hours, it shouldn't come as a surprise that the Center for Media and Public Affairs claims coverage of violent crime has risen over 700 percent since 1993, even while instances of such crime has declined. That's probably why so many people think crime is going up.

All of this means that as a local TV reporter, you are always approaching people who have experienced a loss. I developed a routine. I would walk up and knock on the door, and then step back a few feet so that the people inside could see I wasn't threatening. This is particularly important in places where residents own firearms. Which, in America, is everywhere. I also held my notepad out in front so they would realize I was a journalist and not a bill collector. This is also important in places where residents own firearms. And last, I kept my cameraman a step or two behind me, farther away from the door and with the camera pointed at the ground. I didn't want people thinking I was doing a *60 Minutes* style ambush. On the other hand, if they mistakenly thought I worked for Publisher's Clearinghouse, that could work to my advantage.

I found that if I was on someone's porch, appearing relatively harmless and sympathetic, I had a much better shot of convincing the person to talk then if I called on the phone and asked. There are some times when protocol demands that you phone ahead out of courtesy, but most of the time, you are much better off just showing up. I also found that a lot of what determined whether someone would talk had to do with how I asked. If people kept turning me down, it usually meant I wasn't asking the right way. Usually I said something like, "Excuse me sir (or ma'm), I'm Paul Spelman, from Channel 6, and I want to tell you that I'm very sorry for your loss. But I was wondering if we could talk to you a little bit about what your son/daughter/wife/husband was like?"

Different people react very differently to such a request. For whatever reason, the wealthier and more successful you are, the *less* likely it is you'll talk to the media. I would try to interview someone with a good job, a safe and healthy family, and plenty of insurance on the house that burned down and they wouldn't give me the time of day. "Please leave me and my family alone to grieve." Whereas an uneducated fellow who lost his life's savings when his barn went up in smoke will talk to me till the cows come home (and find they have no place to stay). Perhaps it is because the less fortunate need more help, or perhaps because they don't have much else to brag about, so a reporter willing to put them on TV and listen to their troubles seems like a consolation prize for life's many hardships.

I am not exaggerating, though, in saying that it is much harder getting comments from someone with money. Whenever I would head out on a story where I knew I was going to have to knock on doors, I was very happy if the address turned out to be in the less fashionable part of town. Call it the trailer park rule — the more trailers, the more likely I'd get a sound bite.

No matter where it was, though, it did take a while before I became comfortable at door knocking, whether I was there for a victim's family's comment or for something less serious. Door knocking is an essential skill for a TV reporter; you knock on more doors than the Jehovah's Witnesses. I had days when I literally knocked at 30 different homes before I found someone who would talk to me. I've knocked on the door of accused child molesters, fugitives, and shooting suspects. One time, I knocked on the door of a man wanted for killing two people in a Knoxville office massacre. Police had a manhunt going on all over the city for him, so it seemed unlikely he'd be at home. But I had to find out.

So I knocked on the guy's door, held my breath for 10 seconds and then happily walked away. It was a long 10 seconds. But I had to see if he was home and would talk to us. What if he turned out to be one of those cooperative criminals who actually likes talking to the media, or had some sort of manifesto he wanted to make public? I would have been in trouble if he popped up on a competing channel professing his innocence and blaming the shooting on an armaments malfunction.

And sometimes suspects do talk to you. I once got an interview with a bar owner accused of gunning down a drunken customer. He claimed it was in self-defense and took me through what happened, even so far as to point out the pool of blood still staining his floor. I then went to the deceased person's home, explained that I was sorry for their loss, told them what the bar owner had said, and gave them an opportunity for rebuttal. Which they did quite strenuously. I did not enjoy approaching people and making these kinds of requests, but as a reporter you never know whether people will talk to you, so you have to ask.

* * *

"Can we film the operation? Is the head dead yet? You know the boys in the newsroom got a running bet ...."

It is also hard not to become cavalier and insensitive about tragedy when you cover it all the time. I recall one of the first times I was to interview a murder victim's mother and realized I hadn't bothered to learn her son's name. "Tell me about ... um ... tell me about your son," was what I ended up saying. I'm not sure if she realized or not, but I felt terrible afterward. Later on, after I had literally dozens more deaths under my belt, I probably wouldn't have given it a second thought. Which is not a good thing. But I had to develop psychological armor. It was the only way I could handle all the death and grieving I was immersed in on a daily basis. I think most journalists are not insensitive people. It is just that when you cover sorrow and sadness all the time, you have to keep a distance or you can't keep doing the job.

That's probably why there is so much joking around about it in the newsroom. Jokes such as the one I heard after a brutal baseball bat murder where the suspect's last name happened to be Yoda: "Use the force Luke. If that doesn't work, use the bat." One producer I worked with used to joke that she had a "spot-news dance" she could do whenever she needed a show-topping tractor-trailer accident or nursing home fire.

People I worked with at one station played a game called "The Dead Pool," where each participant came up with a list of celebrities they thought might succumb during the coming year. As one player put it, it was his list of people who shouldn't join a record club. If any of the chosen celebs passed away, the player who selected the deceased earned points. It was sort of a fantasy fatality league, and the more obscure the selection, the greater the reward. Strom Thurmond and Ronald Reagan were worth little, since they were on nearly every player's list. Former *Diff'rent Strokes* star Dana Plato, on the other hand, got her selecter a slew of points and some curious questions when she died of a drug overdose. How the reporter knew to put her on his list of the soon-to-be-deceased is unsettling, and I expect that back in the Middle Ages he would have been burned at the stake.

I can honestly say that I never participated in "The Dead Pool." While I was as cynical as the next reporter, I drew the line at actively rooting for someone's demise. But it wasn't as though I spoke out vehemently against the game either. I did keep an eye on the standings.

Some of the apparent insensitivity among journalists no doubt arises as a natural defense mechanism, and some of it probably comes from associating with people who are even more callous about death than you are: law enforcement. Police officers develop a disturbingly disinterested attitude toward the dead and dying. I recall how once, while I was covering a fatal plane crash in which a family of three perished in the Tennessee River, a Knox County deputy remarked, "You know, the real news story today isn't this plane, it's that the [University of Florida football team] Gators lost."

To truly appreciate the Vol-centric nature of this comment, you have to understand that the Gators had not even played the Vols that day, but the Gators' loss that day at the University of Georgia allowed the Vols back into contention for the national title. I guess his reasoning was that people die all the time, whereas the Gators only lose once or twice a year. The really disturbing aspect of his comment was that, in Knoxville, he was probably right.

Meanwhile, his attitude, while unsettling, probably wouldn't even get him in the door at the annual conference of medical examiners. I've interviewed medical examiners that made the most cynical of reporters look like Tiny Tim. One M.E. I dealt with in Knoxville even had a morgue in his home garage. He was considered one of the top examiners in the state of Tennessee, although known for being a bit eccentric (and to be known among M.E.s as "the eccentric one" is surely saying something.). This M.E. was also known for rarely granting TV interviews, but he agreed to talk to me because he was upset that county officials had ignored his findings in a shooting case. He said his examination indicated that a shooting victim had been shot twice and had been shot from behind, and that the bullets had come from two different guns. This indicated, he said, that the victim was likely ambushed, and didn't jibe at all with the shooter's claim that he fired in self-defense.

But for some reason, the D.A. and sheriff in that county wouldn't charge the defendant with murder, which left the M.E. incensed. I called him to ask about the case, and he blurted out that he was really mad about the way it had been handled. "Are you mad enough to talk to me on camera?" I asked, and remarkably, he said yes. So with photog Jason Hensley, I went out to the M.E.'s rural home about 30 minutes east of Knoxville to interview him.

We were talking to him in a small room that seemed to double as his office and TV parlor when I happened to mention an unrelated shooting that had occurred the night before in a different county. "Oh, I'm doing that one too," he said, "You want to see the head films?" I didn't know what head films were, but he seemed eager to display them for me, so I said sure. He then led us back into a garage that he'd turned into a small lab, complete with a cold metal table under a bright, harsh light. On the slab was a naked dead man with a bullet hole in his head and a large thermometer sticking out of his stomach. The M.E. didn't even glance at him. He proceeded past the table to an x-ray screen, where he pointed to a small white fleck in the black mass of skull and said, "Here you can see where the bullet fragmented after it ricocheted off the bone ... ."

Needless to say, I was distracted and had trouble paying attention to his instructive lesson in forensics. I didn't know what to say. There was a dead body lying on the table in this guy's garage. Was I supposed to act like it wasn't there and ask the M.E. a few technical questions about "head films"? Jason was so stunned his camera was pointing at the floor.

"Ricocheted off the bone, hmm, that's interesting," I finally muttered, before giving in to curiosity and turning and staring at the dead body. The victim didn't look real. His face was purplish and bloody, yet he had a very serene expression, almost as if he had no objection to his current plight. He resembled one of those statues at a Madame Tussaud's wax museum.

"That's the guy, huh?" I managed to say.

"Yep. Killed when he was asleep, probably by his son," said the M.E. in a offhand manner, as he came over and forcibly jiggled the thermometer sticking out of the man's stomach. "By his temperature, looks like it was early in the morning."

I told the doc I was surprised that he kept bodies in his garage, to which he commented, "It's very convenient; you wouldn't believe how little my morgue costs. My wife helps me do autopsies, and my daughter, who's in med school, sometimes comes down and pitches in." I would love to see their Christmas photos.

Later, as Jason and I were leaving, the M.E. turned to his wife and said, "I'm a little hungry, I'm going to go get some bread. I figure we can get the trunk done in about an hour, but we'll have lunch first." He then turned to me and added, "It's not like he's going to run off."

I wondered afterward if he was deliberately trying to shock, and I think he probably was. It worked. Although Jason and I didn't throw up or anything, we were in a daze the whole way back to the station. Jason kept shaking his head and muttering, "I'm going to go get some bread …."

When we got back, the assignment editor asked if we happened to learn anything about the previous night's shooting, and we replied, "Oh yes, we met the victim."

"He survived?" she asked, in a surprised manner.

"No. No, you definitely can't say that," I replied.

I guess I should have expected such an attitude from someone who deals with the dead but rarely the grieving. I think this makes it much easier to become emotionally detached. I once interviewed a coroner who told me he couldn't stand to see suffering. "I'd be a terrible ambulance driver," he said, "but if they're dead it doesn't bother me." A few months later I ran into him on the street and asked, "How's business?" to which he replied, "Not so good. No one's died in a while."

As a reporter, I had to deal with the grieving all the time, and whenever I would start to get too nonchalant or uncaring about death, something, or someone, would remind me that good news for me was bad news for someone else. This really hit home one day when I did a story about a man who disappeared while fishing in a rural county west of Knoxville. All the investigators could find were his clothes, neatly folded and lying on the bank of the river. There was also a bloody knife sitting atop the stack.

The whole thing was pretty interesting — a genuine whodunit. But when I tried to contact the investigators, I got stonewalled by the sheriff's department.

"The investigating officer worked late last night and isn't in, and the sheriff's gone," explained the unhelpful dispatcher. "They're the only ones that can talk to you."

"Any idea when they'll be back?" I asked.

"No, they're pretty busy all day. Now if you'll excuse me, I have other work to do." Click.

So photog Jay Kaley and I went out to the riverbank to get video of the scene and see what else we could find. We were hoping we would get lucky and run into a relative, or find another fisherman fearful that he'd be next.

"I always get lucky out in this county," I told Jay, "maybe we'll get lucky again."

When we got there, we did indeed get a break. I spotted a guy fishing along the riverbank, and it turned out he was the same person who had discovered the missing man's clothes and bloody knife. Evidently his discovery hadn't turned him off the local fishing hole. We stuck a microphone on the guy and had him show us precisely how and where he had stumbled on the clothes. Just as he was recounting his tale, we heard people shouting from the other side of the water.

"Hey, there's a body over here!"

"What'd they say?"

"They say there's a dead body over there."

"You're kidding."

They weren't.

It was the missing man. His bloated corpse had floated to the surface after two days under water. So while Jay shot video, I called the sheriff's department again. When I identified myself, the dispatcher said, "I told you before, there's no one here that can talk to you."

"Okay," I replied, "but when they come in, tell them we found their missing guy; he's in the water out here." Amazingly, they became available. So we got some great footage of the sheriff's department investigators arriving on the scene and recovering the body and combing the area for clues. All sorts of good material from a TV news perspective, especially since for a long time, we were the only camera crew on the scene. "I told you we'd get lucky," I said to Jay, as I stood there feeling quite pleased.

A few minutes later, I got another break, as the sister of the victim showed up and I convinced her to talk to us on camera. "He was a wonderful guy," she said in a slightly faltering voice. "I just can't believe this has happened. He had had some problems with his marriage, but he seemed to be working through them."

"You must have been worried about him when he didn't come home," I said.

"I've had a bad feeling ever since he disappeared," she replied, as tears started to well up. "But I was really hoping I was wrong. I guess it's just not my lucky day."

Her grief really put my good fortune into perspective.

Occurrences like that served as a stark reminder that I needed to be genuinely sympathetic and caring when dealing with people who had lost a loved one. I tried to make myself remember that when I left — when I drove away and headed back to the station — their hurt and pain would remain. That wasn't going to disappear just because I moved on to a different news story, on to cover someone else's misery and grief. For me, it was just the story of the day, maybe even of the hour. But for them, it was real, it was their life, and it was forever.

The significance of this struck me another night when I was doing a story about domestic violence. It was one of those march-and-sing vigil things that domestic violence shelters seem to put on every other week. You cover so many of these in local TV news that it's hard not to get cynical about them. But as we were packing up our gear, I noticed one woman sitting alone in her car, crying. Watching her, I realized how lonely and afraid she must have felt. Once our cameras were gone and the vigil was over, she still faced the fact that she couldn't go home again and was, in all likelihood, starting over.

Sometimes the sadness and grief associated with other people's misery really does hit you, even when you've been covering these kinds of events for a while. Oddly enough, it's not always the worst cases that affect you. I did dozens of stories about the senseless murder of a Knoxville family by a group of devil-worshipping teenagers and it only bothered me a little bit. But I got really depressed one day when a man came into our newsroom with a picture of his missing 15-year old brother. The kid had only been gone a couple of days and could have been a runaway, for all we knew, but the brother kept saying, "This is so unlike him; I hope he's all right."

It really bothered me. After just a few years in local news, I'd already seen so many bad outcomes I couldn't envision a happy ending. But compared to some of the other atrocities I've covered, this one shouldn't even have registered. After all, we didn't even know the kid was hurt. Why did this one affect me? I don't know. It didn't affect anyone else. For the most part everybody in the newsroom ignored the guy, and when I came in a few days later and asked whether they ever found him, all I got was, "Found who?"

* * *

"I make my living off the Evening News, just give me something, something I can use ...."

Even after I learned to cope with covering constant death and destruction, what I still found disturbing was the arbitrariness of what gets covered and how much. There is no getting around the fact that the news media views and values different deaths and disasters differently. Actually, it is not all that arbitrary. Another reporter and I once sat around and made up an imaginary point scale you could use to calculate the "newsworthiness" of a tragedy. The more points, the bigger the story.

Start with something violent or tragic. Then add or subtract points depending on whether it is local. Anything local gets a big boost; anything distant needs to be more severe. Foreign tragedies in far-off places need to be about 50 times worse than local tragedies in order to merit equivalent coverage. Take a look at the back pages of a local newspaper sometime; you'll see a two-paragraph blurb describing how 223 people drowned in a ferryboat accident in Turkey or a news brief about 3,000 people missing after a cyclone in Bangladesh. Now imagine if that happened in your city, or in Chicago or St. Louis, or anywhere in America, for that matter. How much coverage would it receive? It wouldn't be in the back of the newspaper or the "global roundup" after the weather. But in local news, it has to be local to get the points.

If the death is the result of foul play, add several more points. Add a point or two if either the victim or killer was very young or very old. A twelve-year-old murderer, or a murderer in his eighties (I covered one of these once in Wilmington; the guy could barely walk, yet managed to shoot his wife) is far more newsworthy than a 25-year-old perpetrator, and the same goes for the victim. Add another point if the victim or suspect is disabled, deaf, or blind. Subtract points if the victim was using drugs or hanging out on a street corner where such merchandise is sold. Subtract a point if the victim is poor or the crime took place in a shabby neighborhood, and add a point if the opposite is true. Add a point if the victim is a tourist or an athlete. In Knoxville, add six points if the victim is a former Vol. Add more points if the victim or suspect is especially photogenic, a la Jon Benet Ramsey or Scott Peterson.

The manner of death can also be worth points if it was especially gruesome or unusual. Dismemberment, for instance, is more newsworthy than a stabbing. If someone is shot 23 times, it merits more coverage than being shot once, even if one bullet did the trick. And to be absolutely honest, you should add points if the victim is white. While it is rarely acknowledged, there is no doubt that white victims get more coverage than minority victims.

If you really want a lot of points, the story should include an animal. Local TV viewers often seem more interested in the plight of a pet than in that of another human being. Maybe that's because animals don't have a choice. If a human falls victim to a crime, we can always think, "Well, not to be overly judgmental, but maybe that guy shouldn't have been in that deserted train yard buying cocaine at three in the morning." Whereas when a puppy gets tortured by degenerate youths, which occurred in Knoxville when I was there, nobody blames the dog.

It was my friend and fellow newsman Jonathan Dienst who tipped me off to the importance of animals. "Always go with the cat or puppy," he told me. "Viewers love animal stories. The important thing is to get the animal's name. You've got to make sure people know it was 'Whiskers' and not just some stray. You'll get more of a response from animal stories than anything else you do."

Jon was right. In two and half years in Wilmington, I covered numerous accidents and hurricanes and city council controversies, yet the story that provoked more viewer phone calls than any other was a Christmas-day piece I did about a lost goat that wandered into the backyard of my friends, the Landsmans. I didn't have much else to cover that day, so I did a story on the Christmas goat. My station got about 25 phone calls from people wanting either to adopt the goat, eat the goat, or speculate as to its possible owner. Weeks later, long after the goat had been returned to its rightful owner (because of our publicity), my station was still getting calls.

In Knoxville, I did so many animal stories I started to get a reputation as the "animal cruelty guy." I did stories about dogs stuck with syringes, about pets skinned and left on the railroad tracks, and about a migrant worker who beat a dog to death with a shovel. That last one was quite memorable because I knocked on the dog killer's door and he agreed to talk to me. He didn't see anything reprehensible about his behavior. I asked if the dog had been threatening him in such a way that he had had to act in self-defense, and he explained that, no, it had been quite friendly because he lured it close with a piece of bologna. That's a lot of points, let me tell you.

I've also done numerous stories about people with too many cats. Unfortunately, this is very common; it's some sort of psychological disorder. People start taking in strays out of genuine kindness and then lose control and can't care for all of them. I did one story about a woman who moved into her car because her four dozen cats had taken over her home. The house was an absolute disaster by the time I did the story, with cat feces and decaying corpses all over the place. Sad story. Lots of points.

Add up your animal points, calamity points, and any of the other factors that apply, and you have a rudimentary system you could use to create an automated assignment editor. Whatever stories garner the most points that day get the most coverage. Stations don't literally do this, of course, but they might as well. Because whether consciously or not, all of these factors get taken into consideration at the daily story meeting when stations decide what to put on the air. Few reporters actually come out and say, "Let's do this story because the victim was a blind woman in a wheelchair living in a nice neighborhood with her three-legged dachshund," but that's what they are thinking. And like it or not, those factors do have an impact on how the public views the story.

Take a story I once did about a fatal accident on a farm near Knoxville. When my assignment editor first told me about it, it didn't sound particularly noteworthy. Not to sound uncaring, but farming is one of the most dangerous professions around, and farmers get hurt all the time. But then it turned out the victim was a young girl, and she wasn't farming, she was taking part in a Halloween hayride as part of a "haunted jungle" put on by a local Boys and Girls club. The ride consisted of a flatbed trailer pulled through a field in the dark. At one point, adults dressed as witches and goblins, one of them being the girl's mother, pulled the girl off the trailer to scare her. When she tried to climb back aboard, her foot caught beneath the wheel. She was run over and crushed, her cries drowned out by the joyful screams of other kids having fun.

That story was worth a terrible amount of points. There were the facts that she was young; kids were involved; it was Halloween; the hayride was put on by a well-known and well-meaning charity; the accident could easily have been avoided; and her mother witnessed the whole thing. As if that doesn't garner enough points, the mother turned out to be a single mom (more points); the girl was her only child (more points); the girl was quite attractive (more points); and she had been her middle school homecoming queen the year before (many, many more points). My story led the newscast.

Would it have been any less tragic for the mother if her daughter had drowned in a swimming pool, or been struck by a car while crossing the street? I don't know, but I know it would have been less newsworthy.

Or take the day some young children were shot and wounded at a Jewish day-care center in Los Angeles. That very same day, in an unrelated incident, several people were found murdered in a private home in the same city. Which made the big headlines? The children, of course. None of them died, but because they were innocent children, and because it was perceived as a hate crime against Jews, it made the front page and led the national newscasts. Meanwhile, the other story was buried on page 26 (in Knoxville's newspaper anyway), and consisted of two or three column inches far below the fold. Same city, same day; yet which was the greater tragedy? From the news standpoint, it was obviously the children. Yet if I were related to the murder victims, I am not sure I would agree.

With so much crime coverage these days, even genuinely tragic stories often need additional pegs or hooks to make them more notable. A story I once did on an elderly couple, victims of a violent home invasion, became much more interesting from a TV news perspective when I noticed a medal on the wall commending the man for enduring three years as a prisoner of war during World War II. I wrote up a script explaining how he had survived horrible atrocities at the hands of the Japanese army only to return to the land of the free and the brave and (years later) get beaten up for his savings by neighborhood thugs. His POW experience had nothing to do with the current crime, but it gave a home-invasion story a hook, and a few more points. As a TV reporter, you're always looking for these things.

You can't always find them. I once had a woman beg me to do a story about a child molester arrested on her street. She was very upset, and it quickly became apparent that the child was her daughter. In TV news, you don't do stories about every child molester because there are too many of them. But I felt bad for the woman and her daughter, so I spent about 20 minutes searching for a hook. "How old is the guy who was arrested?" I asked. I was hoping he was either 9 or 93.

"He's in his midforties," she replied. No help there. "What does he do for a living?" I asked, hoping for a city official, a police officer, or perhaps a priest. "He's in insurance." Not a good answer.

I searched and searched for something to make this more than your run-of-the-mill molester story but finally gave up. Meanwhile, a few months later, I did a story about a school bus driver who was arrested for the very same crime. It led the newscast.

Chapter 22

The News of the Day

"Paul, what have you got?"

All eyes turn to me. I'm sitting in a WATE conference room with the rest of the station's reporters, photographers, and producers, not to mention the news director and assignment editor. We're holding our daily story meeting, going around the table throwing out ideas. WATE reporters are required to bring at least two new ideas every day, and it's my turn.

"Well, at the county courthouse today," I start off, reviewing my notes, "we've got a couple of fine fellows in attendance. First, there's another hearing for our good friend Almeer Nance. Nance, you'll recall, is a teenager who got life plus 25 years for murder and robbery. He's appealing his conviction because he says that although he was old enough to steal and kill, he was not old enough to know better than to confess to the police about it. Says it should not have been allowed in. My guess is that nothing will happen on this today; the judge will take everything under advisement and issue a ruling at 4:57 on Friday when no one's paying any attention. But I'll call the courts later and check on it. Might be worth a VO for the five or eleven.

"Then we've got James Mellon, who you'll remember was involved in the Cone station robbery and murder. Mellon is the bright fellow who pleaded guilty and agreed to cooperate, then changed his mind and tried to back out of the deal because he was scared one of his cohorts was going to kill him in prison. The judge said, sorry, you already pleaded guilty, and Mellon ended up with the death penalty because he wouldn't cooperate with the prosecutors. Not a smart move. I mean, what's the point of pleading guilty if you're going to get the death penalty. Might as well have a trial and enjoy getting to sit in court for a few days. In any event,

Mellon is now appealing, saying he had inadequate counsel. Considering the result, I might agree with that assessment, but I don't think the judge is going to let him out of jail because of it. I'm not sure what's going to be talked about in court today, but I'll check later to see if anything interesting went on."

Neither of these stories is especially new or interesting, and I would have difficulty turning them into full-length news pieces (packages). But I don't have much else to talk about at the story meeting today so I am dragging them out for all they're worth. Some days I have a lot of story ideas. Other days the well runs dry and I have to stretch. This is one of those days.

"Then from the police blotter, the only thing we've got is a case where a woman reportedly went to her ex-boyfriend's job site, pointed a gun at his groin, and said, according to the report, 'If I can't have it, no one else can either.' Fortunately for her ex, he managed to talk her into putting the gun down before anything untoward happened. I'm not sure we can do a story on this, but thought I should mention it.

"Other than those, I was thinking we could do a story about all those pretty red poppies the Department of Transportation planted along the Interstate, and how they might cause traffic accidents because drivers are slowing down to look at them and take pictures."

"It's been done," says one of the other reporters. "Channel 8 did that on Monday."

"Which doesn't mean we shouldn't do it," chimes in another person. "Nobody watches Channel 8, and if they did, they wouldn't be watching us."

"So our viewers won't know we've been scooped on the poppies," remarks my photog for the day, Jay Kaley.

These are good points, but I stay silent. I'm not going to fight for the poppies. I don't really want to do the poppy story; I just couldn't think of any other ideas.

339

"Oh, well," I reply, turning to Wanda. "What do you have?"

* * *

Morning story meetings are where most of the decisions get made about what gets covered in local news. Pretty much every station in the country has a morning meeting like this, where participants are expected to bring ideas. When I first started out in Whiteville and Wilmington, I found this to be a strain, and would stress out about it. Even years later, I still found it hard to come up with *good* ideas. But after a few years in TV news, I became fairly accomplished in the techniques used to come up with routine local news stories.

One thing that helped me enormously in Knoxville was that I was given responsibility for covering the courts. It was a lot to keep my eye on, but it also provided a constant source of stories. Every day began with a brief trip to Knoxville's City–County Building, which, as its name implies, houses nearly all the government offices for the City of Knoxville and Knox County. Most importantly for me, it also housed the courts.

My first stop was the criminal court desk, to check the daily docket for arraignments, motions, trials, and sentences. When I spotted something interesting, I would write it down and bring it back for our meeting. What I was looking for were major crimes or familiar names. Major crimes meant at least attempted murder. Anything less and my station wasn't interested. Even attempted murder didn't ordinarily merit coverage. As for familiar names, that was often more important than the crime itself. If it was someone well known in Knoxville, a former Vol, for instance, a case might be worth covering even if it was just a misdemeanor. If I saw a name that looked familiar but I couldn't quite place it, I'd jot it down and then search the station archives when I got back. Occasionally, I'd strike gold and find that that unimportant-looking assault case on the docket referred to an incident involving a former city mayor getting mugged by a homeless man.

340

I also took note if docket names were the same as those of famous celebrities. I did this to make sure that the "Jim Carrey" listed on the docket that day wasn't, by some freakish stroke of luck (for me, not him), the same Jim Carrey I had seen getting dumb and dumber with Jeff Daniels. (It wasn't.) Checking the docket every day made me realize how many people have the same names. I couldn't help smiling every time I saw that Gary Cooper had been arrested again; that John Paul Jones had indeed begun to fight and was in trouble because of it; and that instead of dutifully coming home, Bill Bailey had been charged with trying to run someone over with his car.

After checking the crime dockets, my next stop was the civil side of the courthouse to skim through the lawsuits. An interesting claim might provide a good story, but I saw more absurd lawsuits than anything else. There were lawsuits over bad haircuts, bad meals, and bad clothing; lawsuits over corpses in the wrong plots; over children cut from the school golf team; even lawsuits over failed lawsuits. If you are ever curious about how litigious America has become, amble down to the local courthouse and take a look at the lawsuits. It will make you never want to own a car, a dog, or a bathroom. That's because cars crash, dogs bite, and bathroom floors get slippery. All of which leads to lawsuits with alarming regularity.

Car accidents were by far the most numerous. I saw anywhere from five to fifteen car crash suits a day. I got to where I would glance at the front page of a legal filing, see the words "was traveling eastward on" and immediately move on. Car accident suits are boring, unless, of course, a celebrity or Vol was involved.

Another common complaint was for medical malpractice. These suits I could usually tell right away because of the large claim amounts. While a fender bender might prompt a $75,000 suit, malpractice suits were usually for $10 or $20 million. This is because medical suits are much more difficult to prove and thus require a bigger payoff for plaintiffs' attorneys, who generally work on a contingency basis and don't make any money unless they win. It's also because hospitals, physicians, and their insurers have much deeper pockets and more liability coverage than your average bad driver.

Despite the impressive monetary figures, I didn't do a whole lot of stories about medical malpractice suits either, because they were so common and because doctors will almost never talk about these suits on camera. The suits themselves are also usually quite complex, and it can require a medical degree to decipher what went wrong and who's responsible. But if a suit seemed especially unique, I would bring it back for our story meeting. Most of the ones I retrieved involved either an unexpected fatality of someone young (extra points, remember), or an egregious medical mistake that even an English major such as myself could understand, such as a cutting off the wrong appendage.

This sort of mistake occurs much more frequently than you would think. I did one story about a woman who had a double mastectomy, only to learn she never had breast cancer to begin with. She was seeking damages equivalent to the gross national product of the European Union. When I mentioned that lawsuit at our morning meeting, every person in the room groaned in horror. Of course, then I had to do the story. There is an unwritten rule in local TV news that if the mere mention of something evokes audible noises from your audience, it is worth doing. If it gets especially loud groans, it should lead at six.

However, it was rare that I got a really worthwhile story out of the lawsuit stack. Much more common were suits I enjoyed simply for the humor quotient. One of my favorites was a lawsuit between two roller-hockey players for "unnecessary roughness." According to the legal filing, the defendant, just prior to hitting the plaintiff, was heard to comment, "Your ass is mine, motherf----." Said player then proceeded to "go beyond the realm of civilized society" and slam his stick down on the hands of the aforementioned motherf----, resulting in grievous injury. The injured party was seeking $160,000 in damages.

These sorts of lawsuits rarely made it on our air, but at least afforded me some amusement. This was good to have, since the courts could be depressing if you stopped to consider how badly people treated each other. There were so many victims and crimes it could boggle the mind. After I had been checking the dockets for a while, even serious offenses such as aggravated assault with a deadly weapon began to look like child's play; almost a rite of passage for some Knoxville citizens.

Evidently I was not the only one at the courthouse who felt this need not to dwell on one man's inhumanity toward another. I once saw a Knoxville judge, during a lull in the court proceedings, pull out a book of Carl Sandburg poetry and read aloud from the bench about the simple joys of life. I'm not sure if he was doing this for his own amusement, or as intended guidance for his literally captive audience, a group of shackled inmates awaiting their turn on domestic violence charges.

It is hard to describe their expressions; a mix of confusion and contempt. Certainly they were less enthusiastic than they had been just moments before, when listening to testimony from a fellow inmate accused of stalking his ex-girlfriend. She wanted him detained and volunteered that one justification for this was that he had given her gonorrhea. "That ain't true, judge," replied the ex-boyfriend with a smirk. "If she had it, three other girls would have it also." Although this exchange may not have matched the literary merit of the judge's reading, it may explain why *Judge Judy* gets better ratings than *Masterpiece Theater*. But the judge evidently felt that the inmates were in need of poetic enlightenment.

After my daily courthouse rounds, I headed over to the Knoxville police headquarters to see if I could find anything interesting in the police log. The log was a brief summary of criminal activity in Knoxville during the past few days, mostly small-time stuff — domestic disputes, neighborhood assaults, and drunken disturbances; often some combination of the three. The log was a litany of human misery, but most of the really juicy stuff (murders and mass mayhem etc.) never ended up in it.

Occasionally, though, I could find some small incident worth doing a story on solely for its novelty factor, such as the report of a young boy robbed at gunpoint for his Halloween candy, or a report describing how a Knoxville woman "forcibly" performed oral sex on a former boyfriend and then "made him" have intercourse. The former boyfriend felt the need to report this encounter to the police because, he said, he was worried it might violate his probation. The suspect was listed as a white female, 5'6", 220 pounds (which lends a bit more credence to his story), with a "calm, professional demeanor." The reporting officer also noted that the victim had "no visible injuries." It's really too bad most of this stuff never made it on the air.

Checking the log was the last stop on my morning rounds before heading back to the station for our meeting. If my rounds or other sources in the community had generated enough stories, I was set for the meeting. But if they hadn't, and quite often they hadn't, I had to come up with other ideas. In big markets, there is often something going on that day that you can cover. There was a lot more going on in Knoxville than in Whiteville or Wilmington, but still not enough to fill the newscasts by itself. So all reporters had to generate ideas, and the ideas that aroused the most interest at our meeting became our coverage for the day.

It was here that my time in small markets really came in handy, because I'd mastered many of the techniques for generating local news story ideas. These techniques make up the heart of local TV news, even in big markets, and if you watch any station in America, you will see these sorts of stories performed over and over again on a daily basis.

One technique is to propose a local angle to a big national story. This is called "localizing." A big cruise ship just ran into an iceberg near Finland; is there a local connection? Anyone from our area on board? Did a local engineer design the ship's stereo system? Is there anyone from our area who has ever been to Finland, or who can pick Finland out on a map?

Those are the first things local reporters check when they hear of a big national story. That's why, for instance, during the Elian Gonzalez drama, every station in Knoxville interviewed the same Cuban exile living in East Tennessee. She didn't know Elian any better than I did, but hey, at least she knows her way around Havana. That's also why passenger lists are so important after a plane crash or train derailment.

The other way to localize a story is to take a big national issue and redo it locally. That's why, after a student shooting in Arkansas, TV crews in Montana will head to their local schools to make sure they're safe and to see if students are more concerned than they were yesterday. It is also why, after an airplane crashes in Australia, your station in Missouri does a live report from the Kansas City airport about danger signs to watch out for when boarding a plane for Milwaukee.

These are not always bad stories, but they get done over and over and over again, even when there is little need to localize them. It is amazing what stations will localize in the name of informing the public. In Knoxville, we once localized the fatal crash of NASCAR driver Adam Petty (in New Hampshire) by sending a reporter to local dirt tracks to see if amateur race car drivers felt more at risk.

Localizing is such a reflexive response in local news that if I planned to suggest localizing a story as my story idea at the daily meeting, I had to get there early and get a seat just to the left of the assignment editor. That's because we always went around the table in that direction, and if I were too many seats around, someone else would propose the localizing idea before I got the chance.

If there isn't a big national issue to localize, another common story-generating technique is to play off a local issue that, by itself, might not be very interesting. You take a minor issue and use it as a peg for something bigger. For instance, after I mentioned a police report about two neighbors beating each other up, a not uncommon occurrence, someone suggested we do a story about neighborly relations and "what to do if your neighbor builds a big fence, makes a lot of noise, or just turns out to be an ass." You would start out by mentioning the police case, and then go into a long story with helpful suggestions on how to resolve neighborly disputes. I believe this one was shot down.

You can also peg a story to the trusty old "economic impact" angle. How much is the UT–Florida football game worth to local merchants? How much revenue will the fall leaf season generate for area gas stations? Economic impact stories are very common in smaller markets because they sound like genuine hard-news stories, even though most viewers couldn't care less. Most people celebrating the Fourth of July have only a passing interest in how much the hot-dog vendors are earning. And who really cares about the economic impact of National Prayer Day? Yet economic impact stories get done all the time in local news.

As do anniversary stories, another local news staple. It has been exactly one year since the power blackout that crippled the city; let's do a story about how residents and businesses recovered, and how the power company has taken steps to avoid a reoccurrence. TV stations like anniversary stories because it gives them a chance to re-air all that great video they shot the year before. And some anniversary stories are genuinely valid updates, but others are relatively pointless. The latter are simply using an anniversary date as a news peg for something that is not otherwise newsworthy. It's been two years to the day since the local Stein Mart store closed;

let's do a story about how far people are now traveling for discount merchandise. I've done way too many of these kinds of stories.

Even so, that number can't hold a candle to the number of stories I've done about the weather. There is something about weather that just lends itself to TV news. I didn't realize this at first. I had to come to understand that weather doesn't have to do anything to merit intensive TV coverage; weather itself qualifies as something worth covering. It will snow so we will show. This is why meteorologists are afforded huge blocks of valuable news time to describe how a low-pressure system developing over Paraguay could impact our area in four to six weeks.

When I first got into TV, I had just moved from a mountain town in Colorado where it was common to see snow in May and June. When my assignment editor in North Carolina woke me up in Whiteville one morning telling me to go cover a local snow flurry, my reaction was, "Cover what? What's happening?"

"It's snowing."

"That's great. What do you want me to do about it?"

"Just get shots of it, shots of people walking in it, driving in it, throwing snowballs etc."

"Um. Okay."

It was one of the easiest stories I've ever done. I stepped out of my apartment and started shooting video of snow on the ground and on my pickup truck. I walked a block over and got a couple of comments from passersby and from kids building a snowman. I got a shot of a car driving through the slush. Then I went and got breakfast. I was done.

The whole concept amazed me. Why would people want to look at local news to see the same thing they could see by looking out the window? In Telluride, we didn't devote much news time to the weather. Our radio news ran a 30–45 second report from the National Weather Service and that was about it. One day someone called me at the station to learn the forecast, so I peered out the window, saw a few clouds, and confidently proclaimed that it was partly cloudy with a 50 percent chance of snow.

"Fifty percent? I thought it was only 20 percent," exclaimed the caller.

"Sounds like you know more than I do," was my reply.

In Telluride, we only covered weather when it really impacted something, such as the flash flood that tore down power lines or the snowstorm that trapped a woman in labor on the highway. These were genuine news stories *caused by* the weather. But once I got into local TV, I had to understand that weather is a story in and of itself simply because everyone is affected by the weather, if only to the extent that they notice it. I'm not talking about hailstorms or tornadoes that cause genuine damage, I'm talking about your run-of-the-mill rain, snow, and sleet that occurs all the time.

For TV, you can always find a peg. If it is cold outside, you do the "Man, it's cold" story, talking about the dangers from frostbite and space heaters and how rising heating oil prices are putting the squeeze on senior citizens. If it's balmy outside, you do the "Man, it's hot" story, going live from Lowe's to talk about sales of fans and air conditioners and the danger of sunstroke to outdoor workers. Remember to stay hydrated, folks, and take plenty of breaks. If it's neither too hot nor too cold, you can do the Goldilocks story, about how nice it is and how people are enjoying themselves and going to the park.

In Knoxville, we had an official rule that if there was any kind of weather alert (which simply required a small storm front somewhere in our viewing area), it had to lead our broadcast. The president of the United States could have been shot, but if a thunderstorm was somewhere over East Tennessee, we would start our show by going to the Weather Lab for an update. And what exactly is a "Weather Lab"? Makes it sound as if a mad scientist is in there brewing up the weather. "Just two more milligrams of low pressure and we'll have it," cue maniacal laugh.

We did not have a Weather Lab in Knoxville when I first arrived; the weather section of the studio was called the Weather Center. Then we got more elaborate pictures and decorations and it suddenly the center became a lab. These days, nearly every local station has a Weather Lab, Weather Center, Storm Team, Storm Center, Storm Tracker, Snow Tracker, Doppler Radar, Viper Radar (whatever that is), or some variation thereof. Competing stations battle over who has the more accurate equipment and can give you a storm warning 20 seconds sooner.

As for reporters, whenever it hails or snows, you invariably find yourself outside, usually near a highway, talking about driving conditions. In Knoxville, I even did live reports when there wasn't any snow, reporting on snow that had been forecast but hadn't arrived or had ended up somewhere else. "As you can see, there isn't any snow right here. But it's a different story up in Johnson City …" (roll videotape of snow in Johnson City). For that story, I actually drove nearly two hours each way in order to find snow to show.

In local news, you don't wait for snowflakes to start falling before beginning "prep" stories about people stocking up on bread, milk, and toilet paper. I grew up in the Northeast, went to school in the blizzard belt of upstate New York, and lived in the high mountains of Colorado, and yet I can't recall a single time when I had to wait more than a day or two to get to a grocery store. How long do people expect to be snowed in?

I don't think TV meteorologists are to blame for this excessive coverage. Most meteorologists I've worked with take a sensible view of the weather and don't sensationalize it. When I would go to Knoxville's chief meteorologist, Matt Hinkin, and explain that I needed his help doing another snow prep story, he would look at me as if I were crazy. "Why are you doing that? It's only going to be a dusting."

"I know, but management thinks it's important."

Important for ratings, maybe. Viewers pay a lot of attention to weather. Matt was the most popular person on our newscast. People who preferred the news on other Knoxville stations would switch to our station just to watch Matt do the weather and then switch back after he was finished. They just liked Matt's way of explaining things; like why partly cloudy is nicer than partly sunny because in the latter the sky is mostly cloudy and just partly sunny, whereas in the former the sky is mostly sunny and just partly cloudy.

While some weather stories are undoubtedly newsworthy, a lot of the enthusiasm for these stories comes from TV news consultants. Consultants say viewers pay attention to weather, so that's what you should cover. This give-the-people-what-they-are-already-interested-in approach was all the rage when I arrived in Knoxville. A great deal of our coverage was determined by research. Not the kind of research where a reporter digs up facts about county officials pilfering funds, but rather research about what the public wants to see. Our news director at the time was a firm believer in the numbers.

The way this works is that consultants take a poll to see what viewers care about. If enough people say crime, you do stories about crime. If people say education, you do stories about schools and so on. The idea is that if you give the public what they're interested in, they'll want to tune in and you'll get good ratings.

In Knoxville, people told consultants that they were interested in crime prevention, health care, education and religion. So our station created what are termed news franchises. These are special stories that air on a regular basis focusing on a particular topic, such as health or education. Franchises are popular in the TV business, even at the network level. NBC's "In Depth," and "The Fleecing of America" were franchises.

At Channel 6 in Knoxville, ours had similarly catchy names, such as "Six on Your Side" (consumer protection), "Six in the Classroom" (education), and "Focus on Faith" (spiritual issues). The franchises ran on specific days every week so viewers would know when to tune in for their favorites. Nearly every reporter was responsible for his or her own franchise. Mine was called "Fighting Back," and it was devoted to crime prevention. Over the course of a single year, I did close to a hundred "Fighting Back" stories on how police and the community can and do fight back against crime. I covered guard dogs, burglar alarms, bomb detectors, community watch programs, DUI checkpoints, defensive gardening, pawn shop patrols, cop-car cameras, bean-bag bullets, infrared detectors, bike squads, cell-phone cloning, sketch artistry, self-defense sprays, senior citizen safety squads, post-office package detection, forensic dentistry, and a host of other topics that were in some way related to crime prevention.

Some of these made for good stories. Others less so. But doing two "Fighting Back" pieces a week in addition to my regular daily news stories was a burden. Every week I would rack my brain to come up with new "Fighting Back" ideas and try to figure out how and when to shoot them. The franchises used up an enormous amount of station resources that could have been devoted to other news coverage. WATE had only two or three reporters most days to begin with, and when two of them were out shooting franchises, we were left shorthanded whenever a school bus rolled off the highway.

If you have all of your reporters doing franchises, inevitably either the franchises, the regular news coverage, or both, suffer as a result. Yet WATE, guided by its consultants, kept coming up with more and more of them. They even created one called "Legal Lives," to appeal to that all-important viewing demographic: attorneys. "Legal Lives" was supposed to focus on lawyers and what they do. *Boston Legal* and *L.A Law* notwithstanding, the real practice of law does not make for riveting TV. The only entertaining and informative thing to come out of that franchise occurred when our cameras followed a lawyer into a classroom to talk to some students and a sixth grader asked, "My friend shot somebody. What do you think he'll get?"

WATE ended up dropping the "Legal Lives" franchise fairly quickly. But even so, at one point we had something like 10 other franchises airing per week. Some people suggested we change our slogan from "Coverage You Can Count On" to "Franchises You Can Frown On." Another person suggested I combine my "Fighting Back" franchise with Don Dare's "Six on Your Side" franchise and call it "Fighting Your Backside"; a suggestion I endorsed but did not pass on to management.

In addition to the franchises, polling research also played a big role in Knoxville during ratings months. Gimmicks and special stories are popular during sweeps because that's when viewership numbers set station ad rates. To boost ratings at WATE, management and consultants came up with the idea of focusing on one issue each month and devoting an enormous amount of resources to that issue.

The first time we did this, the station called it "Heart Smart" month, and all the reporters did stories about eating, exercising, not smoking, and everything else related to a healthy heart. Really groundbreaking stuff. Unfortunately for the reporters, the station happened to do well that ratings period. So for the next sweeps, management came up with "Cancer Month," where we all did stories related to cancer. That didn't prove as popular with the viewers, and the station scrapped plans to focus on other ailments. Which didn't stop the station consultants and management from coming up with other month-long ideas, such as "Education Month," during which nearly every story had to relate in some way on schools. Even my "Fighting Back" franchise was reconfigured to play into this, as I was directed to do stories about school crossing guards and safety at high school football games. Even some teachers told me afterward that we overdid it.

It was all borne of research. WATE was so devoted to research that at one point show producers had to fill out forms each day describing how their shows were targeting specific viewers. These viewers were labeled by the consultants as the "B-1" and "D-1" demographic, and had somehow been identified as important viewers to reach. B-1 folks were described as having "feelings of social commitment and community ties," being strong supporters of law and order, being "empathetic" (it didn't say to what), and wanting to "be in harmony with oneself and one's surroundings." They also had a "sensitivity or attachment to religious values" and "an openness to the world and to foreign ways of life." D-1 people were fairly similar to B-1ers, but also "enjoyed outdoor activities" and crafts and games. I couldn't wait to meet these people.

I'm not exaggerating any of this; the wording comes straight from the written directives given to our producers by station management. To the producers' credit, most of them ignored these forms when deciding what we should cover and just filled them out afterward in a way that would satisfy the consultants.

In my opinion, this sort of approach doesn't work. You can't decide what stories to cover based on what viewers say they're interested in beforehand. If you ask a viewer if he or she cares about education, the viewer will say yes, of course. And who is going to say that health isn't important? But news stories still have to be interesting and newsworthy. If your big story is boring, people aren't going to watch, even if it's about something they told you they cared about.

If it's genuine news, you don't need to look at the ingredients to figure out whether you should cover it. While viewer research can perhaps assist stations in deciding what areas to focus on, it shouldn't determine the coverage. And just as franchises used up resources, so did the big monthly specials. We had days during Cancer Month when there was big breaking news going on, but the first few minutes of our newscast (the lead, supposedly the most important story of the day) involved our anchors standing in front of a phone bank telling viewers to call in with questions about skin cancer. A noble purpose, but not exactly earth shattering and new. I think more viewers called in to ask why we weren't covering real news.

But the consultants said this was the way to get good ratings. They also told us to "produce-up" our broadcast, in which producers pick one big topic for the day and then everyone else does stories relating to that topic. If the big story is an apartment fire, one reporter covers the "nuts and bolts" — the details of the fire — while another does a sidebar story on fire prevention and why it's so important to put batteries in those smoke detectors, and another reporter might do a story about cavemen and their original quest for fire. According to the produce-up approach, it doesn't matter much what the sidebars are, as long as they're connected to the main story you focus on that day. Then the station labels everything Team Coverage to show viewers what a comprehensive job it's doing.

This technique works very well if the main story is a big one. When a fireworks factory exploded near Knoxville, it was too big for one reporter to handle. We produced-up with one reporter covering the details (what caused it, how many hurt, etc.), another reporter getting comments from neighbors, and another reporter (me) at the hospital covering the injured and getting reactions from their families. A story like that is much better to split up. We ended up winning an award for our coverage.

Producing-up is less effective when the main topic only merits one story to begin with, because you end up with several superfluous pieces providing much more information than viewers ever wanted to know about something. Our finest example of excessive producing-up involved the demolition of an old smokestack in Knoxville. The property owners planned to knock it down, an event that, admittedly, looks kind of cool. We decided to produce-up this story, so I covered the nuts and bolts of the demolition, another reporter did a sidebar about the history of the facility and its smokestack, and another reporter did a piece about stadiums and other big things that have been knocked down (basically an excuse to show cool footage of other big demolitions). I then went live at 5:00, 5:30, 5:45, 6:00 and 6:15 to update the public on the demolition that had taken place around 3:30.

Perhaps not surprisingly, our ratings did not improve despite all this franchising and producing-up and our news director was fired. A new news director came in and, much to the relief of most reporters, stopped paying as much attention to outside consultants and their research.

The only downside to the move away from producing-up was that it meant that reporters had to come up with more stories on their own. Which is why the morning story meetings got significantly more demanding. Even utilizing all the local news techniques I had mastered, it could still be challenging to come up with two new story ideas every day. Some days I drew a blank, in which case, the only option was to aggressively support someone else's idea in lieu of suggesting my own. Basically, I would piggy-back on a previously mentioned story idea and talk for as long as possible about different ways you could do the story and why it might be worthwhile.

Which is very likely what another reporter was attempting to do when she said, "You know, I really think the poppies could be interesting." This reporter was sitting down by the end of the table just to the right of the assignment editor. This is the best position to sit in if you have utterly failed to think up any story ideas that day, because you are the last person to go, and thus have time to hear what everyone else has suggested and see if there is anything you can hitch a ride on.

"I mean, how much did it cost the taxpayers to plant these flowers?" the reporter continues. "And are these the same kind of poppies that were in *The Wizard of Oz*? Isn't that dangerous for drivers? I mean, in *The Wizard of Oz*, they all fell asleep!"

"I don't think those are the same kind of poppies," remarks someone else, "and besides, that scene just never rang true for me."

"Yeah, what was the deal with the snow," pipes in one of the photogs. "Why would that wake you up if you were overdosing on opiates?"

"All right, all right," finally interjects the news director, putting an end to this interesting digression. "It's obvious there's some interest in the poppies. And they're very visual. Paul, you do the poppy story."

So I did.

Chapter 23

The Spaces Between the Trees

It is nine o'clock in the evening and I am running out of time. I have been sent to cover an awards ceremony honoring Peyton Manning, star quarterback of the Tennessee Vols. The ceremony is part of a charity fund-raiser, and hundreds of Knoxville's elite have paid a fair amount of money so they can have dinner in the same ballroom as their football hero.

I've already availed myself of a complimentary dinner, and I'm waiting for the speeches to start. My photographer has plugged his camera directly into the sound system, so as soon as Peyton and the others start talking from the podium, we can record it all and put together a story for the eleven o'clock news. The problem for me is that the dinner started late, and everyone is spending too much time on their meals, meaning that the awards part of the ceremony hasn't started yet. No one is making speeches. They're all eating. And I don't have a single sound bite for my story.

With my deadline getting closer and closer, I realize that I cannot wait any longer. "Come with me," I say to the photog, "Time to dispense with politeness." He unplugs from the sound system, hands me a microphone and we head to the stage at the front of the room. We crouch down behind the long head table, crawling our way down toward the middle where Peyton is sitting.

"Hey Peyton," I whisper from my knees. "Peyton, Hey, Channel 6 news ...." Peyton is eating. He turns and looks down toward me with some food in his mouth, looking a bit startled to see a TV crew crawling behind him as he's having his dinner. "Look, I'm sorry to bother you," I say, "But we've got to go. Mind if we ask you a couple of quick questions?"

"Sure. Fire away," he says, chewing on his salad.

357

I ask him the usual questions; what it means to win this award, what he thinks about the charitable organization, and so on. He gives me a few usable sound bites and I thank him and hightail it back to the station, arriving barely in time to get the story written and on the newscast. Then I go home and forget all about having to sneak onstage and interrupt Peyton Manning's dinner.

*   *   *

In TV news, and especially in *local* TV news, every day is like starting over. No matter what story you did the day before; no matter how great you were or how badly you mangled it; you start work each day with a clean slate. It is almost as if every day's work is a drawing on an Etch A Sketch, and each morning the assignment director shakes it all up and hands it back to you again.

I found this both a benefit and a burden. A benefit because when I went home at night I didn't have a lot of lingering issues to worry about. My story was finished. It aired. I couldn't go back and redo it, so no point worrying about it. And in all likelihood, I would be covering something completely different the next day. So I put the day's story out of my mind almost as soon as I heard the anchor say, "Thanks Paul. And in other news ...." If you asked me on Friday what I covered on Wednesday, I honestly would have had a hard time remembering.

This could also be a burden, however, in that I got up each day without the slightest idea what I would have to cover and whether I would be able to handle it. As I've noted, in local news, the true test of whether someone is a good reporter usually isn't how deeply that person delves into an issue, or how beautifully that person crafts a script, or even how stylish the reporter appears on camera, it's the reporter's ability to handle every story that comes along, and to do it quickly and competently. In local TV news, you've always got to come back with a story, and you are always against the clock.

Despite my early struggles with live shots and tight deadlines, Knoxville is where I hit my stride as a reporter. Everything I'd learned in Telluride, Whiteville, and Wilmington coalesced to the point where I became fairly comfortable as a reporter no matter what the story was about and what it entailed. Part of this comfort level was simply due to experience and repetition. Just as important, however, was an evolution in my approach; a change in mind-set that enabled me to stay calm and adapt to whatever came my way. Unlike early on, when I was always worrying, I reached the point where I got up each morning without any idea of what lay ahead but with the confidence I'd be able to deal with it.

When I started out in TV, I had been secretly afraid. Afraid that a difficult story would expose me as a journalistic imposter. When an assignment editor would tell me, "Paul, a truck carrying nuclear waste overturned on I-40. Go cover it," my immediate reaction wasn't, "Let's go!" or "What a great story," or even, "Are you sure it's safe for me to go out there?" Instead, my first thought was, "What if I can't do it? What if I'm not up to this?" As a result, I would often try to talk the assignment editor out of it. "Oh, that's not that big of a story. Just another traffic mishap."

In Wilmington, I am embarrassed to say, I argued with our assignment desk over whether I should cover, among other things, a gas tank explosion that killed two people, a prison break, and a police department standoff involving a suspected murderer. "Are you sure I need to cover this? I'm kind of busy right now."

My reluctance was not due to poor news judgment but to fear; fear of the unknown and fear of failure. In TV news, it is easy to dwell on all the obstacles that could prevent you from getting a story, especially if it is all on your shoulders, as it is for reporters. After all, you might drive an hour to the scene of some "big story" only to have it turn out to be a false alarm. Or there might not be anyone there to interview, or witnesses and the police might refuse to talk, or the scene might be too far back in the woods to get to, or the marijuana grower might go for his rifle. It's a lot safer just to stay close by and do a story about the economic impact of Arbor Day.

Eventually, though, I realized that the only time I got angry and argumentative with the assignment desk was when I was afraid I couldn't handle something. If I feared I might fail, I would get defensive and fight the assignment. But if I believed I could do it, I would go after the toughest assignment without a word of complaint.

Some of this awareness I figured out for myself, and some of it came from a Knoxville news director, Brian Trauring. Brian was a small unimposing man who didn't say a whole lot and hardly ever raised his voice. He did not have what you would call a commanding presence, and if you walked into the newsroom one day, you would never have guessed that he was the boss. Yet I came to realize that when it came to news, Brian knew what he was doing. He'd let everyone else argue over something for a while, then he'd make a quick decision and move on, and that decision invariably turned out to be the right one (yes, even his decision to have the anchor interview George Bush). And unlike some newsroom bosses, Brian didn't spend a lot of time trying to affix blame or berating you when you did something wrong. But he did chastise me one day for worrying too much about obstacles. This happened after a Tennessee state senator was shot and killed in a town about an hour and a half west of Knoxville. I was actually resisting going out to cover it. I was worried that I would get there too late and the story might be too much for me to handle.

"You know, the senator's family probably won't talk to us, and I expect the sheriff's department is pretty busy right now. Plus it's too far for a live shot and by the time I get out there the scene will probably be clear."

"Paul," Brian said with some exasperation, "Instead of focusing on what you might *not* be able to accomplish, maybe you should focus on what you *might* be able to accomplish."

360

It sounds clichéd to say it, but this single remark changed my entire way of looking at things. That's because it brought to mind a technique I learned in Colorado for skiing in the trees. Often the best snow, and hence the best skiing, is off of the main slopes and in the heavily wooded areas where fewer skiers dare to tread. You can find deep, snowy powder in the trees several days after the main runs have been skied down to dirt and rocks. That's why, in ski towns like Telluride, experienced skiers often ski the trees. And whenever anyone asks, "Aren't you worried about hitting a tree?" the response is always, "You don't ski the trees, you ski the spaces between the trees."

It is absolutely true. If you focus on the trees, you'll freak out and run into problems (literally). That, or you'll never leave the top of the hill to begin with because you won't be able to see a clear way through to the bottom. But if you just start down and focus on the daylight, the spaces between the trees, you can usually make it through and have a lot of fun in the process. Of course, every now and then you sideswipe a branch or two. But if you aren't going 100 miles an hour, it doesn't hurt that much.

When Brian told me to focus on the possibilities, it was like a bell suddenly went off for me. Skiing the trees, I thought, he's talking about skiing in the trees. This recognition ultimately changed my entire approach to TV news reporting. Instead of worrying about all the obstacles that might arise, I came to approach stories by jumping into the fray and seeing what I could accomplish. I found that if I focused on the opportunities instead of the obstacles, I could accomplish far more than I had ever thought possible.

On the day of the state senator's murder, I went out to the scene and did a decent job. I didn't catch the murderer or perform any miracles, but I got enough facts from the sheriff's department to explain what they thought had happened. I managed to interview a couple of neighbors and get some shots of the scene. And I made it back in time to get the story on the air. In other words, I did what I was supposed to do. The next day, I went back out there and my story ended up on CNN.

Completely changing my approach to covering news did not occur overnight. For a long time, I still worried about obstacles and feared that I would fail. But I kept reminding myself to ski the trees, and kept taking stories I previously would have been terrified to try. My development also took a step forward when I devised what I termed my fallback routine, a technique I relied on along with my ski-the-trees philosophy. I would start out shooting for the optimal result — the ideal; my vision of how the story should turn out if everything went exactly as I planned. Unfortunately, it's rare for a story to turn out the way you envisioned it. So when the optimal result proved impossible, I would fall back to my second most desired outcome. I'd give that a certain amount of time to succeed, and then fall back to my third most desired outcome. And so on. I always kept a close eye on the clock and gave each attempt a set amount of time to come through before I fell back to something else. Basically, it was a strategy of hoping to get lucky and then adjusting on the fly.

When I say "lucky," I don't mean having lots of bad things happen to other people. I mean putting myself in position for opportunities and then taking advantage of what came my way. I found that the best way was to keep working and leave myself open to fortune. Take the day I did a story about a man from East Tennessee who had been killed in China. The man had been murdered in his hotel room in Dongguan City during what police believed was a botched robbery attempt. This sort of crime isn't that uncommon, in China or elsewhere, but it was unusual for a man from East Tennessee to even be in China, so it merited a story on our local newscast. This is one of those instances where the circumstances make an event more newsworthy. If he had been killed in a hotel room in Knoxville it would have aroused less interest. But because it occurred in an exotic locale, it garnered a few more points and we decided at the morning meeting that I should do a story about it.

For a story like this, ideally I'd contact the family and set up an interview. Reaction from a victim's family is usually option number one, the optimal result, because the family can tell you the most about the victim and will provide you with the most emotional responses. But in this case, I wasn't able to locate the family in the phone book. All I knew was that the man hailed from a small town called Athens about an hour south of Knoxville, and that an Athens funeral home was handling memorial services. So my photographer and I headed down to Athens. The clock was ticking. It was 10:15 in the morning when we left, and I had to be back at the station by 4:30 at the very latest to get my story on the five and six o'clock newscasts. So not counting driving time, I had about four hours to get the story.

When covering a fatality, funeral homes are often good places to start because the employees are accustomed to dealing with death and mourning and often understand how to approach the bereaved. While most funeral home workers I've met respect the family's privacy, they also understand that reporters are just doing a job, as they are, and they generally won't spit at you or take offence at your presence. Sometimes they'll even volunteer to act as intermediaries.

In Athens, the funeral home put us in touch with a few family members. I approached them, expressed my condolences, and explained why we were there and what we were looking for. Unfortunately, they didn't want to talk to me. This left me in a bit of a bind. I couldn't interview the police, because they were in China, and I don't speak Mandarin. I couldn't get video of the crime scene, because, again, China was out of my driving range. And with the family declining to talk to me, all I had was a single photo of the victim, which, at most, would use up about 10 seconds of airtime. I still had more than a minute of airtime to fill.

So using my fallback method, I fell back to my second option: get comment from co-workers. A co-worker's recollection would not be as intimate as that of a family member, but at least he or she could tell us something about the man who died.

It was now a little past noon.

The factory where the man supposedly worked was 20 minutes farther south, but we drove to the gates and I stood outside, jumping in front of cars and stopping workers as they exited. Unfortunately, nobody knew him, so I spent about 40 minutes and nearly got run over for nothing. Strike two. It was now 1:30, and still all I had was a photograph.

At this point, I fell back to option three and focused on the general response in the community. We drove back to Athens and my photographer got video of the town so we could show where the man was from and what sort of a place it was. We went into a restaurant and talked to a few customers. I stopped some people on the street and asked what they thought.

It was here that I finally got a break. After stopping several people, one told me she worked with a woman who had known the man. We tracked that woman down at a local store and convinced her to talk to us. She had not been extremely close, but her children and his children played together. Was she the designated spokesperson the family would have selected? No. Would she even be invited to the funeral? Who knows. But I had to get something, and this woman could tell me a little bit about the man who'd been killed. By this point, it was after 3:00 and I'd run out of time.

We packed up our gear and headed back. In the car, I replayed the tape of everything we had. It wasn't much. We had a photograph of the man, some shots of his hometown, and a few short comments, including one from a woman who knew the man slightly. I scribbled down a script about how this small town in Tennessee might be a world away from the Far East, but how distant events felt disturbingly close following the sad and unexpected death of one of its own. I wrote about how residents were reacting to the news; how some said it was hard to comprehend, while others noted that when a death occurs in a small community, everyone feels the loss. I included a few comments from the woman in the store, who described him as an active family man and a good father to his children. We got back to the station with just enough time for me to get it on the air.

It wasn't Woodward and Bernstein, and wasn't going to win any awards. It was probably not even my best work that week. But it told a story and filled a few minutes of airtime. That's all I could hope for. I had spent about six hours working on it, more than three of that driving around in the car. I'd come back with a photograph, video of the man's hometown, and a few brief comments from people who lived there. We were the only Knoxville news source to get that much. I don't know if the others tried. It was hardly a huge news coup, but it was something I would not have been able to get a year or two earlier. I might not even have tried. This time I hadn't been afraid, and I'd made the best of what I could get. It's what you do as a local TV reporter.

Sometimes it is better to thoroughly plan everything out beforehand and prepare for every obstacle that might arise. But often you don't have that option, and the point for me was that after Telluride, Whiteville, Wilmington, and now Knoxville, I'd reached a level where I could almost always figure out a way to come back with something. I might be a local news hack, but at least I had become a fairly competent one. I could stop worrying about whether I could do the job. I could stop being afraid. I no longer felt as though I was impersonating a TV reporter.

Chapter 24

Farewell Knoxville

After three and a half years at WATE, I decided to leave Knoxville. This was not a difficult decision, because my station left me little choice. They told me I had to either sign another multiyear contract or find another job. They had bent the rules and let me work there for a year after my contract expired, but now they wanted a commitment. Other reporters were pointing to my no-contract situation and asking for the same latitude, and management felt it was starting to destabilize the newsroom.

I understood their thinking and didn't hold it against them. But the thought of a few more years in Knoxville wasn't something I could stomach. It wasn't that the city or the station was so bad, or that they treated me unfairly. I was just burned out on being there.

For one thing, no matter how good my Southern drawl became (quite convincing, according to my Northern friends and family), I never quite fit in in the South. Even after six years below the Mason-Dixon Line, I still felt like a Yankee-in-exile.

Just as importantly, I'd gone about as far as I could go in Knoxville as a TV reporter. I had done almost every kind of story you could cover there and learned an enormous amount about writing, reporting, and going live. I'm not saying I was the best reporter in Knoxville or even the best on WATE's staff, simply that I had reached a point where the work didn't challenge me very often. I might do one story a month that seemed interesting or different. My pace of improvement had slowed to a crawl.

Sometimes, to make things more interesting, I found myself taking ridiculous risks, waiting until the very last minute to work on a story just to see if I could get it finished in time. When you start deliberately making things harder for yourself, it's time to think about a change. The only TV challenge left for me in Knoxville would have been to try and make it as an anchor, something I had little interest in. I've tried it a few times and can tell you that anchoring isn't my forte. Besides, I still had dreams of making it to the big time as a reporter, and staying at WATE another few years wasn't going to further my cause.

So, with some trepidation, I started making plans to depart, even though I didn't have another job lined up. It's not as though I hadn't tried to land another reporting position. I had done pretty much everything possible. I had sent out tapes for more than a year and a half, with some 75 Spelman reels making their way to stations in Atlanta, Baltimore, Boston, Charlotte, Chicago, Cincinnati, Cleveland, Dallas, Denver, Detroit, Indianapolis, Los Angeles, Milwaukee, Minneapolis, New York, Orlando, Philadelphia, Pittsburgh, Sacramento, San Diego, San Francisco, Seattle, and Washington, to name just a few. I had exhausted an enormous amount of money, energy, and vacation time looking for a job. Yet from all those stations and cities, I had garnered four job interviews and one underwhelming offer from a Long Island cable station. I turned it down. The pay wasn't much better than what I was earning in Knoxville, whereas my cost of living would have been three times higher.

I finally decided it wasn't going to happen by sending out tapes from Tennessee. So I decided to do what I had done before — back when I moved to Telluride — go somewhere and look for work once I arrived. I figured that sometimes you need to get in their face and force the issue, so to speak. I needed to put myself in position to get lucky.

By this point, one big thing had changed in my life. Amazingly enough for a nomadic TV reporter, I was now in a serious relationship. My girlfriend was a UT veterinary student named Erin. She was the first long-term girlfriend I had had in several years; the first time in ages I had allowed myself the liberty of not worrying about when I might have to leave, where I might have to go, and whether she could or would come along. We met at a Christmas party hosted by a colleague, and five months later, things were going pretty well. I knew it was serious when I agreed not to run a story Erin inadvertently leaked to me about one of the UT football mascots.

The University of Tennessee has several mascots, some human, others of the animal variety. It turned out that one of the canine mascots, "Smokey," had swallowed a sock and needed medical assistance at the UT veterinary hospital. This would have been a big scoop in Knoxville and probably would have led the newscast. "Vol Hero in Peril!" "Dog Days for Gridiron Legend!" But as a UT veterinary student, Erin wasn't supposed to disclose the school clinic's patients, and when I started making excited noises about setting up a live-truck outside the vet school emergency room, she begged me not do it.

I was conflicted, and immediately thought back to that career-influencing film *The Year of Living Dangerously*. There is a critical scene in which British Secret Service worker Sigourney Weaver reveals classified information to reporter Mel Gibson after they've just spent the night together. Sigourney tells him he can't do a story with the information and Mel replies, "Then you shouldn't have told me," and goes ahead and does it anyway.

In Knoxville, I reluctantly agreed to forgo the story. This was a big step for me; an allegiance in my personal life taking precedence over the news. Then again, Mel's story involved communists smuggling guns to overthrow the government; my story involved a dog swallowing a sock.

Perhaps because of my courageous decision, or more likely because I kept cooking her dinner, Erin decided to take a big step as well. When I explained that I would have to leave Knoxville and get a job in another city, she simply asked, "Where do you think you could go?"

368

"I don't know," I replied, "maybe Washington, D.C. I've heard there are a lot of opportunities there for freelance reporters." The next thing I knew, Erin was applying for postgraduation veterinary jobs near the nation's capital. She committed to D.C. before I did.

Erin landed a job in Maryland, and we came up with a plan to get an apartment equidistant from Washington and Baltimore. Hopefully, I could show these big-city news directors that I had what it takes; that I was a solid reporter who worked hard and could ski the spaces between the trees with the best of them. Freelance reporting would lead to a full-time position. I would make it to the big time. Fame. Fortune. Glory. That was the idea, anyway. If I wasn't able to find freelance work, I'd have to either head back to another small market or switch careers. But I didn't want to stay in Knoxville and figured taking a chance was better than accepting my lot.

So Erin and I packed up everything we had and moved to Maryland. We brought Lenny the cat along with us. Lenny had adopted me, not the other way around, but as he was my main source of companionship during my solitary years, I couldn't leave him behind.

We arrived in Maryland in the summer of 2000 and I started making the TV news rounds. I called up all the news directors at Baltimore and Washington stations, explaining how fortunate they were to have such an accomplished newsman as myself move to their area. I called up bureau chiefs for all the Washington news organizations and dropped off my resume tape. Whenever they asked about my reasons for leaving WATE and Knoxville, I said I moved after my girlfriend got a new job in Maryland. Like most misleading statements, it was technically accurate.

But none of my efforts seemed to bear any fruit. My tape just didn't seem quite good enough for big-time TV. I was getting to that point where I'd have to make a major decision – give up on TV news, or move away from Erin.

How do you know when it's time to throw in your hand and call it quits? How do you know when to give up or when to keep trying for your shot at the big time? I was starting to consider that question when Cissy Baker and Tribune offered me a one-day tryout.

Epilogue: Fall of 2000

When my truck Proud Mary broke down on the way to the Tribune tryout, I gently coaxed the truck over to the side of the road to get it out of the traffic. It was about 6:20 in the morning, and I was on a two-lane road on the outskirts of Montgomery County, about 25 minutes from the nearest subway station, Shady Grove, which is itself a 35–40 minute subway ride from downtown Washington. I didn't have any tools for fixing the truck; I didn't have a cell phone; and I didn't have the foggiest idea of what I was going to do. But after a decade of dealing with daily deadlines, obstacles, and setbacks, at least I knew how to approach the problem from a practical perspective. So I pushed down the rising panic and went into fallback mode, looking for a way to ski through the trees.

The truck doesn't run. What are my options? Let's go through the checklist. First fallback – try to restart it. This was pretty much pointless, I knew, but I went through the motions anyway, turning the ignition a few times and pumping the gas. Nothing. I could have generated more noise from a tricycle.

Okay, next step. I got out and popped the hood. As I've said, if the engine isn't missing, I won't normally be able to diagnose the problem. But since this battery slip-and-slide thing had occurred before, I had a general idea what to look for. It was as I had feared. The battery, slick with motor oil, had shifted from its normal position and ripped the wires connecting it to the truck. They weren't pulled free so much as torn in half. On one side, the ends were still bolted to the battery; on the other, they were still wired to the truck. In the middle, there were shorn and frayed shreds.

I wasn't dressed properly for automotive maintenance, but I took off my suit jacket, threw my nice tie over my shoulder to keep it from brushing against the omnipresent motor oil, and leaned over the still scalding engine to try and jam the battery back into its regular position. I could only push it part of the way. It may have been loose enough to slide when the truck went around a sharp corner, but it was still bolted tightly enough to keep me from moving it far under my own power.

This meant that the two ends of the battery wire were just barely touching, and only if I held them in place. There wasn't enough slack to twist one wire end around the other. As it was, the wires were very stiff, and when I tried to forcibly jam them together, I ended up cutting my fingers as the sharp wires dug into my skin.

I spent about 10 minutes trying to force the battery and wires back together, but to no avail. It must have been a comical sight for passing motorists. Here I was, all decked out in my best suit, and I'm standing on the side of the road next to an old pickup truck pretending to be a Pep Boy. While there weren't a lot of houses around, the road was fairly busy, with commuters whizzing by on their way to work. Nobody stopped or offered to help, and I didn't ask for it. I hadn't reached that level of desperation yet, although I knew that was coming. My last fallback option would be to jump in front of another vehicle and plead with them to take me to D.C.

First I decided to search the inside of my truck cabin and see if there was anything that could be of use. I knew I didn't have any real tools, but maybe I had some wires or jumper cables or an extra engine in there somewhere. I didn't find much. Behind the seat I had a tire iron, of little help in this situation unless I felt like rotating the tires while I was waiting. I also found my Club antitheft device, again of little use in this situation. If I couldn't start the truck with a key, it wasn't likely a thief could get very far either. If one could, I might not object. Take my truck, just drop me in D.C.

There was also a flashlight, a pen, a few coins that had fallen from my pockets, an oil soaked rag, and a full quart of unopened motor oil. Even in my desperate strait, I recognized the priceless irony of that last item.

I did, however, spot one small twist tie, over on the floor on the passenger side. It was the sort of twist tie you get in a bunch of 40 with your garbage bags. It was small and bent and a bit worn, and looked as though it had been there for a few years. Why it was there, I don't know. I don't make a point of carrying twist ties in my truck, and to this day I have no idea where it came from. But I started thinking. Hmm. Maybe. It was worth a shot.

Feeling much like MacGyver, I jammed the two ends from the metal battery wire together and wrapped the twist tie around them a few times. It took me quite a number of tries before I could get the ends to stay in place, but when I finally let go, lo and behold, the wires held. They didn't look like they were going to hold for long, but they held long enough for me to walk around to the driver's side, gingerly climb back in, and turn the key. Proud Mary started back up. Hallelujah. I couldn't believe it. But I didn't have a lot of time to sit and admire my resourcefulness. I was now running late and had a sneaking suspicion that it was just a matter of time before the twist tie broke and the engine went south again. So I closed the hood as gently as I could and worked my way back into traffic.

Everything seemed fine. The blinkers functioned, the lights turned on and off, even the radio was working. It was like a resurrection. Even so, I was terrified it wouldn't last. I tried to accelerate as gradually as possible, and took every turn like a granny transporting the queen's fine china. I figured that any sharp turn or bump and my twist-tie remedy was history. I was still far too far from D.C. to start congratulating myself.

I drove about a mile and pulled onto Interstate 270, heading south toward the capital. I didn't plan to drive the whole way, I just wanted to make it to a subway station before the twist tie snapped. Unfortunately, I didn't make it. I got about halfway there when my truck bounced over a pothole. The radio suddenly cut out and the familiar red warning light came on again on my dashboard. The wires must have pulled apart again. I cursed and started to look for a place to pull off. I was, however, still going about 50 miles an hour, fast enough to keep the engine running. I knew, though, that if I had to slow down, the truck would shut off completely again. And for all I knew, my twist-tie savior was lying in that pothole a half a mile back. I didn't have any other miracle cures. I had to keep moving for as long as possible.

I wove my way through traffic, trying to stay at speed. I was fortunate in that it was still fairly early. 20 minutes later and I-270 traffic slowed to a crawl. As it was, I had to take the exit ramp for the Metro a bit faster than the posted speed limit sign recommends. But I had to keep moving. Every minute still driving got me a little bit nearer, and I figured if I got close enough and the truck died, I would leave it there and walk to the station. I could leave a note and come back for it later.

I didn't have to. After a few more minutes of tense, frantic driving, I pulled into the Metro train station. I got really lucky in that there were open parking spaces right near the entrance. I spotted one and headed straight for it, reducing my speed dangerously low as I did so. The engine shut off a couple of seconds before I made it, but I was able to coast into the spot. Fortunately, I was perfectly aligned and didn't have to reposition the truck, which was, again, dead as a doornail. No need to hook up The Club, this vehicle wasn't going anywhere. I couldn't worry about that now, though, I would deal with Proud Mary when I got back. The important thing was to make it to Washington.

I jumped out of the truck and ran for the train. About 40 minutes later, I hurried into Tribune's Washington bureau, panting and sweating profusely. I was about 10 minutes late. I launched into an explanation of my commuting difficulties, but stopped when I realized they weren't mad and had barely noticed my late arrival. They were just getting started themselves. It was 7:40 in the morning. They offered me some coffee.

We had a brief meeting to discuss what story I would cover. To this day, I have no recollection of what it was. I was so wired and jittery from my nerve-wracking commuting experience that the story I did that day passed in and out of my consciousness without registering. I must have done something relating to the president, because at 1:00 p.m. I found myself standing on the White House lawn doing a live shot for WGN in Chicago. I was actually inside the White House gates, looking around in a daze at all the big-time network reporters, strolling around the White House grounds as if it were their backyard. A few photographers were asleep nearby, resting in portable chairs with paperbacks on their laps, just a few steps from the door to the White House pressroom. Meanwhile, crowds of tourists peered through the gates and took my picture. I looked down and realized my hands were still stained with motor oil. The whole experience felt surreal.

I guess I did an okay job, because when I arrived back at the bureau afterward, Cissy Baker complimented me and booked me for a few more days of freelance reporting. I knew I still had a lot to prove, and my continued success in D.C. was hardly assured. But I was in the door.

Aftermath

It's been several years since that hectic day when I got my foot in the door in D.C.'s TV news scene. I wrote much of this account during my first winter in D.C., when the freelance reporting market slowed to a crawl after the drawn-out presidential election of Bush versus Gore. Washington stations and news bureaus spent so much money covering that election that they ran out of funds for freelancers. I didn't work for a long time.

Eventually, though, the freelance business picked back up, and I managed to survive, if not necessarily thrive. I worked as a TV reporter for four years in D.C., working mostly freelance for capital news bureaus and the fledgling cable channel Tech TV. For a year and a half, I had a full-time staff job as a reporter with the Washington bureau for Hearst-Argyle TV, a company with 26 local TV stations around the country.

Working for Hearst and other D.C. news bureaus was not like working in local news. For one thing, it usually meant that I only did one story a day, as opposed to doing three or four. But I had to do that one story for every station affiliated with the news bureau. I'd end up reciting the same lines 15 or 20 times in a row, and the hardest part was sounding fresh each time and remembering which station I was talking to. Sometimes I got confused and ended up saying, "Back to you in Boston" when I was going live for Baltimore. Other times I went back to "Laura and Steve" only to be gently reminded that I was talking to "Lorraine and Ken."

For Hearst, I had to carry around two dozen different microphone cubes — called mike flags — one for each station in the Hearst-Argyle empire. Right before a live shot for a particular station, I'd put that station's flag atop my microphone so that viewers of that station would think I was one of their local reporters. I also had to memorize each station's individual outcue, or "tag," so

I could end each report with the appropriate "Eyewitness News 5" (Oklahoma City), "KOAT Action 7 News" (Albuquerque), or "Channel 4 Action News" (Pittsburgh).

As a D.C. bureau reporter, you do your fair share of live shots, whether the real or pretaped kind. Sometimes I'd start out doing live shots for East Coast cities at 10:00 p.m. and work my way west, ending with Seattle, Sacramento, or Los Angeles at 1:00 in the morning. I also went live for a few New York City stations, much to the enjoyment of my mother there, who had never seen me live on TV. She was headed out to a restaurant for a late dinner the first time I called to let her know I would be on in New York. It was too late for her to alter her dinner plans, but at 10:00 she marched into the restaurant bar and demanded they change the channel so she could view her TV reporter son. Fortunately, the bar patrons weren't watching anything important, just the final game of the NCAA men's basketball tournament. But March Madness takes a back seat to my mother when she's determined, and they dutifully complied. My mom claims people in the bar actually applauded at the end of my report, although if that's true, I suspect they were applauding the fact that they could switch back to their game.

For the most part, I enjoyed reporting for the Washington news bureaus, but it is a very different animal from working in local news. You don't cover many murders and fires and three-car crashes, since this sort of local story doesn't "travel" well. Viewers in Kansas City don't care about a D.C. subway problem or a Maryland resident with 50 cats. So instead, you do stories about congressional hearings and national issues, and spend a lot of time interviewing senators, congressmen, cabinet secretaries and other "important people."

This may sound exciting, but calling these encounters "interviews" is a bit of an overstatement. Most of the time you get two or three questions in and the VIP's responses are straight out of their media handler's guidebook. Listen, answer, bridge.

A perfect example of D.C. bureau reporting is what takes place at the president's annual State of the Union address. I covered this event for Hearst in 2002. Along with about 50 other TV crews, I crowded into the Capitol's Statuary Hall, directly outside the chamber where the president delivered his speech. Each TV crew was designated a spot near one of the statues of "important people in American history." Before the speech begins, you contact the offices of the respective senators and representatives in your viewing area to let them know you'll be set up by, say, Sam Houston, or a few feet to the left of King Kamehameha. Then, about 15 or 20 minutes into the speech, long before it's over, politicians start streaming out of the chamber to give you their "reaction" to the president's speech.

As a bureau reporter, my task was to get one usable comment from at least one elected official from each of my respective viewing areas. Since Hearst had over 20 stations, that meant I had to get comments from a lot of people. In the course of an hour and a half, I "interviewed" nine senators, 27 congressmen and one governor. These folks are normally treated like royalty, but in Statuary Hall they were literally standing in line waiting to get their comments in. Occasionally a brief squabble would break out over whether a senator should get to jump ahead of a congressman, or whether senior senators deserved priority over junior ones. I heard audible grumblings when we let Ted Kennedy cut in line.

My in-depth interviews generally amounted to a "What did you think?" followed by "That was super, thanks. Next please ...." A lot of the time, I wasn't even sure who I was talking to. I'd studied their pictures as best I could beforehand, but they were coming so fast it was hard not to get confused. At one point I asked a woman to state her district so I would have it on tape, only to have her reply, "My district is the state of Arkansas. I'm a senator." "Of course you are, Senator. Congratulations on that. So, what did you think of the speech?"

As for President George W. himself, I never did get a chance to interview him in person. Maybe he was reluctant to chat with someone he remembered as a lowly Knoxville news intern. His staff certainly didn't roll out the welcome mat for me. When I called to inquire about obtaining a permanent White House press pass, I was put through to a very junior staffer who asked who I worked for. "Well I work for a lot of different news organizations," I replied. "I'm a freelancer. I've been in D.C. for over a year, and have done stories for Tribune Broadcasting, Hearst Argyle TV, Conus Communications, and others."

"Well, I've never heard of you," she replied. "So you probably won't get it." She was, unfortunately, correct.

My closest encounter with any of the White House occupants came one day when Barney the Bush dog strolled by on a bathroom break (his, not mine) while I was shooting a stand-up on the White House lawn. I went over and petted him for a bit. I was kind of hoping he might bite me and the president would have to personally apologize, but Barney seemed friendlier than the rest of the administration. What was it Harry Truman said, if you want a friend in Washington, get a dog?

Despite that, I have to admit that working in D.C. can make you feel mildly important every now and then. Walking the halls of Congress; getting to talk to powerful politicians; going live from the White House about the latest presidential pronouncement — you end up feeling sort of important by association. Tourists take your picture when you're leaving the White House, and people always ask you what it's like inside. Since I was only allowed in the White House press area, I couldn't tell them much, but I explained that the bathrooms were sparkling. In this I was being kind; they're really kind of dingy. In fact, the whole press area is pretty rundown. The carpet is old and worn, the chairs are literally falling apart, and the pressroom has that stale coffee-and-microwaved-food smell of an airplane cabin after a long flight. The pressroom looked much worse in person than it did on the TV show *The West Wing*, probably because viewers wouldn't believe it if the show depicted the pressroom in its true state.

I'm sure the rest of the White House is quite nice, but I never got to see it. Apart from the pressroom, I was only allowed to go to small area of the lawn nicknamed "Pebble Beach," where all the camera crews set up. If I left that area and wandered 15 feet across the lawn I would have been tackled by the Secret Service. So much for my insider access. I did, however, once manage to take a nap in the White House pressroom by pushing together a couple of chairs and putting a shirt over my eyes. So at least I can truthfully say I've slept at the White House.

I also did get to cover some big events, like the D.C. Sniper shootings, the Anthrax Attacks, and the Chandra Levy disappearance. I did dozens and dozens of stories about Afghanistan, Iraq, and other conflicts in the Middle East. On the other hand, I did all of these reports from Washington; it wasn't as if I was out there tracking down Saddam Hussein.

I also went to New York on 9/11 and reported from near ground zero. That was an unnerving experience, especially that first day when there was so much uncertainty about what was going on. People I'd never met before wished me luck when they heard where I was going, and I recall riding north up the New Jersey turnpike toward New York City while every other car seemed headed in the opposite direction. I had no idea what I was heading into and what it would be like when I arrived. I tried not to be afraid, and thought about skiing the trees.

When a photographer, a producer, and I arrived outside New York around midnight, we couldn't get into Manhattan because the bridges and tunnels were closed, but by five in the morning I was doing live shots from the town of Kearny right across the Hudson River. I did about 30 live shots on the morning of September 12th, and after the bridges opened up, we moved the live shots into

Manhattan itself. A few days later I found out that several people I knew from high school and college had been in the World Trade Center. Another had been on one of the planes that crashed into the towers. Leaving the live-shot location a few days later, I bumped into two classmates headed to a memorial service for another college friend whose body had yet to be found.

I spent two weeks reporting from New York after 9/11, doing live shots for over a dozen stations. But even this reporting was very removed from the hands-on news gathering I did in local TV news. I had to do so many live shots that I rarely had to time to go out and interview anyone or cover anything myself. So instead, I remained at the live-shot location and put together stories from interviews and video footage that other people collected. My story might have video footage that had been gathered by a CNN crew and sound bites picked up by a local New York station, all sent to Atlanta and rebroadcast over CNN's satellite feed before being picked up by the Tribune bureau in D.C. and dropped into my story. In some ways, I could have been back in a studio in D.C., but then, of course, I wouldn't have been "live on the scene" in New York.

* * *

So did I make it to the major leagues in TV reporting? That depends on your definition, I guess. I probably made it further than 90 percent of the people who start out dreaming of making it to the big time in TV news. On the other hand, I was just one of dozens of Washington bureau reporters, and for much of the time, I wasn't full-time, just a freelancer working day to day. I also still got paid less than many educators (although I did finally earn enough to buy a new car, giving Proud Mary a much-needed break after 210,000 miles). I guess you could say I reached a level in TV news where there were still plenty of reporters above me, but I was high enough where I could at least run into them every now and then. They looked like they were having a good time.

As for me, I wasn't having as good a time covering news as I had early on. It's strange, I know, because in D.C. I was a lot higher up than I'd been in Tennessee or North Carolina. I didn't have to one-man band, give roadside weather reports, or localize an important story happening somewhere else. A lot of the time, I was doing a story on the big story.

But covering relatively big-time news in Washington was in many ways less interesting than covering local news in smaller markets. I learned a lot less and got to experience far fewer new and unusual things. I'd come home from work and Erin, who by that point had agreed to marry me, would ask what I did that day, only to have me reply, "Ah, some hearing on the hill. Nothing exciting." I had little interest in rehashing my day as a D.C. bureau reporter. But at the same time, I wasn't eager to go back to local news and cover the animal abuse story of the week.

I also came to realize that the TV news business gets harsher and, in some ways, more superficial the higher up you go. You're judged more and more by how you look and come across as opposed to the quality of your writing, reporting, and ability to come back with a good story. It is very disheartening to work hard on a story, track down all the right sources, make sense out of confusing and contradictory information, and write a sharp and entertaining script, only to have a news executive tell you that it wasn't any good because you "lacked energy" in your live shot. That happened to me more than a few times as a D.C. bureau reporter. No matter how hard you work as a TV reporter, if you don't have enough on-camera charisma, you're probably not going to make it to the major leagues. And the people who make judgments about your "energy" are often on the business side of the industry — executives deciding whether you can help pull in an audience.

Perhaps most significantly for me, however, was that I simply got tired of always being a neutral observer. Working as a reporter, no matter what level and what medium, means going through life as a professional spectator. You are always watching historic events but are never involved in the outcome. You're not supposed to. Some reporters are so intent on remaining impartial that they don't even vote, and take pride in this fact. I came to find this disinterested detachment frustrating, and felt that I was not adding much real value to anything.

On the contrary, I felt that I was probably taking something away. I would take a complex and important issue and reduce it to a 75-second story, merely skimming the surface of the topic and moving on. I would interview an expert for 25 minutes and use six or seven seconds on the air. It was almost the reverse of what I did when I created something out of nothing. But I didn't have the option of going more in-depth. At Hearst, I had a strict 75-second time limit for my stories, and if a story came in at 77 seconds I was told to cut out enough words to shave off two seconds. You wouldn't believe how many hours I spent trying to cut seconds from my scripts.

All of this finally convinced me to make a change. In 2004, 15 years after I graduated from Colgate, I headed back to school, this time to study law. I had always had an interest in legal cases, and a modest knack for covering them, so I decided I would try doing them instead of just watching them. I was accepted to the University of Maryland School of Law, graduated in 2007, and became a practicing attorney.

Would I still jump at the chance to be a network correspondent if it were offered? No, I really wouldn't. Oh, sometimes I still think about what it would be like to cover the big story, or to go live for the Nightly News. I invested so much time and effort to make it in TV, it was hard to turn my back on it. I can still hear a stubborn voice saying, "Don't give up. Keep at it. You don't want all those years of striving, of enduring, to be for nothing." But then I remind myself that what you do to get somewhere doesn't make it worthwhile once you're there, and I really have no interest in going live from some disaster site or covering the latest presidential imbroglio. The other day I asked myself, if I could have any job in TV news, would I take it? The answer was no. It is a very strange feeling to realize you no longer want something that you dreamed of, and sacrificed so much for, for such a long time.

But you can't ignore things you don't like about TV or the news in the hope that you'll love it when you reach the top. You have to love reporting at whatever level you're at, and be happy even if you never make it higher than a well-run local station in a place where you can afford to pay the rent. Because if you sacrifice solely on the premise that TV reporting will be worth it in the end, what do you do if you never make it, or if the end isn't as glorious as you had imagined? The old saw that it is the journey and not the destination really does apply to TV news. You can't look at reporting as a means to an end because it's mostly means. You have to enjoy where you are, not where you want to be.

Still, looking back on it now, I don't think I would have done much differently. I met a lot of very interesting people along the way, saw some unusual events, and learned an enormous amount about lots of things, and about myself. When I set out to be a TV reporter, I wanted to see real life and real people. I wanted to tell genuine stories, to get down and dirty and view America closer to the trenches. I think that to some extent I did that. While in some ways my journey through TV news was even worse than I had hoped, in other ways it was better than I had feared. So even though I ultimately left the news behind, I'm glad I was a TV reporter.

Acknowledgments

Thanks are due to many many people for helping me in one form or another, and I will not try to list them all. But I need to specifically acknowledge the aid of Sara Corbett, Eric Krell, Chris Reed, and especially my sister Erika Spelman, who reviewed drafts and provided me with valuable insight and encouragement. Thanks are also due, whether they want it or not, to Cissy Baker, Peter Barnes, Jonathan Dienst, Jon Evans, Jeff Goldblatt, Lynn Heinisch, Leigh Powell Hines, Jon Kovash, Stephen Stock, Marta Tarbell, and Brian Trauring, all of whom either helped me break into the news business or helped me survive as long as I did. I also need to thank Larry Spelman, Jill Spelman, Dorothy Spelman, and Richard Gallagher for always supporting my choices, no matter how strange or irrational they seemed at the time, and Len and Viv Landsman for becoming my family when I moved to North Carolina. And finally, I am eternally grateful for the help, encouragement, love, and companionship of my wife Erin, who believed in me more than I believed in myself.

About the Author

From 1994–2004, Paul Spelman worked as a TV news reporter in North Carolina, Tennessee, and Washington, D.C. His news stories appeared on more than 40 TV stations around the country, including WPIX–New York, WCVB–Boston, KTLA–Los Angeles, and WGN–Chicago. He has also reported for the cable channel Tech TV, worked as a newspaper and radio reporter in Telluride, Colorado, and written articles for various publications. A native New Yorker, Paul graduated from Colgate University in 1989 and from the University of Maryland School of Law in 2007. He is now an attorney in Washington, D.C., and lives in Silver Spring, Maryland with his wife Erin, their twin sons Billy and Jeremy, and their sleepy cats Jacob and Marvin.

To learn more about Paul or the book, or to contact the author, please visit evenworsethanwehadhoped.com.